TERROR TRIALS

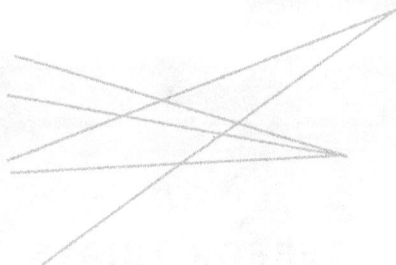

THINKING FROM ELSEWHERE

TERROR TRIALS

Life and Law in Delhi's Courts

MAYUR R. SURESH

FORDHAM UNIVERSITY PRESS NEW YORK 2023

Fordham University Press has no responsibility for the persistence or accuracy of URLs for external or third-party Internet websites referred to in this publication and does not guarantee that any con- tent on such websites is, or will remain, accurate or appropriate.

Fordham University Press also publishes its books in a variety of electronic formats. Some content that appears in print may not be available in electronic books.

Visit us online at www.fordhampress.com.

Library of Congress Cataloging-in-Publication Data available online at https://catalog.loc.gov.

Printed in the United States of America

25 24 23   5 4 3 2 1

First edition

For Amma and Appa

CONTENTS

ABBREVIATIONS AND GLOSSARY

affidavit: This is a written statement that is sworn to as truthful by the person making it. In some courts, such as the Supreme Court, affidavits are used in place of oral testimony.

ahlmad: This is an official in the court bureaucracy. There is usually one *ahlmad* for each court, who is in charge of the records of the court, ensuring that the day's files are given to the reader (see below) and that the reader returns the files in good order. The *ahlmad* holds the keys to the court's massive filing cabinets and signs off on a number of things from stationery requests to witness reimbursements. The *ahlmad* also ensures that the court's orders are followed and acts as the link between that particular court and other courts.

ATS: Anti-Terrorism Squad. In some states (such as Maharashtra and Uttar Pradesh) the police have constituted Anti-Terrorism Squads as special police units to investigate terrorist crimes.

ASJ: additional sessions judge. This is the highest criminal court in a district.

charge sheet: Officially known as a "Report under s[ection] 173, CrPC [Code of Criminal Procedure]," this document is filed by the police in every criminal case. It outlines the narrative, the evidence, and charges against accused persons.

cognizance: This is the process by which a magistrate takes official notice of a charge sheet.

committal: This occurs if, after taking cognizance of a charge sheet, the magistrate comes to the conclusion that the charges made against the defendant are triable only by a superior court (i.e., the Court of Sessions). The magistrate is then said to commit the case for trial before the Court of Sessions.

cross-examination: This is the process by which the witness produced by one party is questioned by the opposite party in a legal dispute. In criminal trials, most of the witnesses are produced by the prosecution, and the cross examination is done by the defense lawyers. The cross-examination of witnesses takes place after the examination-in-chief (see below).

CrPC: Code of Criminal Procedure, 1973. India's main law that deals with the procedure of criminal cases.

DD: daily diary. These are diaries kept by each police station. They are meant to record significant events at police stations.

examination-in-chief: This is the process (also known as "direct examination" in some contexts) by which the witness is questioned by the party who produced the witness. In criminal trials, most of the witnesses are produced by the prosecution, and the examination-in-chief is done by the prosecutor. The examination-in-chief takes place before the cross-examination (see above).

ExPW: exhibit prosecution witness. This abbreviation is written in courtroom depositions, often followed by a number, indicating the witness, and letter, indicating the document being referred to in the deposition. For example, "ExPW9/A" refers to the document marked A exhibited by prosecution witness number 9.

fard makboojgi: seizure memo. This memo is produced by the police during an investigation. It documents that the police have seized certain physical items as a part of their investigation.

fard nishandehi: pointing-out memo. This is a memo produced by the police during an investigation to document that a witness has pointed out a particular person or object of relevance to the investigation.

FIR: first information report. This is the first record of a complaint made to a police station. It is a written document.

IPC: Indian Penal Code, 1860. The main criminal legislation in India.

JC: judicial custody. After the period of police custody (or PC, see below) is complete, defendants are taken out of the custody of the police and are said to be sent to custody of courts. In effect, they are sent to the local jail pending their trials. The presiding judge has the option to release the defendant on bail, but this is virtually impossible under the Unlawful Activities Prevention Act (UAPA, see below) because of the restrictive bail provisions of the statute.

magistrate: This is the lowest criminal court judge in India's judicial hierarchy. Magistrates are given the powers to deal with pretrial motions pertaining to arrest, disclosure of evidence, cognizance of charge sheets, and committal to Sessions courts. They also have the power to conduct the trials for lesser offenses. In cities, they are known as metropolitan magistrates (MMs, see below).

MLC: medico-legal certificate. This is a document produced by doctors recording injuries sustained by patients and other medical information pertaining to those injuries.

mukhbir: secret informer. In many cases, the Special Cell (see below) claims that it received information about terrorist crimes from a secret informer, whose identity is not disclosed to the court or to the defense.

MM: metropolitan magistrate. This is the lower level criminal court judge in a metropolitan area.

naib court: A police officer who acts as the Delhi police's representative in court and is the channel of information and paperwork between the police and the court.

NIA: National Investigation Agency. This is a specialized antiterror police agency set up under the National Investigation Agency Act, 2008. Unlike other police agencies, which are governed by state governments, the NIA is governed by the Central Ministry of Home Affairs.

panch witness: An independent public witness to a police investigation, who is meant to certify that portions of the investigation occurred in the way that the police said that it did.

PC: police custody. After the police officially arrest a person and that person is produced before a magistrate, the police will ask that the person be placed in police custody to aid with the investigation. The magistrate may grant this request or send the person to judicial custody (JC, see above) or release the person on bail. In most terror cases, people arrested are sent to police custody.

PCO: public call office. This is a payphone facility. These are not coin operated and are usually staffed with an operator.

PUCL: People's Union for Civil Liberties. Founded in 1976, this is one of India's largest human rights organizations.

PUDR: People's Union for Democratic Rights. This is a human rights association based in Delhi.

POTA: Prevention of Terrorism Act, 2001. India's anti-terror law, which was enacted after September 11. Though it was repealed in 2004, most of its provisions were grafted onto the Unlawful Activities Prevention Act (UAPA) via an amendment made in the same year.

PS: police station. The abbreviation usually appears before the name of the police station, as in PS Gole Market.

reader: An official in the court's bureaucracy who organizes the judge's calendar and manages the daily case files. Each court has a reader.

rukka: This is a summary of information about an offence that, in some criminal cases, is given to the station house officer (SHO, see below), who then registers a first information report (FIR, see above).

seizure memo: This is a memo written by police listing the articles of evidence that they have taken into their custody.

Sessions Court: This is the highest criminal trial court in a district. Often abbreviated to ASJs, or additional sessions judges (see above), these are given the jurisdiction to conduct trials under India's present anti-terror law, the Unlawful Activities Prevention Act (UAPA, see above).

SHO: station house officer. The officer in charge of a police station.

SIMI: Students Islamic Movement of India. It is banned as a terrorist organization by the government of India.

Special Cell: The unit of the Delhi police that deals with terror investigations, as well as other investigations that the government assigns to it.

TADA: Terrorist and Disruptive Activities (Prevention) Act, 1985. India's anti-terror law that was ostensibly enacted in response to the Khalistani movement. It lapsed after ten years.

UAPA: Unlawful Activities Prevention Act, 1967. India's current anti-terror law. The main legislation, enacted in 1967, was meant to deal with separatist threats from around the country. In 2004, anti-terror provisions were grafted on via an amendment. A significant amendment was made after the terrorist attacks in Mumbai, in November 2008.

vakalatnama: A power of attorney given by a client to a lawyer, which enables the lawyer to act on behalf of the client in a particular case.

                    chorus
                    should we discuss your
                    philanthropy
                    prometheus
                    I went a bit too far
                    chorus
                    how do you mean
prometheus
I stopped them seeing death before them
                    chorus
                                who
                    prometheus
                    human beings
                    chorus
                    how
prometheus
I planted blind hope in their hearts
chorus
why
                    prometheus
                    they were breaking
                    chorus
                    you fool

                    from 4NO's *Prometheus
                    Rebound*
                                —ANNE CARSON, *RED DOC>*

INTRODUCTION

Early in 2008, I took the opportunity to assist a lawyer and good friend, Jawahar Raja, in Delhi in the defense of the Students Islamic Movement of India (SIMI). The government of India had banned the organization on the allegation that its members were conducting terrorist acts throughout the country. These included what we might readily call "terrorist" acts, such as causing explosions in civilian areas, along with acts that stretched the concept of terrorism (if there is one) beyond recognition: putting up posters that questioned the legitimacy of the Indian state, protesting discrimination against Muslims, downloading Islamic sermons, peddling fake currency, and merely possessing a copy of the *Rubaiyyat* by Omar Khayyam. If anything, this confirmed my preconceived ideas about the law: It segued with Hindu nationalism to create a climate in which minorities and opposition groups were persecuted.

At that time, I was convinced that the law was an inherently violent institution. I disagreed with those who believe that the rule of law is an "unqualified human good" (Thompson 1990, 266).[1] The repeated arrests of obviously innocent people on terrorism charges, whose potential sentences could span decades, only confirmed this for me. Before I started research for this book, I understood the state and the law as entities that viewed human rights as a constant threat. As I wrote in 2007, "A condition of emergency activates the idea that the body of the citizen is dangerous and intractable, and that the 'rights' that adhere to the citizen function as loaded weapons, cocked and ready to be used against the state. The emergent citizen, much like the terrorist, is thus the figure that threatens to shatter the sovereign order" (130). The law, I thought then, was an institution that was

aimed at destroying human freedom or, at the very least, conditioned to suppress it.

Moreover, five years of law school and internships had put me off courts.
In my younger eyes, courts were places of humiliating hierarchy, endless
waiting, boredom, and frustration. While theoretical ideas and the intricacies of legal doctrines excited me, I thought of courts as places where ideas
and ideals met slow, agonizing deaths. Imagine my trepidation when I found
myself entering a courtroom to engage with the law—with institutions that
I thought were inherently unfair and unjust.

Before my first day in court, at Jawahar's office, I felt as if I were being
snowed under by a blizzard of papers and files. These paper drifts were so
massive that burlap bags and a steel trolley had to be bought to move
them. I took a tentative stab at one of these files and opened it up—it was
like reading a different language. I recognized the words as being mostly in
English, but I was frustrated by their opacity. How was a "161 statement"
different from a "164 statement"? Was the accused discharged or acquitted,
and what was the difference? And what on earth was a "pointing out
memo"? Some words were entirely alien and incomprehensible—*rukka*,
fard makboojgi, *nishandehi*. It was clear that I would have to work hard as
I had much to learn.

Before my first day at the tribunal's hearings, I met a former member of
SIMI, Mohammed Yaseen Falahi, or Yaseen bhai,[2] as I came to call him.
Yaseen bhai said to me, with feigned pride, that of all the hundreds of terrorism cases brought against former SIMI members at the time, he was the
only ex-SIMI member who had been actually convicted of a terrorist offense.
His crime? The police alleged that he had put up a poster in a predominantly
Muslim area in south Delhi at a busy intersection in broad daylight. The
poster, as described in the prosecution's charge sheet, had an "anti-national"
slogan—"Destroy Nationalism. Establish Khilafat"[3]—in big lettering, with
a picture of a closed fist crushing the flags of Russia, the United States, and
India. For putting up this poster—something he denies he did—he was convicted of sedition and of membership in a terrorist organization. Yaseen
bhai told me of his life in jail, of the indignities he had to put up with, but
also the moments of laughter and even friendship. At the time, while I had
only a vague understanding of legal processes, it was clear that he had an
intimate knowledge of the law from his experiences of trial processes. He
spoke with easy familiarity of the *mukhbir*, or secret informer, who alleg-

edly told the police that he was putting up posters, the absence of *panch*, or public witnesses, and the convictions under 124A IPC and s. 20 POTA. He said these words to me, assuming that I understood them completely. Yaseen bhai clearly knew more about the law than I did. My five years at law school had left me unprepared for life in courtrooms.

SIMI was first banned by the government of India in 2001, and the ban lapsed every two years. Each time the government banned the organization, the banning order had to be adjudicated before a tribunal. The association was banned again early in 2008, and the tribunal that was constituted was housed in the Delhi High Court building.

The morning of my first day at the tribunal was a hurricane of activity: files had to be tied together and packed, motions had to be printed off a stubborn printer, and thick books had to be flagged with post-it notes and piled into bags. Jawahar, Anand Singh (Jawahar's clerk), Yaseen bhai, and I scurried around the office trying to make sure that we had not forgotten anything in our last-minute dash to the courts. As we were late, Jawahar asked Yaseen bhai and me to park his car as he ran into the court complex lugging a massive bag, his lawyer's gown billowing behind him, with Anand pulling a trolley carrying files close at his heels.

It was then left to Yaseen bhai, a person who had been convicted of terrorist crimes, to guide me through the courts. After we parked the car, we walked toward the court compound. As we passed through security at Gate No. 5 of the court compound wall, a security guard asked me to deposit my cell phone with the reception. Yaseen bhai raised his voice: "Can't you see he is a lawyer?" and with that I was allowed to keep my cell phone with me. He shepherded me through another security kiosk toward the court building and explained that there were two entries into the court building: one for lawyers and one for the general public. I was to go through the lawyers' entry and meet him inside at the courtroom. He then rapidly shot out directions, telling me to go to the Annexe building, first floor, courtroom number 35. I nodded blankly. Half an hour later, I arrived at the courtroom in the middle of the proceedings, having got lost in the seemingly labyrinthine corridors. I tentatively entered the courtroom and sat down next to Yaseen bhai at the back of the courtroom. These chairs, wooden and without cushions, were meant for the general public and were apparently unworthy of lawyers. He teased me: "Go to the front! Sit with the lawyers! You're supposed to be a lawyer!"

These early days in the courts were confusing. I saw Yaseen bhai hug the police officials who had arrested him and greet the government officials who had banned his organization as if they were old friends. I assumed that Yaseen bhai would be angry with them, but instead it was evident that eight years of regular meetings had led to a certain type of camaraderie that I could not immediately understand. While part of what happened before the tribunal was centered on bigger narratives about the freedom of association and how successive governments had used the law to oppress minority groups, what I found was that most of the time in court was spent going over the minutiae of legal processes: Had the evidence been properly submitted? Were documents properly attested? Could certain questions be allowed during cross-examination?

This new encounter with the courts allowed me to look at this world with fresh eyes. After the SIMI tribunal came to an end, I decided to stay on in Jawahar's office for the next four years. In doing so, not only did I have to learn the language of the law but also how to navigate files and court records. I learned which court officials deal with what types of issues, as I tentatively tried to navigate through the bureaucracy of courtrooms. I learned that persuasion was a subtle art and was jealous of those with the ability to grease palms with ease. I was taken to the best canteen in the court complex and was told where to get the cheapest photocopies. The rhythm of the court and the language of the law began to structure my life, right down to sleeping and eating, my wardrobe, and my gestures and modes of speech. I became fully ensconced in the world of the court. While once I had seen the law as an instrument of oppression and persecution, I now began to see it as opening up a field through which one had to find one's way.

I hope this brief autobiographical foray hints at the direction of this book, but let me explain it explicitly here. Building on the long theoretical association of law and force, certain strands of sociolegal scholarship and critical legal thought have centered on the state's attitude to human life and its exclusionary discourses and practices. At its most benign, the law is seen as an instrument that can affect society by imposing external sanctions and inducements or by shaping social meaning (Sarat and Kearns 1995; Lessig 1998; Sunstein 1996; Goodman 2001; Pound 2002). The law's close association with force means that it is imbued with the ability to determine which lives are worth living and which can be killed. (Agamben 1998, 2005; Gupta 2012; Mbembé 2003). Accordingly, other strands of legal theory have focused on how the law discursively constructs ideas of a life that is worth living and produces images of its subjects. The law here is seen as the harbinger of material as well as epistemic violence. It colonizes the world, destroying life in the process. Imagining the law as violence or coercion leaves us with no way to respond to it—we must either submit to its power or resist it. It leaves no room to account for the ways in which people creatively use and inhabit the law. It has no place for everyday discourses about the law, in which it may also be seen as vulnerable and negotiable in addition to being violent and overwhelming.

To imagine the law purely as a form of physical and epistemic violence is to elide over the significance that it holds in people's everyday lives. As we will see in this book, it is the law's technicalities—the paperwork, legal language, and investigative and courtroom processes—that enables modes of participation and negotiation in the trial process. This is not to say that the lives of my ethnographic interlocutors were not disrupted by their arrests, trials, and detentions. On the contrary, several of them faced brutal torture at the hands of the police, and their years—sometimes more than a decade— in detention during their trials exacted enormous economic, social, and personal costs. Despite these experiences of life-destroying violence, the law's technicalities enabled life to emerge within courtrooms.

Throughout a trial, the law does not operate in a singular, authorial manner. It is a world of various rules, people, institutions, materials, modes of speech, and processes—all of which I refer to as legal technicalities. In focusing on the technicalities of the legal process, this book looks at quotidian aspects of courtrooms that are often passed over by critical theories of law. It understands legal technicalities as enabling modes of participation in the trial process. In doing so, this book departs from ways of thinking about the law as an instrument of social force or as a product of society (Bourdieu 1987; Pottage 2014). These technicalities can be used not only instrumentally to intervene in the trial processes but also as ways to enable participants in the trial to find a footing in courtrooms.

THE TIS HAZARI COURTS

The terrorism trials that I follow in this book took place mostly in Delhi's bustling Tis Hazari Courts Complex. In scholarly works on trials, courtrooms have often been described as theatrical spaces where the state performatively constitutes its own power (Felman 2002; Ertür 2015), while the architecture of courts has also been seen as bearing a visual language symbolizing sovereign authority (Haldar 1994; Mulcahy 2007; Khoraki-wala 2020). Given that it stands on the north side of Delhi's old city, abutting the crumbling walls that once enclosed the former Mughal capital, one could also imagine that the Tis Hazari Courts Complex conveys the sovereign authority of the state through its history as well. The court complex was built on an old ground called Tis Hazari, meaning thirty thousand. I was told by lawyers that that the name recounted the history of the place as the camping ground of thirty thousand troops from the Sikh kingdom before they attacked Delhi and enforced a treaty on the Mughal emperor in the late eighteenth century. As a site of bloody violence and enforced peace-making, this would seem like ideal ground to convey the authority of the law.

Tis Hazari itself does not live up to these grand ideas. It would be difficult to describe these courts as theatrical or dramatic, as scholars of political trials and courtroom architecture might, or as living up to the dramatic history of the ground it is built upon. It is a three-story building in the middle of a larger compound, built in what upper-class South Delhi residents might call "a Public Works Department style." Once Delhi's only district court, the Tis Hazari building presently houses the courts for two of Delhi's nine judicial districts with 136 criminal, civil, labor, family, and traffic courts (Delhi District Courts 2014). It is popularly known as Asia's largest court complex, and by some estimates, about fifty thousand people visit the complex every day. According to statistics available for 2008–09, a total of 357,221 criminal cases were initiated in Delhi's trial courts in that year (Judicial Committee District Courts of Delhi 2008). While judicial districts have been recently redrawn, easing the case burden on the Tis Hazari courts, a total of 69,624 criminal cases were initiated in the year ending November 2019.[4]

Another ethnography of the Tis Hazari courts describes it as a "place of dirty dealings of all sorts" (Mody 2008, 113), where corruption, violence, prejudice, and injustice are endemic. While I did see and hear of a number of underhand dealings, injustices, and acts of violence perpetrated there, the courts could be described in other terms as well. Lawyers would often wistfully talk about the old days, when "sab kuch milta tha" (you could get anything)—from files and law books, to alcohol and *ganja*—in Tis Hazari.

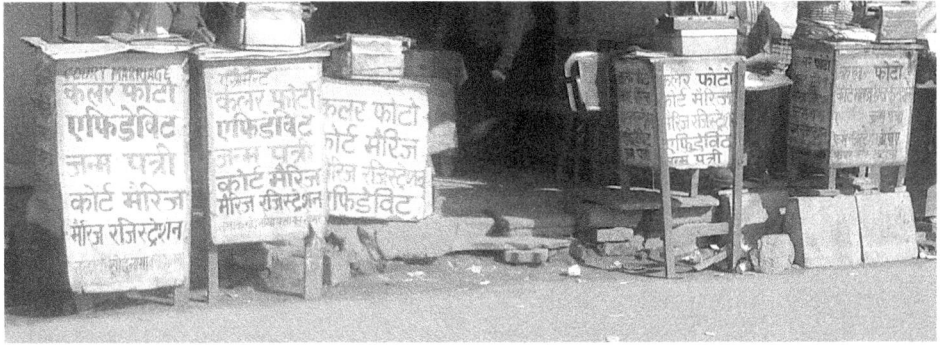

FIGURE 1. Boards adjacent to the Tis Hazari Court building advertising "Colour photo, affidavit, birth certificate, court marriage, marriage registration."

Parts of the compound resembled a marketplace, while other parts looked like the unplanned residential neighborhoods that can be found all over Delhi. This was a space where people plied their trade—from lawyers and court staff to shop owners and canteen workers—and also made their lives (Nigam 2004).

Parts of the compound hold lawyers' offices that seem to have grown over time, like rabbit warrens. Immediately outside the court building, there are large jumbles of steel desks, set up by lawyers, with crude typewriters and tattered files; they sit alongside rows of ramshackle sheds set up by typists and notaries, with advertisements that read "Color Photo, Court Marriage, Affidavit, Birth Certificate, Marriage Registration" (see Figure 1). The compound also holds numerous bookshops, photocopying centers, and stationery shops, as well as small restaurants, chai shops, and *chaat wallahs*. The food attracts monkeys, which enter the courtrooms and not only damage the "court's records but sometimes [also] files and documents [that] are found strewn in the corridors and power cables [that] are found snapped" (*Deccan Herald* 2012).

Depending on where you enter the court compound, you can find yourself either lost in a maze of lawyers' chambers, facing the rush from Delhi's metro rail, or being harassed by local touts offering to conduct all manner of legal paperwork. You may also encounter the court's famous "lock-up," where those under trial are held before and after their day in court. Police vans lumber in from Delhi's two principal jails—Tihar and Rohini—making their way through the anxious crowds streaming into the court.

Once inside the compound, you can enter the main court building through defunct metal detectors and, on occasion, be perfunctorily frisked by a police officer. The building itself is three stories high and is built around a 250-meter-long single corridor that forms the central spine of the building, with courtrooms and offices running along either side of it. The court building also houses the public prosecutors' offices, a police station, a canteen, a lock-up, a bank, an accounts office, record rooms, and a number of judicial and bureaucratic offices.

The courtrooms themselves are often crowded, noisy, and hot, with litigants, officials, and lawyers walking around and talking. Animated families of those facing trials also sometimes add to the unruly atmosphere. As I awkwardly discovered in the Delhi High Court, here, too, the front seats are unofficially reserved for lawyers, while witnesses, police officials, and the accused waiting for their cases occupy the seats at the back of the room.

When you enter a courtroom, your gaze is probably first drawn to the judge's desk. In the Tis Hazari courts, the desk is placed on a raised platform at one end of the courtroom. There is usually a door behind the platform that leads to the judge's personal chambers. Next to the judge's desk there are two or three people, usually men. One is the reader: this person organizes the judge's calendar and manages the daily case files in the court. Another is a stenographer (a senior judge may have two stenographers), who usually sits behind a computer with an attached printer. The stenographer's job is not to transcribe everything that happens in court, but rather to take down the judge's orders and witness depositions. In an effort to get through their heavy caseloads, it is not uncommon for judges to conduct two trials simultaneously, with witnesses and lawyers crowding around the stenographers at either end of the platform, while the judge deals with a third case, interjecting in the recording of evidence only if there is a dispute between the lawyers. As a result, lawyers, witnesses, police officials, and litigants stand huddled at the front of the courtroom near the judge's podium. In some of the smaller courts, there is barely half a meter between the judge and the lawyers. I was told a story about how a lawyer was so angry with a magistrate that he leaned over and slapped her—they were that close to each other.

The fact that all testimony has to be transcribed and that there are no juries means that lawyers are less inclined to perform, and the proceedings are usually quite technical, though often contentious, affairs. What this also means is that since you often cannot see through the crowd, you need to get as close as possible to hear what is being said. Sometimes there are gaps in my field notes regarding arguments or witness depositions simply because I could not get close enough to hear what was being said. A common question that I have been asked in court is "Unhone kya kaha?" (What did they say?)

If you turn your gaze away from the front of the courtroom, where all the "action" is, you begin to notice that there are other people who are alternate centers of activity. One of these, called the *ahlmad*, is in charge of the records of the court, ensuring that the day's files are given to the reader and that the reader returns the files in good order. The ahlmad holds the keys to the massive filing cabinets that store the court's files and signs off on a number of things from stationery requests to witness reimbursements. The ahlmad also ensures that the court's orders are followed through and acts as the link between that particular court and other courts. Among the court's bureaucrats, it is the ahlmad who is given the most bribes; since he controls the files and the court's paperwork, he can determine how quickly summonses are issued, hand out unofficial copies of court papers, and occasionally "lose" or "forget" to deliver a file.

Criminal courts have another official called the *naib court*, a police officer who acts as the Delhi Police's representative in court and is the channel of information between the police and the court. Often, the naib court will issue (on the judge's order) summons for witnesses, coordinate with jail authorities regarding the production of people in custody pending trial, and prepare warrants of arrest. Since he is the link to the Delhi Police and because important police paperwork goes through him, the naib court is another important informal channel of information.

It is in this quotidian world of courtrooms that terrorism trials also take place—a fact that often takes people by surprise. I am often asked, "How did you get access to the courts?" This question imagines terrorism to be an exceptional crime, which is tried in specialized trials screened off from the public and marked by special procedures. As I show later, far from being "exceptional," the terrorism trials that I follow in this book, like other criminal trials, take place in this milieu of ordinary criminal courts. In this book, I seek to move away from thinking about courts as the spectacular staging of sovereignty and of terrorism trials as enacting a state of exception to thinking about courts as everyday spaces marked by mundane legal processes. In doing so, I do not contend that there is no violence, hierarchy, or semiotic power in the structure of the Tis Hazari courtrooms or that there is no performative element in the everyday business of courts, but rather that there are less dramatic and more subtle, contested, and fluctuating ways in which legal power works in the courtroom space. In order to make this argument, this book focuses on legal technicalities.

WHY FOCUS ON LEGAL TECHNICALITIES?

During my time in Delhi's courts, when I asked terror-accused[5] how they felt about their trials, they often narrated their cases in technical terms: Several spoke of how the police had not notified their next of kin of their arrests or had not presented them before a magistrate within twenty-four hours of their arrests, others told me of how the police had fabricated the daily diaries of the police station, one said that the main witness against him had "turned hostile" against the prosecution, while others narrated how the police were not taking proper "sanction to prosecute" before bringing charges under the Unlawful Activities Prevention Act, 1967. Any discussion of the trials immediately turned very technical.

Technicalities are sometimes referred to as "procedural law," which is often distinguished from substantive law. While substantive law is said to deal with the content of particular rules, procedural law deals with how substantive law should be administered. For example, the definition of the crime of murder in a statute as killing a human being with the intent to kill is matter of substantive law. Procedural law, on the other hand, will tell us how a person accused of murder is to be put on trial, the evidentiary processes involved, and how to determine whether this person is guilty of murder. The philosophical distinction between procedural and substantive law in the common law tradition can be traced back to Bentham (Risinger 1982). What accompanied this scholarly separation of procedural from substantive law was the diminution of the latter in favor of the former (Main 2009–10). Substantive law came to be seen as a sphere of worthy scholarship and debate, while procedural law was seen as being mechanical. To use a gendered metaphor sometimes employed by judges and scholars, whereas procedural law can be described as the handmaid, substantive law is said to be the mistress.[6]

While the artificiality of this distinction between substantive and procedural law in legal scholarship has been recognized (Main 2009–10), the hierarchy between these two ostensible categories remains. Often, technicalities are seen as too trivial to warrant attention and are dismissed as "mere technicalities"; they are seen as insignificant when compared with substantive law. This approach stands in marked contrast to the experience of going through a trial, which is dominated by technical questions.

As we will see in this book, technicalities lie at the heart of a trial. Mundane questions occupy lawyers, judges, witnesses, and terror-accused during case hearings: Did the prosecution obtain permission to prosecute a person for terrorism offenses in the proper manner? Were the registers that the police are meant to keep regarding their own movements maintained properly? It was these sorts of technical questions, which asked whether a process was properly followed, that were integral. From a purely instrumental point of view, the reason these technicalities assumed significance is that an eventual conviction or acquittal often depends on how they unfold.

In a legal system that claims to be guided by the rule of law, the ostensible aim of these technicalities in a trial, according to the conventional view (Burns 1999), is to ensure factual accuracy while simultaneously restraining arbitrary governmental action. The technicalities are meant to ensure that the facts brought by the police and prosecution against the defendant are not simply conjured by them. Thus, the police and prosecution must follow certain procedures, both when collecting evidence and when presenting it. As we will see in chapters 4 and 5, it not merely that facts are presented to the court, but rather that investigative and courtroom procedures fabricate the facts. Consequently, any failure to follow these mundane procedures means that certain facts will not be produced, and this can have important consequences at the time of judgment. As these chapters also demonstrate, something as seemingly insignificant as the police's failure to properly fill out a register can lead to an acquittal, and the loss of a file can lead judges to determine that a killing of a "terrorist" by state officials was not a murder, but an accident.

Further, these technicalities do not just produce facts but are also an essential part of determining the meaning of what is known as substantive law. Once facts are produced, the court must then determine whether the facts constitute acts that are prohibited by a criminal statute. To do this, the court has to impart meaning to words used in these enactments. Take

Yaseen bhai's case as an example. The court first determined that he had put up a poster as alleged by the police (a claim that Yaseen bhai contests) and that the poster contained certain words and images. The judge then had to determine whether the act of putting up that poster constituted certain crimes. Was the act of putting up posters that said "Destroy nationalism" an incitement to "hatred," "contempt," or "disaffection toward the Government of India" (i.e., a crime of sedition, under Section 124A of the Indian Penal Code [IPC]) and a display of his "member[ship] of a terrorist organisation" (criminalized under Section 20 of the Unlawful Activities Prevention Act [UAPA])? While the conventional view holds that the words used in a statute have an obvious meaning, and that it is clear whether a particular action falls within a rule, outside of it, or in some gray zone, in Chapter 3, I argue that there is no such thing as an obvious meaning and that legal meaning is constantly produced through the technicalities of legal reasoning. The ethnographic scenes from the book highlight the falsity of the distinction between substantive and procedural law, showing that the issues ostensibly germane to substantive law are also highly technical.

In this book, I build on modes of scholarship that approach technicalities on their own terms. In trying to account for the role played by the technicalities that characterize a trial, this strand of scholarship seeks to understand the *"agency of the technocratic legal form"* (Riles 2005, 980; emphasis in original). Taking a cue from the methodological approaches developed by science and technology studies (STS) and actor-network theory (ANT) and their focus on scientific tools, this approach argues that scholars ought to look at the role of mundane routines and legal technicalities to understand how knowledge is produced. Latour (2010), for example, looks at the how a quintessential legal technology, the file, along with counselors and judges, gradually creates, frames, and decides a legal dispute. In the same vein, Riles (2000, 2005, 2011) argues that legal knowledge is produced by a variety of actants: legal doctrine itself, practitioners of the law (lawyers, judges, bureaucrats, court officials), and the materiality of legal processes. In this view, legal knowledge is an artifact of networks composed of material and nonmaterial and human and nonhuman actants. Riles argues that scholars interested in law ought to study the technicalities of the law to explore how legal processes take on a life of their own in producing juridical truth and how the law is not just a reflection of "wider cultural trends" (Riles 2005, 980).

By focusing on legal process, these scholars have drawn into focus the mundane technicalities that are so often erased in legal studies and highlighted the importance of studying the law on its own terms. They show us that the prosaic rules of procedures and technicalities can be understood beyond their relationship to ideas of social power and that the study of legal processes can be framed beyond the "politics, culture, history or personalities surrounding it" (Riles 2005, 1029). As Pottage (2014) suggests, in this mode of scholarship, the stripping "away [of] the modes of sociality" of law enables us to see the law as a "vehicle for instances and agencies" (150) only for itself.

Riles (2004, 2011) notes that sociolegal scholarship has understood the technicality as both as a means to social control and as a way of solving problems closer to the ground. Accordingly, the legal technicality has been understood as "a tool, a technology for doing something, a means to an end" (Riles 2011, 68), which occludes an appreciation of the means themselves. This mode of scholarship aims to bring attention to how legal tools are actants in their own right, and not just a means to an end.

However, in locating legal technicalities in a wider constellation of actants, the ANT-inflected mode of scholarship deprives these "tools" of any sort of vitality. By locating technicalities within wider assemblages of actants, this mode of scholarship imagines these tools almost as objects that come together with other human and nonhuman actants to produce certain effects. What is missing is an account of the processes of growth, development, and formation of the tools themselves.

This book looks at how terror-accused persons and their lawyers worked with legal technicalities and discovered the potential of these legal tools. As we will see, the significance of legal technicalities and the possibilities they hold are rarely self-evident. Instead, by constantly working with them, the accused and their lawyers revealed the importance and the capacities of these legal technicalities. The terror-accused and their lawyers were co-interpreters of legal texts, actively participating in the construction of the file and becoming comfortable in modes of legal writing. Though seemingly mundane, these technicalities are fraught and highly contested and acquire urgent ethical qualities in the course of a trial—legal language becomes a way to speak in the trial, the file becomes a space in which the world can be made and unmade, the petition becomes a way of imagining a future, and investigative and courtroom procedures become facilitators of unexpected close relationships between the police and the terror-accused. The itineraries of technicalities are important, because they not only determine the outcome of a trial, but also chart possible paths through the lifeworld of the courtroom.

THE TEKHNE OF LAW

In the chapters that follow, I provide an account of the importance of technicalities in the lifeworld of courtrooms. Unlike the conventional idea of the lawyer or judge who learns the law from formal instruction, this account shows that all participants in the trial—the lawyers, judges, police officers, and terror-accused—acquired legal knowledge by actively watching, feeling, listening, reading, writing, and speaking in courtrooms. Theirs is a mode of "knowing from the inside" (Ingold 2013, 1). They had to learn how the law worked, and in turn, how they could work the law. While these technicalities concerned the ways in which things were done by the police or in the courts, they were also the modes through which the terror-accused and their lawyers engaged with the trial process. Technicalities were forms of practical knowledge that constantly emerged through working with the law.

The terror-accused I met in Delhi's courts were not abandoned souls who had been left adrift by the legal process. Instead, they actively participated in the courtroom procedures. In the words of one of my interlocutors, while they may not have had formal training as a lawyer (or *akshar gyan*, literally "letter knowledge"), they had *anubhav gyan*, or experiential knowledge of legal processes. Their knowledge of the legal process "gr[ew] from the crucible of practical and observational engagements with beings and things" (Ingold 2013, 6) around them. The basis of this experiential knowledge was the technicalities of the trial process—legal forms, texts, and doctrines; paperwork; and police and court procedures—that are central to the activity in trials.

Through theoretical insights from ecological approaches in anthropology, I look at legal technicalities as the *"conditions of possibility of life"* Ingold 2011, 85; emphasis in original) in a courtroom and specifically at the ways in which these technicalities enable terror-accused persons to intervene in their trials and find their footing in the courtroom. In bringing the "dwelling perspective" (Ingold 1995, 2000) to the legal process, this book argues that the law—through its procedures, materials, and personnel—

provides the means through which terror-accused weave themselves into the fabric of life in the courtrooms. To think of legal technicalities as providing avenues of participation is to depart from understanding the experience of law solely as a process of loss of meaning and a deprivation of the possibility of justice (Parmar 2015; Mertz 2007).

An ethnographic understanding of legal technicalities draws us close to the etymological root of "technicality"—namely, *tekhne*, which means "to craft," "to weave," or "to fabricate." Tekhne involves knowledge practices that reveal themselves the more they are engaged with (Heidegger 1977). Accordingly, this book imagines legal technicalities as materials worked upon by craftspeople, who learn their trade as they work with these materials. Like craftspeople, who do not simply impose form upon their materials,[7] but rather see what forms emerge through their work, the terror-accused constantly work with legal technicalities as a way of intervening in their case. This book seeks to highlight how creativity and improvisation with legal technicalities lie at the heart of the trial process.

This way of understanding a legal technicality emerges from an intimate, dexterous relationship with the law, allowing knowledge to grow from working with people and things—police officers, legal texts, files, and modes of speech and writing—involved in the investigative and judicial processes. Such knowledge is gained through a slow process. Rather than being deliberate or intentional, knowledge of the legal process emerges through contingent and tentative attempts at using and responding to legal technicalities and through experimenting with legal technicalities to see what possibilities emerge. It is almost as if engaging with the legal process has a tactile element to it—we feel our way around to see what range of movement is possible. In this book, I look at how some terror-accused slowly taught themselves the ins and outs of investigative procedures, which enabled them to show that the police had fabricated the evidence against them. I provide an account of how the terror-accused slowly and collaboratively learned legal language and produced meanings for legal texts, how they learned to produce facts through the court file, and deployed various modes of legal writing.

The reason why terror-accused persons engaged with legal technicalities should be obvious: They were seeking ways to avoid a conviction. They learned the law, understood how the police are supposed to prepare and file their paperwork, and how court processes occur, thus engaging with a variety of different technicalities. They sought to develop skills to engage with legal technicalities to offset the very real threat that they might be convicted and spend the rest of their lives in prison. At the same time, working with technicalities enabled the terror-accused to find a footing in the lifeworld of the trial. Legal procedures and technicalities were modes of inhabiting the courtroom in order to escape it.

This is not to suggest that any of the participants in the trial had a mastery of the law and that they knew the potential of every legal technicality. Far from it. Among the various experiences narrated in this book, we will encounter judges who do not know the law, a prosecutor who gets trapped by his own words, and documents that can be read against themselves. Uncertainty is at the heart of any engagement with the law. Moreover, any engagement with the police, the file, and legal texts is risky, as one can never determine what the result of such an engagement might be. Hence, while the cultivation of tekhne of the law was in response to the threat, the engagement with legal technicalities also perpetuates this threat (Weber 1989). As the itineraries of legal technicalities can never be known in advance, they had equal chances of harming or helping the terror-accused.[8] As we will see in this book, even as the terror-accused and their lawyers creatively used technicalities to intervene in the trial process, the police and prosecution used these same technicalities to exclude them from it.

TEKHNE, VOICE, AND EMBODIMENT

Following Cavell's injunction to bring the human voice back into philosophy (1994, 58), this book similarly attempts to bring the human voice into the law. This voice is tethered to human lives, with all their passions, demands, and vulnerabilities. In this book, I hope to show the ways in which voice emerges through the work with legal technicalities and how technicalities emerge as a way through which voice is embodied. Amid the grind of courtroom procedures, I found letters written to judges appealing for justice, which conveyed both intimacy and vulnerability; a knowledge of legal procedure that was deployed with hope and trepidation; a cautious faith in the courts and a deep sense of betrayal when this trust was belied.

Implicit in the idea of tekhne is the idea of a future, of a future that has not arisen as yet, but could come to be. Importantly, it is a future that is demanded. The terror-accused engaged with technicalities in an effort to be let out on bail, and eventually to be acquitted by the courts. They engaged with technicalities to show that witnesses were lying, to demonstrate that documents were fabricated, in the eventual hope that the judge would be persuaded by their claims. To engage with technicalities, is therefore to confront, to demand, and to persuade in an effort to obtain a particular future. This highlights what ordinary language philosophers might call the perlocutionary dimensions of the law.

In Austin's influential text (1962), the perlocutionary utterance, which is understood as a speech act that produces certain affects, is distinguished from the illocutionary, which is a type of utterance that does something. In Austin's text, the illocutionary act is largely associated with the idea of the performative, on basis that both are largely conventional (Austin 1962, 103); this implies that in order for an illocutionary utterance to be successful, it must be uttered in certain settings and in a certain form (Cavell 2005, 187). The utterance of a judge who says "I sentence you" will be successful (or "felicitous," to use Austin's phrasing) because of the institutional settings in which this statement is said.[9] The success of the perlocutionary, which is something that is dismissed as irrelevant in Austin's text, is contingent on the effects it produces upon the listener. Thus while the success of the illocutionary depends on convention, the perlocutionary is understood through the effects that it produces.

Though the illocutionary has received widespread discussion in political thought, the perlocutionary has only recently received the attention of scholars who have attempted to understand the central significance of this category of utterance (Cavell 2005; Lorenzini 2015, 2020; Laugier 2020). As we will see in Chapter 3, a focus on the illocutionary has meant that some theorists have understood Austin to be showing us how speech acts may be successful. However, as Cavell (1995) notes, Austin is drawing our attention to the ways in which speech acts may fail and we may become vulnerable to language. The focus on the illocutionary has been at the cost of neglecting passionate aspects of speech, where human desires and vulnerabilities come into play.

In working with technicalities, the terror-accused and their lawyers are making demands of the police and prosecution and are seeking to persuade the judge to accede to their claims. This is not the language of the illocutionary, but of the perlocutionary. The perlocutionary is the site of confrontation, persuasion, and human frailty. The perlocutionary draws attention to our demands, desires, frustrations, failures, and vulnerabilities. It is the perlocutionary that constitutes the "textures of human existence" (Laugier 2020, n.p.) in the courtroom. The law becomes a mode of confrontation and making claims, but also a way of expressing human vulnerability. By understanding how the terror-accused worked with technicalities, we can attend to the ways in which human voice emerge through the law.

In focusing on embodiment and voice in legal technicalities, this book departs from two types of scholarship: One focuses on the "exceptional" nature of terrorism laws and the other on the location of trials in society. Regarding the first, many accounts of terrorism laws are thought of as enacting a state of exception, whereas my time in the courts shows that terrorism trials often looked like ordinary criminal trials, albeit marked by certain technical differences. Regarding the second, trials are often viewed as extensions of social hierarchies and conflicts and as providing a unique vantage point from which to study society. In the next sections, I engage with these arguments.

ANTI-TERROR LAWS AND THE "STATE OF EXCEPTION"

When I first began thinking about this project, my aim was to flesh out the idea of the state of exception ethnographically. I was interested in how the idea of the emergency played out in terrorism trials. I wanted to look at how courts understood legal texts and procedures, in the context of the perceived existential threat posed by terrorism. At that point in time, I was taken with Agamben's (1998, 2005) juridical genealogy of the state of exception and bare life. In his works, the state of emergency lies at the heart of the modern state; this idea is echoed by some histories of the Indian state (Hussain 2003; Samadar 2006). In Agamben's work, the paradigm of modern political life is the concentration camp and not the city. Whereas in the city, citizens are governed by laws, in concentration camps, where there is no law, humans take the form of bare life, and their lives can be taken away at will by the sovereign power. Indeed, given the impunity with which the police appear to deal with terror-accused persons and the costs exacted by anti-terror laws on the lives of the terror-accused and their families, it was difficult for me not to be taken in by this nihilistic vision. The condition of vulnerability in which life exists in the face of state power in terrorism trials initially confirmed Agamben's theses for me. But as we will see in the next section,

I found it difficult to sustain this view after my encounters with the trial courts.

Far from responding to emergency situations, the history of pre- and post-independence India shows us that the enactment of anti-terror statutes is cyclical, with anti-terrorism and security laws being periodically enacted, struck down, repealed, and reenacted (Kalhan et al. 2006). The persistence of such legislations belies the idea they are responding to exceptional events that are temporary. Despite this, the "state of exception" is the predominant way in which such laws have been thought of in colonial India as well as after independence in 1947.

In colonial India, the state harnessed the idea that revolutionary violence demanded an emergency legal regime (Ghosh 2017; McQuade 2021). Anxieties over what such violence may mean for the stability of the state led colonial administrators to argue that "ordinary" laws were not enough to deal with extraordinary violence and that emergency legislation was required to ensure that trails were over quickly. What was necessary to deal with such violence, colonial administrators argued, were special rules of procedure and evidence.[10] In other words, the "state of exception" presented by this violence was responded to not with a withdrawal of law (Schmitt 1985), but with an attention to legal technicalities.

Special legal technicalities populate many laws that attempted to tackle revolutionary violence in colonial India. Take, for instance, the Criminal Law Amendment Act 1908, which was enacted in response to the attempted killing of a magistrate in Bengal and a series of other bombing conspiracies (Ghosh 2017, 42; McQuade 2021, 117). The first part of the 1908 act provided for special procedures (such as prohibiting bail for accused; trial by judges rather than by jury; and special rules of evidence) ostensibly aimed at ensuring a quicker trial.[11]

As De (2014) points out, these special rules often went hand in hand with the creation of special courts and tribunals. Special courts with special rules of evidence and procedure were created in various colonial jurisdictions to deal with revolutionary violence in different parts of the British Empire. These special courts were set up to isolate these trials from the public view and to deal with them quickly and effectively (De 2014; McQuade 2021).

For example, in 1917, the Indian colonial government set up a special committee known alternatively as the Sedition Committee, or the Rowlatt Committee (named after its chairperson Justice Sidney Rowlatt), to "investigate and report on the nature and extent of the criminal conspiracies connected with the revolutionary movement in India" (Sedition Committee 1918, iii).[12] The committee recommended special rules of evidence and procedure that it believed would make convictions in such cases easier to achieve: allowing confessions, removing the need for corroboration of accomplice testimony, modified procedures including the removal of commitment proceedings and a jury, and very limited grounds of appeal. While it created no substantive crimes, the changes recommended were highly technical: it recommended that certain classes of general crimes in notified disturbed areas be tried with these modified rules of procedure and evidence.[13]

The Anarchical and Revolutionary Crimes Act, 1919, was enacted following the Rowlatt Committee's recommendations.[14] It allowed for the governor general to declare "the whole or any part of British India" as areas in which "anarchical or revolutionary acts are being promoted."[15] Once that declaration was in place, the act allowed for the setting up of special courts[16] that would try specified offenses under the Indian Penal Code, 1860, and other criminal statutes.[17] In other words, it did not create new crimes, but created new courts and new procedures to deal with ordinary, yet specifically designated, crimes. Once such a declaration was made, the act allowed warrantless search, seizures, and arrests and prescribed a summary procedure for people accused of general crimes in notified areas. The government was given the power to determine when and in which cases this modified procedure should be followed.[18]

Independent India has followed a similar trajectory by focusing on technical aspects of the trial. While the enactment of the constitution in 1950 changed the way in which exceptional procedures (such as referring the trial of specific people to special courts) could be effected,[19] postcolonial anti-terror laws also created special courts and enacted special rules of evidence and procedure. In the logic of the state, these "exceptional" procedural and evidentiary laws are necessary to ensure that terrorists are "speedily tried and punished" (Malimath et al. 2003, 226).

The Terrorist Affected Areas (Special Courts) Act, 1984 followed a tactic adopted under the Anarchical and Revolutionary Crimes Act, 1919. Enacted during the insurgency in Punjab, the Special Courts Act enabled the government to declare parts of the country as terrorist-affected areas and to set up special courts that had modified procedural and evidentiary rules and that curtailed the right of appeal. These special courts, again, would adjudicate specified offenses of generally applicable criminal law.

While previous legislations provided for different procedures to try terrorist acts, which were charged as general crimes, they did not define the meaning of the word "terrorism."[20] This changed with first the enactment of the Terrorist and Disruptive Activities (Prevention) Act (TADA), 1985,[21] and then the Prevention of Terrorism Act (POTA), 2002.[22] These two legislations (which are no longer in force) created a new crime of "terrorist act"[23] and reprised similar themes of special evidentiary and procedural rules. They allowed ordinary courts to deviate from the Indian Evidence Act, 1872, and the Code of Criminal Procedure, 1973. TADA and POTA allowed confessions made to a police officer admissible in evidence in a contentious departure from the Indian Evidence Act, which barred such confessions.[24] TADA and POTA both created designated courts and allowed for extended periods of up to 180 days in pre-charge detention and permitted in-camera trials (i.e., with only witnesses, lawyers, and the defendants present), the withholding of witnesses' identities from the accused, and interceptions of electronic communication. Under both acts, the prosecutor had to consent to the granting of bail to suspects. Both acts also reversed the burden of proof in some instances.

India's current anti-terror statute—the Unlawful Activities (Prevention) Act, 1967[25]—includes many of the same evidentiary and procedural provisions as TADA and POTA. It contains an expanded definition of what constitutes the crime of terrorism (including damage to the "monetary stability of India by way of production, smuggling or circulation of" counterfeit Indian currency). It also enacts punishments for other terror-related offenses (conspiracy, harboring, and so on) and allows for the designation of terrorist organizations. And it also repeats the special procedures and evidentiary rules for terrorism trials. These include an extended period of permitted custodial detention with the police (of up to thirty days, instead of up to fifteen days for ordinary crimes); an extended period of pre-charge detention (of up to 180 days, instead of up to ninety days for ordinary crimes); special rules regarding bail that make it virtually impossible for a person accused of terrorist crimes to be granted bail pending the trial; and the concealment of witness identity from the defendant and the defense lawyers.

A subsequent legislation—the National Investigative Authority Act, 2008—reprises procedural moves to deal with the "emergency" caused by terrorism. Enacted in the wake of the attacks in Mumbai in November 2008 and anxieties over an emasculated state,[26] it authorized the central government to direct that the investigation and prosecution of terrorism offenses be taken out of the hands of the state governments and transferred to a special agency: the National Investigation Agency (NIA). The constitution accords primacy to the state governments to prosecute crimes and to maintain public order. One minister for the government justified the transferring the prosecution of terrorism crimes to the central government by placing terrorism on a different footing: as a war against the nation and a threat to every citizen, not merely a problem of law and order.[27]

In what was by now a well-worn tactic, the NIA Act also set up special courts and modified the procedure where the NIA is the prosecuting agency by authorizing the special court to act simultaneously as a Court of Sessions and as a magistrate. It repeated the provisions for in-camera trials and non-disclosure of witness identities that were found in the colonial legislations, TADA, POTA, and the UAPA.

Given that anxieties over the "exceptional" threat posed by terrorism crystalized in the form of legal technicalities, it is unsurprising that contemporary scholars and activists locate the locate the "state of emergency" in the technical provisions of anti-terror statutes (Pandey 2020; Singh 2007). It is these minutiae of anti-terrorism laws that, according to activists and academics, have allowed the governments and police to oppress peoples' movements, target minority populations, violate citizens' fundamental rights, and undermine the constitution. It is these mundane technicalities that allow governments and the police to act with impunity (Chatterjee 2017). Technical deviations from ordinary criminal laws have enabled the targeting of minority populations, civil society organizations, and peoples' movements (Balagopal 1989; Suresh and Raja 2012; Suresh 2019).

For human rights activists in India, these "extraordinary" anti-terror laws—and the special rules of evidence and procedure within them—represent a "silent emergency," as they effectively criminalize fundamental rights by granting immense powers to the police and executive and allow the police to commit acts of violence such as torture, arbitrary detention, kidnapping, and extortion under the cover of legality (Human Rights Watch 2011). Human rights groups and academics have drawn our attention to the fact that the aim of anti-terror laws is not criminal sanction, since few terrorism trials ever reach a conviction;[28] rather, the technical rules of anti-terror laws (especially related to bail) show that they are intended to keep people in jail for as long as possible to suppress democratic activity and minority groups (Navlakha 2003; Krishnan 2004; Kalhan et al. 2006). There is ample evidence that anti-terror laws are used to target religious and ethnic minorities (such as Muslims and Dalits) as well as to stifle forms of democratic dissent.[29] In bringing this to light, human rights activists see these laws as fundamentally anti-democratic and as an assault upon constitutionally enshrined fundamental rights and the separation of powers (Singh 2006, 2007; Coordination of Democratic Rights Organisations 2012).

BEYOND THE "STATE OF EXCEPTION"

However, paying close attention to the arguments made by activists and some academics reveals that they understand the exception differently from those theorists who argue that the rule of law is actually the state of emergency lurking in disguise.[30] Unlike Agamben, who argues that the inherent nature of the law itself leads to the state of exception, human rights activists have argued that "exceptional" terrorism laws should be repealed and, by implication, that "ordinary" criminal laws should be used to prosecute acts of violence (Balagopal 1994; Coordination of Democratic Rights Organisations 2012; Jamia Teachers Solidarity Association 2014). These laws are exceptional not just because they reveal that the "purpose of sovereignty is to produce bare life" (Agamben 1998, 181), but because they pose a fundamental challenge to the idea of the rule of law and constitutionalism. In casting these laws as exceptional, scholars and civil liberties organizations are not seeking to upend all law but to return to a form of law that is democratically accountable and protects constitutional principles.[31]

Furthermore, from the perspective of everyday life in courtrooms, viewing the terrorism trial through the idea of the emergency is difficult to sustain. What I found in courts was that there were many different types of criminal trials, each marked by its own special procedures and evidentiary laws. While it is true that anti-terror laws prescribe some different procedures and evidentiary rules, this is also true for other statutes. A number of enactments—the Scheduled Caste and Scheduled Tribe (Prevention of Atrocities) Act, the Prevention of Money Laundering Act, the Narcotic Drugs and Psychotropic Substances Act, and the Protection of Children from Sexual Offences Act, to name a few—all contain departures from the generally applicable Code of Criminal Procedure, 1973, and the Indian Evidence Act, 1872.

Instead of being exceptional, anti-terror laws, like these other statutes, are instances of what Hussain calls "hyperlegality" (2007a; 2007b). According to Hussain, modern law is based not on the universal applicability of a uniform set of laws, but rather on the separation and classification of people and offenses and the application of differential sets of laws to them. Instead of the emptying out of law in the state of exception, "we find not an emptying out of law but an abundant use of technical distinctions, differing regulations, and multiple invocations of authority" (Hussain 2007a, 740). Where Agamben would see a state of exception, other scholars would see a typical form of classification, where different laws are applied to different circumstances (Eckert 2009).

Although terrorism trials stand apart from other criminal trials in certain aspects such as bail, pretrial detention, and the admissibility of certain forms of evidence, terrorism and other criminal trials are also based on the same technicalities. The investigative processes are the same for terrorism offenses as they are for other offenses, and the police have to fill out the same paperwork. The trials for the terrorism cases included in this study were no different: Witnesses had to be sworn in, stenographers had to type out witness depositions, and the modes of argumentation by lawyers and judges were similar. While judges can hold terrorism trial proceedings in camera, they often also do the same for cases involving sexual assault or children.

As an example of the different types of trials that are linked by common technicalities, we can point to the idea of jurisdiction. In arguing that terrorism laws constitute a permanent state of exception, some may point to the fact that laws have created special courts to try terrorism offenses[32] (Singh 2007, 72). Often, however, these special courts are merely ordinary courts that have been given different jurisdictions. For example, the designation of one of the judges whose courtroom I frequented during my fieldwork reads "ASJ-07/TADA/POTA/MCOCA/POCSO/SEBI." This means that this judge, the Additional Sessions Judge No. 7, had other criminal jurisdictions conferred on his court apart from his regular criminal jurisdiction under the Indian Penal Code—that of TADA and POTA, the Maharashtra Control of Organised Crime Act (MCOCA), the Protection of Children from Sexual Offences Act (POSCO), and for economic offenses under the Securities and Exchange Board of India (SEBI) Act. In a day, typically, this judge would handle several cases, and hence, may be sitting in several jurisdictions. For example, he may sit as a Sessions Court judge for general offenses under the penal code, but he may also sit as a designated court (with the modified procedures) under TADA or as a special court under POSCO and have special powers conferred on him by virtue of other laws. It is the same ordinary trial court that sits in different jurisdictions and has different powers in each jurisdiction.

The idea of the exception also hides how legal technicalities enable the terror-accused and their lawyers to actively participate in the trial. For example, in Chapter 2, I look at how the police fabricated a charge against several Kashmiri men. The police claimed that the men had planned to cause explosions in parts of Delhi and that they had been arrested just as they entered the city. The men, on the other hand, claimed that they had been kidnapped by the police and that the police had planted evidence and in some instances blatantly lied to the court in the pretrial proceedings. It is tempting to understand this event as an instance of an exception, where, using the cover provided by anti-terror laws, the police framed and charged several innocent men, who had to wait in jail for eight long years to be acquitted by the trial court. The men in this vignette could be understood as forms of bare life, upon whose bodies the state of exception had been enacted. This framing, however, elides over what happened after the men had been charged by the Delhi Police—that is, they slowly and collaboratively taught themselves legal procedures and used the police's own paperwork to show that the police had fabricated the case. As I show in that chapter, their investment in learning legal technicalities was built not just on the idea that paying attention to the technicalities could help them demonstrate how the police had lied, but also on the hope that the law could be a path to justice.

To be clear: I am arguing that terrorism trials *are* different from other criminal trials in several specific ways. As stated above, they have different rules regarding bail, pretrial detention, and the admissibility of certain forms of evidence. They are also used to target minority populations and democratic rights activists. In practice, they permit a near-indefinite detention and are marked by unfairness. But they are not "exceptional" in the sense that Agamben uses the term.

Further, terrorism laws are different in another way—namely, because of the modes of sociality that are engendered by their technicalities. The fact that it was virtually impossible to get bail in terrorism trials meant that the terror-accused were all kept in detention—before and during their trials—for years on end. During this period, they got to know each other, police officers, and court officials quite well. Different terror-accused individuals from different cases often shared the same lawyers. They knew the same police officers, and the same few designated judges presided over their cases. As the ethnographic narratives presented in this book show, the terror-accused worked collaboratively to understand the specific rules that governed their trials. They shared information about various judges and police officials, and they also shared strategies on points of law.

Framing terrorism trials through the idea of the exception hides this everyday life in trial courts. I could easily describe the lives of these men and other terror suspects in terms of bare life that exists in a perpetual emergency, with their personhood on the brink of an apocalypse. However, this would entail a failure to attend to the quotidian complexities of everyday life in courtrooms. I would then have failed to describe the multiple ways in which terror-accused persons creatively use legal technicalities in inhabiting the courtroom. It would have meant ignoring how terror-accused individuals, in collaboratively understanding and deploying legal technicalities, slowly built ways of being together. I could also describe the law as inherently and unchangeably violent, as a totalizing force, but that too would not take into account the hope placed in the law and the disappointments with the law when it fails us. In short, framing terrorism trials through the state of exception would occlude any view of the tekhne of the law.

THE LAW'S RELATIVE AUTONOMY

In this book, I look at legal technicalities as ways in which participants in the trial make their way through courtroom processes. In doing so, I depart from modes of law and anthropology scholarship that look at legal processes as ways of understanding society. There are two ways in which this has been done: The first looks at legal institutions not as separate from but as firmly located in society, and the second looks at how discourses emerging from within courtrooms produce society. In both these modes of scholarship, the processes that occur within legal institutions are inextricably linked to society.

The first mode enmeshes courts and other legal institutions in society and looks at legal rules and processes as being penetrated by social relations and power structures outside of these institutions. Most ethnographies of courtrooms in India operate within a legal pluralism framework (Berti 2011, 357). Reflecting trends in global scholarship that seeks to understand the place of law *in* society (Starr and Collier 1989; Nader 2002; Berti 2009; Goodale 2017), these ethnographies understand courtrooms as a node in the broader social and political environment. For example, an early work by Cohn (1965) looks at how courts, lawyers, and other officials are enmeshed in wider social networks. Cohn outlines the various ways in which the lower courts are extensions of society, which is evidenced by the use of community-based networks inside courts to channel information and bribes or the use of the courts by people from lower castes to challenge upper-caste dominance. Similarly, Galanter (1968–69) aims to move the understanding of the Indian legal system away from questions of legal doctrine to looking at the people who inhabit the lower levels of the judiciary in order to understand "who they are, what they do, how they interact with one another and with other social groups" (202). He also argues that the law is a path to study modern India and that legal ethnographers should look at court cases as windows into aspects of, and conflicts in, Indian society (Galanter 1992, 3). Likewise, Berti (2011) argues that court cases are not just important to study the unfolding of legal rules by which disputes are settled, but also highlight the workings of society from the "vantage point of litigation and arbitration" (355).[33]

This mode of thinking about legal institutions, as being entirely colonized by society and politics, has been extended to writings about terrorism trials as well. Terrorism trials in India have been looked at as shedding light on the fractures in ideas of Indian citizenship, communal identities, and anxieties over the strength of the state. Terrorism trials are not just about adjudicating the guilt or innocence of the accused, but also form a way of thinking about subjectivity, social identity, citizenship along the lines of religious, caste, or ethnic identity, and the nature of the Indian state and security apparatus. Writings about anti-terror trials in India have highlighted the idea of citizenship as being distributed unequally through society, with Muslims and Dalits bearing the brunt of anti-terror laws. While some authors have framed India's anti-terror laws in the context of the global "war on terror," others have also sought to look at them through the lens of the rise of Hindu majoritarianism, a recurring theme through India's recent history (Balagopal 1994; Chomsky 2005; Mukherji 2005; Sengupta 2006; Roy

2006). According to these works, the social and political world intercedes in court processes, making the latter contingent and negotiable. Further, the law is seen as a tool for understanding the contours and fault lines that run through society. Here, anti-terror trials are seen as symptomatic of nationalist politics, where religious, caste, and economic minorities are targeted using anti-terror laws.

The second way in which courtrooms have been understood as extensions of society has been by examining how the discourse employed in trials constructs the social. Here, the emphasis is not on how the trial is inflected by local social networks from the outside but how social categories are discursively constructed and deployed within the trials. While for the first strand of scholarship, the social flows into courtroom processes, for the second strand, the social is an effect of the courtroom (Philips 1994, 2000; Bunt 2008; Ran-Rubin 2008; Rubin 2008). This approach to a trial asks how representations of social categories emerge through various courtroom processes.

This is not to say that these modes are exclusive of one another. For example, Baxi's (2014) work on rape trials in Gujarat shows how identity, social hierarchy, and criminal culpability are constructed through courtroom processes, even as social pressures from "outside" buffet courtroom processes. It demonstrates how the trappings of official legal procedures are used to cover social pressures that enter the trial, as well as the ways in which the trial discursively constructs the identity of the rape victim and her relationship with her own body and with the perpetrators of the crime.

Both modes of scholarship thus look at trials as microcosms of society. These two ways of understanding the trial make important contributions to theorizing the law. They challenge the law's self-image of being based purely on rules and show that legal processes are not immured from the outside world but are intimately connected to it. They also show how courtroom processes feed off, reify, and duplicate forms of public discourse and, in doing so, construct an imagination of social categories and relationships.

However, the issue I take with these modes of understanding legal technicalities is precisely this: Within them, either society enters legal processes from the outside or social categories are produced within the courtroom and are articulated through legal procedures. These views argue that courtroom trials are social and political conflicts that have been translated into a legal dispute. These modes of scholarship assume a preexisting society—with structures, hierarchies, and conflicts—to which the court case is merely affixed. It is almost as if the "social" can be used to explain everything that happens within courtrooms.[34] This sort of understanding reaches an analytical limit, however, when one ascribes a certain type of politics to every type of legal technicality. For example, is it always possible to see communal politics and ideas of the security state in mundane judicial questions such as, say, verifying whether a document had been properly attested and certified?

This sort of argumentation—of seeing the law through wider society and politics—rarely comes up in courtrooms. It is almost as if the courtroom space is evacuated of larger social and political questions and is focused solely on technicalities. While looking at anti-terror trials in India through the lens of Hindu majoritarianism and the expansion of the security state helps us to locate these laws politically, to understand the social and human costs of these laws, and to belie the "independence" and "rationality" of the law, it comes at the cost of occluding what happens in these trials.

Instead, this book's focus on technicalities shows how the law is both an extension of politics and society and independent of it. In focusing on the technicalities, this book does not argue that the law is entirely independent of society (as some ANT-inflected scholarship, discussed earlier, might argue). Nor does it argue that legal processes are nothing but extensions of society, as those approaches described above might contend. Rather, echoing Skocpol's (1985) argument about the relationship between state and society, this book argues that legal processes are relatively autonomous. This is to say that while politics emerges through legal technicalities, they are not entirely subsumed it. By focusing on legal technicalities, we are able to look at legal knowledge not as being entirely colonized by society and politics outside of the courtroom, but as emerging through and being simultaneously limited by legal processes. For example, in Chapter 4 we will see how the state used the technicalities around paperwork to fabricate a narrative in which the army's killing of a man in Kashmir was an accident. While the approaches outlined above might have settled at narrating this case as one where the oppression in Kashmir extends into the courtroom, I also try to highlight the (ultimately unsuccessful) technical maneuvers that the man's widow and her lawyers used to try to push back against the state's narrative.

In looking at how various individuals work with legal technicalities, we can also see how modes of sociality emerge within the courtroom. For instance, in Chapter 2, I consider how the terror-accused collaborated with each other to produce legal meaning, while in Chapter 3, I provide an account of how a judgment in one terrorism case was repurposed by other defendants in their own trials. While other scholars (Cover 1983; Baxi 1999) have provided accounts of how the narratives built around foundational legal texts provide a basis on which communities may be built, this book looks at how working with technicalities is a collaborative process that creates temporary communities of legal knowledge.

Following legal technicalities as they unfold in the trial process also helps us see the law as tekhne and to explore both its embodied and affective dimensions. For instance, in Chapter 1, I show how the detention of terror-accused mandated by the UAPA led to unexpected forms of intimacy emerging between the police and terror-accused individuals. In Chapter 2, I look at how the ability to produce legal meaning gives the terror-accused the ability to find a footing in the space of the courtroom. In Chapter 3, I look at how the ability to tie the state to its word gives terror-accused persons hope that they may be released, and in Chapter 6, I look at how petitioning writing enables certain forms of voice to emerge.

ETHNOGRAPHY AND THE KAFKAESQUE

Another way in which terrorism trials have been framed is through reference to Kafka (Ahmad 2014; Duffy 2018; Herbert 2006; Sethi 2014; Wax 2008). Literature about the legal response to terrorism, in India and elsewhere, often invokes Kafka to describe the violent, absurd, and disorienting nature of terrorism trials. Terrorism laws and trials that are marked by "arbitrary detention, secret evidence, secret allegations and brutal interrogation methods" (Duffy 2018, 50) are seen as Kafkaesque. These writings draw attention to the fear and alienation that terror suspects often face when confronted by the "gigantic juridical machinery" (Ahmad 2014). In understanding Kafka to speculate on the inscrutable anonymity and monstrous machinery of state power, these writings can be seen as gesturing toward theological and metaphysical readings of Kafka's works.

While the terrorism trials I witnessed could be described in these terms, there are other ways of understanding Kafka and the trials. That is, rather than reading Kafka's works as allegories of political power or philosophical abstractions, I read them as ethnographies in that they call attention to the temporalities of waiting, to the grim comedies and petty hierarchies of bureaucratic life. In this understanding of the Kafkaesque, the law is characterized not by its transcendence, but by its localization. In many of his works, Kafka is concerned with the everyday life of the law. Those of his protagonists who engage with the law spend their time waiting, reading, writing, filing, bribing, and punishing. These actions are far from boring or incidental as they are crucial points in the movement of plot. In this version of the Kafkaesque, the law is not an enigma, but a field of continuous intensities, marked by desire, experimentation, comedy, and confrontation (Deleuze and Guattari 1986).

It is this latter idea of the Kafkaesque that this book draws on. Indeed, the start of my fieldwork was marked by a minor bureaucratic comedy. Through my involvement with practicing lawyers and human rights groups, I knew of three terrorism trials. However, since I wanted to follow all terrorism cases being heard in Delhi, I filed a right to information application asking for details of terrorism cases and their forthcoming dates of hearing.[35] The response I received ostensibly provided me a list of all the terrorism trials then currently underway in Delhi. This list of fourteen cases did not include the three trials that I previously knew about.

In total I followed eighteen cases for fourteen months between December 2011 and March 2013. In addition to the cases mentioned above, I also followed one case (which I discuss in Chapter 1) in which an accused terrorist shot and killed a police officer. While the defendant—whom I call Shahid—was not charged with terrorist offenses in this trial, terrorism formed a part of the narrative presented by the prosecution.

Once I found out about the cases, I found myself, like the protagonists in Kafka's work, doing a lot of waiting in courtrooms. These cases would not be heard every day, and they were usually listed once a week or once a fortnight. When the cases were listed, I would head to the courtroom and wait in back with the terror-accused for the case to be called by the reader. While lawyers, police officers, and the terror-accused often said that waiting in courts for cases to be called was a waste of time, this seemingly pointless period of waiting often proved to be the most productive for my fieldwork, since it was during this time that I was able to speak with many of the terror-accused and their families. In some of the cases, I was able to meet and speak with the terror-accused as often as twice a week. Since I had been following these cases for several years, I had built a close rapport with some of the defendants, their families, the defense and prosecution lawyers, and the policemen dealing with the cases. Sitting at the back of the court, with a pen and notebook in hand, I wrote down conversations I had with terror-accused, police officials, and lawyers. The accused told me how they had been arrested and what their experiences of the trial process had been. We also traded gossip about lawyers and judges—which lawyers were good, which ones were not, which judges were thought to be close to the Delhi police and which ones were honest and upright. Because terror-accused individuals had to wait years—sometimes more than a decade—for their trials to be completed,[36] they also told me about how networks of terror-accused persons grew in jails during their long years of incarceration and how information, knowledge, and strategy were shared among those in these networks. They also told me about their lives in jail, their pasts, and their plans for the future. Police officials and lawyers also shared narratives of their work with me, including experiences of their work and rumors about other police agencies. All these conversations—with terror-accused, lawyers, and police officials—usually took place in Hindi, which I transcribed into my notebook. In this book, I have translated these conversations into English, while retaining some of the words spoken in Hindi to give the reader a flavor of what was being said.

For my part, I occasionally became their link to the outside world. Sometimes, they would give me letters to post. But more often, they would ask me to pass on messages to family members who had missed the day's hearing. At times, since they knew about my legal training and experience in law, they would ask me what I thought about how their case was going or to explain to them what had happened in court. However, as I discovered, they usually knew much more than I did about the intricacies of their cases.

In addition to following ongoing cases in the trial courts, I met with people whose trial process had completed or who had managed to secure bail. One of them was Yaseen bhai, mentioned earlier in this chapter, who was convicted but was on bail while the appeal was making its way through the High Court. I regularly met and interacted with a couple who were trade union workers and had been accused of belonging to a banned communist party. Three others whom I met with varying degrees of regularity had all been acquitted of their crimes: two were Kashmiri men whom I met in Srinagar and one was a man from Delhi who has recently published a book about his experiences as a terror-accused person (Khan 2016). I conducted more formal, recorded interviews with these men. I was keen to get accounts of what their experiences were as terror-accused persons: what their life was like in jail, how they made their way through the court system, and how they lived their lives in the aftermath of this experience.[37] These recorded interviews were conducted in Hindi, which I have translated to English for the reader.

I conducted my research in this everyday world of trial courts, and it is a sense of this world that I seek to convey in this book. To use Das's pithy phrase, this book is an attempt at a "descent into the ordinary" (2007) of the law. Accordingly, it charts four modes of descent into the everyday world of the trial courts: the police (Chapter 1), legal language (Chapters 2 and 3), paperwork (Chapters 4 and 5), and writing (Chapter 6). In each of these chapters, I look at how terror-accused individuals engaged with the technicalities of the trial process. Each of these chapters revolves around one or two cases. In telling the story of these cases, I track the affects and practices surrounding legal technicalities.

In Chapter 1, I think about the intimacy that a sustained engagement with the legal process cultivates by looking at the relationship between the police and the terror-accused. From the moment of a suspect's arrest to the investigative and then the judicial process, the police are the first and the most constant presence for the terror-accused in their entanglement with the law. In recounting narratives of the growth of relationships between the two, the chapter considers what it means to engage with the legal process through the idea of intimacy. This relationship could resemble friendship, but it was also one in which the police could take on monstrous forms. Chapters 2 and 3 engage with questions of legal language. In these chapters, I discuss the law as language, as a way of making oneself at home in the world and as a way of imagining a future. In Chapter 2, I offer the term "recycled legality" to account for the ways in which terror-accused persons make legal language their own. They learned the law, not by instruction, but by a slow process of collaborative translation and reading. They did so not to more correctly obey the law, but to be able to articulate their own demands through it. In Chapter 3, I look at how legal language is something that the state "said." As an utterance of the state, it signaled its power as well as its vulnerability. In Chapters 4 and 5, I look at the next encounter in the trial: the file. This part of the book seeks to account for the feeling that many terror-accused persons have when they approach the file: that it produces truth. In Chapter 4, I look at the ability of the file to hold not just one, but multiple truths. I think of the files as *hypertextual* artifacts, not just because they reflect reality, but because of their capacity to produce multiple realities. Chapter 5 looks at the technicalities of producing truth—that is, the certificatory procedures that accompany paperwork. The procedures through which the file produces truth are simultaneously the ways in which this truth is undermined. Finally, in the last chapter, I look at writing practices by the terror-accused. By focusing on petition-writing practices, I look at the ethical stakes in their writing.

In all of the cases that appear in this book, I have used pseudonyms for the terror-accused, police officers, and lawyers and have attempted to remove anything else that could identify the cases (such as dates and places). While I have copies to all the official documentation that I draw upon in the chapters that follow, I have changed case numbers and other identifying markers. In a book that seeks to return human voice to the life of the law, I reluctantly had to strip people of their names and identities. I can only hope that I have done justice to stories of their lives—lives that they have generously opened up to me. I have retained the names of Mohammad Amir Khan, who has since written a courageous book about his experiences, and Yaseen bhai, who almost insisted that I use his real name. Yaseen bhai has given several interviews about his own case and the trials of SIMI and has never shied away from expressing himself. In his many conversations with others, and me, he has used his cutting humor to speak about the cynical machinations of the Special Cell. To work humor into sadness is to find hope in the midst of despair. This perhaps is how one lives in the world of terrorism trials.

1

CUSTODIAL INTIMACY

Law and the Police in Two Parts

In this chapter I think about the place of the police in the lives of people accused of terrorist crimes. The police were the first contact that the terror-accused had with the legal system. In Delhi, anti-terror investigations were usually handled by the Special Cell.[1] Most of the cases that I follow in this book were investigated by this division of the Delhi police.

Initial encounters with the police narrated to me by the terror-accused with narratives often included violence and deception on the part of the police. Many of the terror-accused whom I met spoke of being kidnapped by the police: One person, now acquitted of terrorist crimes, told me that he had just turned seventeen years old when he was shoved into a white van and kept in a basement for about ten days before he was "officially" arrested and brought before a magistrate; another told of how Special Cell officers barged into his house at about 3 A.M. and hauled him away in front of his wife and children only to be officially arrested three days later. One person—a trade union activist—told me how the officers of the Special Cell came to her house in the evening and she served them tea. The police claimed that they were doing an investigation about some petty thefts in the neighborhood and needed her help. She went along with them to the police station, ostensibly to help them, and they asked her to stay at the police station to help out. It is only when she told them that she wanted to leave, did the police actually tell her that she had been arrested.

A consistent theme of these narratives of first encounters with the police is the presence of an initial period of "illegal detention." Most terror-accused individuals told me that they were taken to police stations, occasionally the Special Cell's building. A few told me that they were taken to other buildings that they later realized were not police stations—because there were no uniformed police officers, signs, or other trappings of the police bureaucracy. This period of illegal detention was marked by verbal or physical threats and, at times, what they described as torture. The period of illegal detention could last from a few days to more than a week; after this period, they were finally "officially arrested" and brought before a magistrate. Subsequently, defendants would usually remain in the custody of the Special Cell, at their lock-up at the Lodhi Road Police Station. The reason given for this latter period of custody—officially known as "police custody," or PC—was usually that the accused were necessary to aid the police in their investigation. The fiction produced by the police was that since the accused had supposedly just been arrested, the Special Cell needed to interrogate them, and thus needed access to the accused for ongoing help with the investigation. The period of PC could last—depending on the number of investigations proceeding against the accused—from several weeks to several months. Police custody means just that—that the accused are held in the lock-up that is part of the police station. For both legal and illegal periods of police custody, the accused and police are constantly in one another's presence.

After the period of PC came to an end, the police usually requested that the terror-accused "be remanded to JC," or judicial custody[2]—in effect the terror-accused went to prison while they waited for their trial to commence. Most of the terror-accused whom I met in the courts said they were all kept in JC in the same "high security" ward in Tihar Jail. The period of usually JC extended till the end of the trial. While judges had the option of releasing people from JC on bail pending trial, this was extremely unlikely—almost impossible—in terrorism trials. As a result, terror-accused often spent years, if not more than a decade, in JC.

While the trials proceeded through the courts, officers from the Special Cell were a constant presence. One or two police officers from the Special Cell were given "charge" of particular cases and were expected to be present in the court every day that the case under their care was being heard. It was these police officers that the terror-accused, their lawyers, the prosecutors, the judges, and I would see at every hearing of each particular case. Seeing the same person over such a long period of time—first at the time of arrest, then over the illegal and legal periods of police custody, and then for years afterward at every court hearing—meant that a relationship of sorts grew between the terror-accused and the police. As a result of the technicalities of the investigative and courtroom process, the terror-accused and the police officers assigned to their cases were a constant presence one another's lives over many years.

Defendants from different terrorism cases were often kept in PC at the same time and thus knew each other. They also often knew the same police officers and regularly shared stories about them. As a result, conversations in courts were filled with rumors about the police. The police were not just physical presences; they were also continually evoked through the narratives told about them.

I spent almost no time with the police outside the court complexes and had little opportunity to observe their everyday lives. I could neither be a part of the police's daily routine (outside the courts) nor be present at the Special Cell police station. Yet, in the courtrooms, I did see unexpected relationships between terror-accused and police officers. I was also privy to the numerous stories about the police that constantly swirled around the court complexes. And I was able to glean some understanding of how terror-accused and police related to one another by participating in courtroom conversations, through stories they told about themselves in breaks between court hearings, and from narratives told by those who had come into direct contact with the police. These helped me observe how relationships between police officers and the terror-accused unfolded.

To describe the relationships between police and the terror-accused, I propose the term "custodial intimacy." In adopting the idea of custodial intimacy to describe these relationships, I join scholars who have departed from looking at the police solely through the lens of violence (Comaroff 2013; Jauregui 2011, 2016).[3] Intimacy is not just a question of physical proximity, but also about how one locates one's place within the life of another, or how one imagines the place of another in one's own life. From this perspective, violence is not in opposition to intimacy, but is a potential part of it. I use the word "intimacy" here to describe the ways in which one produces knowledge of and behaves in relationship to another. Intimacy can as readily signal love, friendship, and care as it can violence, betrayal, and anxiety. In the everyday lives of the terror-accused, the term "custodial intimacy" speaks to the difficulty of discerning the form of intimacy that interactions with the police will take on.

Through the idea of custodial intimacy, I seek to describe two aspects of the relationship between police and terror-accused. On the one hand, the police appear to have a monstrous presence. Rumors about the police circulate widely, and in them the police come to be imbued with fantastical powers. On the other hand, I witnessed the emergence of what could almost be described as friendship between the police and the terror-accused. So there were times in which the police appeared to be friendly, while at other times they appeared threatening. The idea of custodial intimacy seeks to understand these two forms of intimacy as enmeshed in one another.

Custodial intimacy between police officials and the terror-accused is engendered by technicalities of the investigative and trial processes. Extended periods of detention and the near constant presence of particular police officials in courtrooms not only allow for observation of how police and the terror-accused relate to one another, but also shed light on how the terror-accused conceptualize the legal process through their relations with the police. I would like to think of what I present here—through the stories told by and about the police and the terror-accused—as a way of understanding the intimate place the law had in the lives of the terror-accused.

As we will see in the rest of the book, this uncertain intimacy with the police also characterizes the relationship between the law and the terror-accused. In order to work toward an acquittal, terror-accused individuals sought to develop greater knowledge of the technicalities of the trial process. This knowledge, however, led not to certainty but to an opacity. As the terror-accused could never foretell the consequences of working with technicalities (that is, whether it would help or harm their cases), any engagement with technicalities was necessarily an ambiguous one; it is both a response to and a perpetuation of a threat. As with custodial intimacy, cultivating an intimate knowledge of the law was fraught with uncertainty.[4] Looking at the forms of intimacy that emerge between terror-accused and the police can also help us understand the intimacy that terror-accused cultivate with legal technicalities.

In the first part of the chapter, I look at one aspect of this custodial intimacy: the relationships that emerged between terror-accused and police officials from their close physical proximity both when the terror-accused were in police custody and during the long periods spent together during the trial. I ask what forms of relationships are made possible beyond the poles of oppressor-oppressed, or perpetrator-victim. Further, while violence certainly simmered just beneath the surface in these relationships, what emerged is something that tends toward friendship. I use the phrase "*tends toward*" advisedly. As in differential calculus, where a variable tends toward a certain value but never reaches it, any closeness forged here could never be named "friendship" as such. In fact, while police violence can be captured in words, my ethnographic interlocutors could not find the vocabulary to fully describe their relationships with the police. Certainly, they could speak of the violence they faced at the hands of the police—torture, assault, or illegal detention; but they could not precisely name the relationships with police officials that went beyond violence.

In part two of this chapter, I look at another aspect of custodial intimacy. The police were not just physically present, but were made into an intimate presence through the rumors told about them. Rumors about the police circulated widely in the courts, among lawyers and the terror-accused, and one could barely have a conversation in criminal courts without the police being brought into the conversation. As forms of knowledge, these rumors blurred the boundary between fact and fiction, and they rendered basic categories of life unstable. The rumors produced knowledge about the police that was both created and reinforced in their retelling. In the milieu of a terrorism trial, these rumors imbued the police with near-fantastical powers. I argue that these rumors made the police a constant, intimate, and monstrous presence. In this way, for the terror-accused, the police existed as intimate, yet spectral powers, present at all times, even when were not physically proximate.

In the next section, I present the story of Nadeem and Faheem as a way of showing how these two forms of custodial intimacy emerge through interactions with the police and the fundamental uncertainties these involve. Are the police an entity that can be trusted, or do they mean harm? The relationships forged with the police take place in a milieu of police violence. When the terror-accused are entangled with the police they constantly face the question of whether the police will be friendly or monstrous.

In the following story of Nadeem and Faheem, the police are caring and protective, as well as callous and duplicitous. The story comes from several sources: others who had been accused of terrorist crimes, several activists, a friend of Nadeem, Nadeem's lawyer, and Nadeem himself. You could also read parts of this story in newspaper articles or in nonfiction books. I imagine the story as having two functions—first, as demonstrating how relationships between the terror-accused and the police evolve through an investigation, and second, as a way to gesture toward how ideas of police power are produced in part through the proliferation and circulation of rumors.

THE STORY OF NADEEM AND FAHEEM

The first time I heard about Nadeem and Faheem was through a conversation between a Special Cell police officer and a defense lawyer, whom I will call Bhandari and Sheikh, respectively. I had gotten to know them during my time in Delhi's Courts. At the time, Bhandari had been recently promoted and was rising through the ranks of the Special Cell. Sheikh was representing an increasing number of terror-accused who were being prosecuted by the Special Cell. From what I could tell, they had a friendship that was steeped in competitive machismo. They often traded stories about their experiences with the terror-accused and with other investigative agencies. They went on smoke breaks between court hearings, and they went drinking together after court. On several occasions, when they both came to court in the morning, the smell of the previous night's alcohol-induced camaraderie still lingered on their breath.

One muggy day in July, I went to court to attend a case. On reaching Tis Hazari, I discovered that there was a lawyers' strike and no cases were going to be heard on that day. Outside the courtroom, I bumped into Sheikh having a smoke with Bhandari. Sheikh was telling Bhandari about how the National Investigation Agency (NIA, a central agency set up in 2008 to investigate terrorist crimes) was, in his view, entirely incompetent. Sheikh wholeheartedly agreed and said they did not know the basics of an investigation. With no small amount of bravado, Sheikh told Bhandari that one night when he was "poori talli," or totally drunk, an NIA officer came to his house with a notice telling Sheikh that he had to accompany the officer to a police station, in order to help with an investigation.

> I told him, "Do whatever you want, I am not coming with you. Arrest me." Then I took his phone and called [his superior officer] and told him "arrest me." Then he said that they should not have sent the notice, it was wrong. Then the next day, I went there and they asked me where [my client] was getting money from to pay me. I told him, how am I supposed to know? He gets it from somewhere, what's my connection to where it's

coming from? They he asked me "are you taking it in cash?" I told him, "Whatever I have taken, I have taken in white [i.e., legally]." Then do you know what he asks me? He says you must have got at least 1 crore [Rs. 10,000,000] for this case.

At this point Sheikh burst out laughing at the thought of having received such a massive amount for this case. Bhandari joined in with the laughter. He then told us how it was not just the NIA that was incompetent, but that Mumbai Anti-Terrorism Squad (ATS) was equally so.

Some months ago, I was sleeping at home, when I got a phone call saying that the [2011 Mumbai blast] accused had been caught. I thought wow, Delhi police has done something good. Then I heard that the Mumbai police had arrested them.

He turned to me, and as he laughed at the Mumbai police, he asked,

You know about how the [Mumbai] ATS had created a case against those brothers? It was in the newspapers also. They tried to arrest one of the brothers here, but the [local] police stopped them. It was some months ago. The ATS-waalon [ATS people] don't even know how to arrest people properly.

Sheikh then interjected, saying authoritatively, "Bilkul farzi case hai" (It's an entirely fake case).

Bhandari agreed with Sheikh and mocked the Mumbai police for their inability to parse fact from fiction. At the same time, though, in hinting that the person the Mumbai police had tried to arrest was an informer for the Special Cell, Bhandari understood the ATS's confusion, as a terror suspect could actually be simultaneously helping another law-enforcement agency:

One time do you know what happened? Interception pe hua tha [I was on an interception] on some Kashmiri. I was just listening, listening, and listening. Then suddenly I understood that he was an informer for the police in Kashmir. Maadharchod [Mother fucker]. He told the police there, "I have four Pakistani's with me. Unko goli chala doon? [Should I shoot them?]" Then the police said, "Okay, but what name do we give them?" Then the Kashmiri said, "Say they are Pakistani. What difference does a name make? Give them any name. Abu Hamza, Abu Jundal—what difference does it make?"

While both Bhandari and Sheikh laughed at what they saw as the incompetence of the Mumbai ATS (how could they mess up something as basic as an arrest?), Bhandari also understood why the ATS was confused about the identity of the person they had tried to arrest, as he himself might have been in such a position. Still, I was confused about the contours of this case against the two brothers. Who were these two brothers? Why did the ATS arrest them? And why did the Delhi police intervene to prevent the arrest of one of the brothers?

As I could not follow up on the details of this case with Bhandari, that evening I searched online editions of newspapers to find out more about this case. It arose from a series of explosions in Mumbai in 2011. According to one newspaper report, Faheem was arrested by the Mumbai ATS in early January of 2012. According to this report, the Mumbai ATS believed that Faheem, on the orders of the "elusive Indian Mujahideen chief Yasin Bhatkal, [had] stolen two bikes a day before the blasts and fitted explosives on them for triggering explosions." Another newspaper, quoting sources within the Mumbai ATS, claimed that Faheem was the "mastermind" behind the blasts.

However, several other newspapers quoted the Delhi Police's doubts about the claims made by the Mumbai ATS. Leading with the headline "Cops Doubt Mumbai ATS Claim of Solving Blast Cases," one newspaper reported that Faheem and his brother Nadeem were actually informers for the Delhi police's Special Cell and the central government's Intelligence Bureau. The report also quoted a Delhi police officer who questioned the strength of the Mumbai ATS's evidence against Faheem. According to the police officer, all of the evidence was "indirect" and was far from conclusive. He told the newspaper that the fact that Faheem was working with the Delhi police would "prove to be a stumbling block for the Mumbai police."

Several days later, I asked Manisha Sethi, an academic and a human rights activist who is well known for her work on anti-terror trials, about the case. She explained that the Mumbai ATS and the Special Cell were in a "competition" to show the media that they had "cracked" terrorism cases. According to her, the Delhi police had been using the two brothers as informers and had taken Faheem to Mumbai. There, the Mumbai ATS arrested Faheem as one of the prime accused in the Mumbai blast case. Faheem and another brother (Imran) had been held in illegal detention for several days, after which Faheem was officially arrested and Imran was released. She told me that the Special Cell had washed their hands of the two brothers and that the Mumbai ATS were harassing not just Nadeem, but his two other brothers as well.

Manisha then told me of the events subsequent to Faheem's arrest. Several days after they learned that Faheem had been implicated in the case, Nadeem, Imran, and their fourth brother, Iqbal, attempted to take control of the situation by holding a press conference in Delhi. They demanded that Faheem be released and that the officers who held him illegally be charged and punished. They also released a statement detailing the help they provided the Special Cell: they provided dates of meetings and travel to Mumbai, as well as the names of the Special Cell officers with whom they were in touch. The press release ends with the following statements:

> This is a case where the competition between two investigative agencies—the Special Cell of the Delhi police and the Maharashtra ATS—has claimed more innocents. The fight against terror has been reduced to victimization, harassment of Muslims, and violation of the due processes of law. Anti-terror agencies pick up and detain people at will, in this free-for-all race to prove their anti-terror credentials.
>
> We demand an immediate stop to this sort of terrorization of Muslim youth and their families. The process of investigation and questioning must be transparent, and the due processes must be strictly adhered to. All those arrested must be produced before a magistrate within 24 hours and illegal detentions and interrogations in such detention must be strictly punished.

Manisha then told me of a bizarre turn of events during the press conference. Some officers from Mumbai's ATS went to the press conference seeking to arrest Nadeem. They seemed entirely unaware that they were about to step into a room filled with cameras and journalists. After they entered the hall, the Mumbai police asked Nadeem to come with them to his house. He went with them, but he was accompanied by Manisha Sethi. The ATS claimed that they had come to Delhi to collect evidence about Faheem from the brothers' flat. Manisha described the following scene that unfolded in the car ride from the press conference to Nadeem's flat, a scene that she later narrated in her book titled *Kafkaland* (2014, 2):

> The ATS team had arrived in the middle of a press conference. This effectively frustrated their simple enough plan to carry away Nadeem for

uninterrupted interrogation in the comforts of their police station. Slightly irritated at our presence, and shivering from the assault of the Delhi cold, the Assistant Commissioner of Police (ACP) who headed the team began to inquire from this young man. The gist of his inquisition was this:

"What did your brother tell the Special Cell?"

"Wouldn't it be simpler to pose this question to the Special Cell?," we asked.

"Protocol."

Apparently, the protocol is to whisk away suspects, or even their brothers.

"Why do you illegally detain suspects?" I turned to a less pleasant topic. "How would it hurt to send summons to those you wish to interrogate?"

The Inspector looked genuinely hurt. "Illegal detention? Never. We always take the person out for a walk after 23 hours."

It was one of those tragi-comic moments when one isn't sure whether to laugh or to cry. Here was an officer of law telling us that the legal requirement of producing an arrestee before a magistrate within 24 hours could be circumvented "legally."

Not only had the Mumbai police come unprepared to deal with the media attention on the case, but according to Manisha they were also unprepared for the frigidity of Delhi's winter and the Delhi police's attitude toward them. At the flat, some Delhi police constables joined them. The ATS searched Nadeem's house and said they were looking specifically for a camera and a laptop. Nadeem told them that these were stolen some months before—a claim that the ATS refused to believe. Luckily for Nadeem, an officer of the Delhi police who was also there confirmed that the laptop and camera were indeed stolen and that a complaint had been filed. It was obvious to all that the Delhi police were in no hurry to help the Mumbai ATS.

Manisha gave me Nadeem's telephone number. I contacted him, telling him that I got his telephone number from Manisha, and asked him if we could meet. Nadeem was clearly wary of me. He asked me several times how I got his number and who I was. He seemed so hesitant that I did not press him. Some months later, however, I was introduced in person to a very nervous Nadeem at a gathering of human rights activists and academics who had come together to discuss the persecution of people by the Special Cell. After this in-person introduction, he agreed to meet me the following weekend.

He asked that we meet in a public park that was close to a university and was surrounded by shops. I arrived early and sat at a concrete picnic table. I looked around at the park, noticing how open it was to the surroundings, and the steady stream of people that went from the university gates at one end to the shops at the other. He had clearly chosen this park deliberately. It was almost as if he was scared to meet people away from the gaze of witnesses.

He arrived on a single motorbike straddled by two male friends. One of his friends shook my hand and greeted me, while the other appeared to size me up through a silent nod in my direction. Nadeem was evidently nervous about the meeting and had brought his friends along in case I was not who I said I was. Given that he was so apprehensive, I did not feel comfortable asking him if I could record the interview. When I asked if I could take notes, the friend who shook my hand said I could do so.

Over the next several hours, Nadeem told me the story of his and his brother's entanglement with the Mumbai ATS and the Special Cell. In addition to Faheem, he had two older brothers, whom I call Imran and Iqbal. All four of them were engaged in the leather business. They sourced leather products—bags, belts, sandals, briefcases, suitcases—from their home in Darbhanga in the eastern state of Bihar. Nadeem and Faheem had set up a shop in a "Muslim" locality in south Delhi, while Imran and Iqbal had set up a shop in Mumbai.

Nadeem told me that early in December 2011, Imran landed in Delhi's airport on a trip to see his two younger brothers. He hailed an autorickshaw and got in. As soon as he sat down in the back seat, two men forced their way into the rickshaw and sat on either side of him as if to trap Imran inside the vehicle. Imran haggled with them, thinking, perhaps, that they were trying to steal his luggage or commandeer the rickshaw. One of them told him that they were with "Intelligence," threatened him, and told him to keep quiet, while the other told the rickshaw driver to continue to the main bus stop near Nadeem and Faheem's flat.

When they reached the destination, the police told Imran to call Nadeem down to where the rickshaw was parked. Nadeem came down and saw a badly shaken Imran, surrounded by these two men. The two men immediately approached Nadeem and asked him who he was and what he was doing there. Nadeem said was taken aback by their aggressive questioning and asked the two men if they had lost their minds. As Imran told Nadeem to calm down, the two men told Nadeem that they were policemen. Nadeem said that they identified themselves as police officials with the Special Cell, Lodi Colony Police Station.

The police, Nadeem said, wanted to know if he knew someone, let's call him Suri. Nadeem, a bit flustered, said that he did not know Suri, but he knew that his brother Faheem knew him. Nadeem said he spoke without thinking, but it was too late. The police now demanded that Faheem be brought to them as well. Nadeem asked Faheem to come down to meet the police officers.

Faheem confirmed to the police that he indeed knew Suri and had "social relations" with him. Faheem said he was friends with Suri's house mates. They asked Faheem if he had helped Suri get accommodation in Mumbai. Faheem told the police that all he had done was put Suri in touch with a property broker whom Faheem knew in Mumbai. The police then told both Nadeem and Faheem to come to the police station with them. The brothers said they had no inkling of Suri's activities and begged the policemen to leave them alone. All to no avail. As they left in an autorickshaw, the policemen told their brother Imran that no harm would come to his brothers if he kept his mouth shut.

They arrived at a police station that they would later come to know as the Special Cell. Nadeem recalled how they were pushed through the front offices full of large filing cabinets, registers, and empty desks, down a corridor, past a room glowing with the hum of old computers, to the dank cells at the back of the police station. The dark cells had the stench of urine. They pleaded with the police, begging to be let go. Instead, they were pushed into an acrid cell and were brought face to face with Suri. Nadeem could not believe that that the police had him all this time. If they had already arrested him, why did they need to bring in Nadeem and Faheem?

The two policemen asked Faheem if he knew this man they were facing. Faheem said he did and named him as someone he knew as Kamal Suri. While Suri looked forlorn and remained silent, the brothers were shown photos that the police said were taken from Suri's house. The brothers recognized the photos as they were of the opening ceremony of their shop. They showed Nadeem, Faheem, Suri, and some others on their first day of sales.

The police pointed to one of the men in one of the pictures and asked if they knew him. Nadeem said that Faheem told the police that he thought that the man's name was Rizwan. According to Nadeem, the police started saying that "since we knew terrorists, we also must be terrorists." Nadeem said the brothers pleaded their innocence, saying that they did not know that Suri was involved with terrorist groups, and barely knew who Rizwan was. In narrating this story, Nadeem seemed simultaneously incredulous at and understanding of Suri's silence. On the one hand, he felt betrayed by the fact that Suri did not tell the police that they were innocent and were not involved in any of his activities. On the other, Nadeem asked rhetorically, "Who knows what pressure he was under?"

That evening, the police at the Special Cell let Nadeem and Faheem go and said "nothing would happen," if the brothers agreed to cooperate. The next day, Nadeem said, Faheem and the two other policemen flew on a 10:30 A.M. flight to Mumbai to find the house that Suri had rented and to see if Faheem recognized anyone there. Faheem helped the Special Cell officers find the property broker and eventually to find the house. It turned out that it was empty, even though it was still being rented. While the brothers were initially told that it would only be a one-day trip, the Special Cell forced Faheem to stay two more days, reminding him of their arrangement. The Special Cell had a flat in the "target area," as they called it. The three of them stayed there for the next two nights and returned to Delhi after they got tired of waiting for someone to show up at the house.

Nadeem said he hoped things would return to normal after Faheem came back from Mumbai. After all, Faheem had helped the Special Cell. Over the next couple of weeks however, the harassment by the Special Cell increased. Nadeem said that they were summoned without reason to the cell's headquarters and sometimes made to wait hours on end. At times they had to close their shop for entire days and lost business. Once both brothers were asked to leave their cell phones with the police for two days. More than anything else, Nadeem said, it was the stress that they could be called at any time that really unsettled him.

In the middle of January of the next year, Faheem received a call from the Special Cell saying that he should come to the police station immediately. There, he was told that the Special Cell had received "secret information" that the occupants of the flat in Mumbai had returned and that he had to accompany the police to Mumbai. Nadeem said that Faheem tried to avoid getting in deeper with the Special Cell. "What else could he do?" asked Nadeem. That evening, Faheem and the Special Cell officers took a fast train to Mumbai.

The next evening, Nadeem received a phone call from Faheem. Faheem told him, "Kaam ho gaya. Kal vaapas aaunga" (The work is done. I'll be back tomorrow). He told Nadeem that he would stay the night at their brother Imran's house.

However, Faheem did not call Nadeem again. Nadeem said he expected his brother to call when he reached Imran's house, but Faheem failed to do so. He tried calling Faheem but kept getting a "switched off" notification. He tried calling his brothers Imran and Iqbal, but their phones were also returning a "switched off" notification. To his horror, he discovered that one of the employees in the Mumbai store—named Mohammed—had also gone missing and was not reachable on his cell phone. None of the cell phones of these people was switched on.

When Nadeem telephoned the Special Cell officers, they refused to pick up his phone calls. In his desperation he ran to the station, where no one would speak with him. For four long days he did not know where his brothers were or what had happened to them. He said he was paralyzed with fear. During this time, the ATS had visited his parents in Bihar, made them sign some papers, and took away a motorcycle belonging to one of his brothers. He called the Special Cell officers again, but they did not answer their phones.

Finally, on the fourth day he received a phone call from the ATS saying that his brother had been arrested and that Nadeem was being informed of the arrest in compliance with the law. By this time, Faheem, his two brothers, and their employee, Mohammed, had been in illegal custody of the ATS for at least three days. "Why? What about Imran and Iqbal?" he asked, but they had already put down the phone. Soon after, Imran, Iqbal, and their employee, Mohammed, were released. From Imran, Iqbal, and Mohammed and later on, upon speaking with Faheem, he was able to piece together what had happened over the previous four days.

After Faheem telephoned Nadeem saying that "the work has been done," Faheem received a call from Mohammed, saying that Imran and Iqbal had been arrested. Faheem telephoned the Special Cell's officers asking why his brothers had been "picked up," when they knew that Faheem was helping them. Why had they betrayed him? The Special Cell police said they had no clue what he was talking about and that they had not arrested anyone, let alone Imran. And with that they put down the phone. A few minutes later a panicked Faheem received a phone call from one of the officers saying that it had not been they who had arrested Imran and Iqbal, but it was likely that Mumbai's ATS had arrested him. The officer hinted toward a lack of cooperation between the two agencies and said that there was little that they could do. He told Faheem to return to the flat, promising Faheem that he would be safe with them in the "target area."

A few minutes later Faheem received a call from Mohammed, who told him that they should meet at a place called Hotel Sagar. Unknown to Faheem, Mohammed had already been detained by the ATS and was making the phone call from under their thumb. Faheem went to Hotel Sagar and was kidnapped by the ATS. Four days later, Imran, Iqbal, and Mohammed were released, and Faheem was named as a prime accused in the case. Soon thereafter, Nadeem and his brothers held the press conference that I wrote about earlier.

After the press conference in January, things were quiet for several weeks. Nadeem said that his brother had a lawyer and that the only thing that was happening with the case was that it was moving "tareekh pe tareekh" (from one date to the next). According to Nadeem, the Mumbai ATS had fabricated evidence in order to add additional charges under other special security legislation. All contact with the Special Cell ceased.

One morning in February, however, while Nadeem was in the leather shop, two officers from the Mumbai ATS arrived and told him that he was being arrested. They said that he had ignored two prior notices summoning him to the ATS police station in Mumbai. Nadeem said that he tried to reason with them, telling them that he had not received any notices. He managed to call the local police and began telling his neighboring shopkeepers what was happening. A scuffle then broke out when one of Nadeem's employees physically intervened to prevent his arrest. Soon a crowd had gathered and a squad of the Delhi police arrived.

Subsequently the two ATS officers and Nadeem went to the local police station where human rights activists and local politicians had also gathered. A newspaper report of the incident—that I later found—helpfully explained that the ATS could not arrest a person outside its jurisdiction and quoted a Delhi police official saying that such an arrest was illegal. The same officer told the reporter, "The two ATS officers vanished from the scene soon after they met the local officers at the police station." The Mumbai ATS seemed to have been tripped up, if not chased away, by the Delhi police. This is the event that Bhandari and Sheikh were laughing about earlier.

Nadeem said he feared his own arrest and had become frustrated that efforts to secure his brother's release had failed. Soon after this attempted arrest, Nadeem said he got in touch with one of the Special Cell officers who initially approached them and who had taken Faheem to Mumbai. He told me that he first believed that the officer had felt bad about putting them in that situation. And then immediately he wondered if the help he was given by the Special Cell was aimed at poking the Mumbai ATS in the eye. In any event, the officer told Nadeem that he could put him in touch with a trusted lawyer. He even advised Nadeem to file a habeas corpus petition before the Supreme Court asking for both the release of his brother and a stay of his own arrest.

The lawyer who was suggested by the police officer was none other than Sheikh—who was so friendly with Inspector Bhandari of the Special Cell. Nadeem went ahead and agreed to meet Sheikh. He said he met Sheikh but he felt there was something wrong with him. After speaking to some people involved with terrorism trials, he discovered that Sheikh was well known in Delhi and represented many "terrorists" against the Special Cell. Nadeem's friend interjected to say "daal mein kuch kala hai" (literally: there is something black in the daal). Sheikh, a lawyer who fought cases *against* the Special Cell, was being recommended to him *by* the Special Cell. After speaking with his friends and family, Nadeem said he decided not to proceed with hiring Sheikh.

Nadeem said he decided to hire another lawyer—Sanjeev Khanna—recommended by a family friend and filed a petition in the Supreme Court against both the Mumbai ATS. In the petition he asked that Faheem be released and that the Mumbai ATS be prevented from arresting him. After filing the petition, Nadeem telephoned the officer of the Special Cell, urging him to use this opportunity to clear his and Faheem's name by filing a reply supporting Nadeem's claim. The officer gruffly replied, "Hamare upar ilzam lagaya" (You have made allegations against us)." Nadeem said he tried to explain that he did not make any allegations against the Special Cell and that they ought to tell the court that the brothers were working with the Special Cell, and that Faheem was not a terrorist, as the Mumbai ATS alleged. But the Special Cell officer hung up the phone and refused to answer any subsequent calls. Nadeem said, "They have cast so many injustices on me and my brother, the least they could have done was to help us." Nadeem clearly felt betrayed and let down by the Special Cell's refusal to help clear his and Faheem's name.

Nadeem said that in the Supreme Court, the Mumbai ATS said that he (Nadeem) was not a suspect, only a witness, but kept quiet about Faheem. The Special Cell did not even file a reply. "I have read the constitution and know that what both the Special Cell and the ATS did was absolutely wrong," Nadeem told me. Though he technically "won" the case, the court was silent on the fate of Faheem. Instead, the court merely told the ATS that it must give Nadeem a week's notice if they wished to arrest him. "What is the use of that?" Nadeem asked. "If they want, they can arrest me immediately and my brother is still in jail. Nothing has happened to the police officers who trapped us in this."

Several days later, I met the lawyer whom Nadeem eventually hired—Sanjeev Khanna. Mr. Khanna showed me the petition that was filed for Nadeem and Faheem. It narrated the events that led up to Faheem's arrest by the Mumbai ATS and detailed how Nadeem and Faheem were helping the Delhi police and had been arrested on false charges. The petition told the court of an ugly "war" between the Delhi Special Cell and the Mumbai ATS and that Faheem and Nadeem were caught in the middle. The ATS arrested Faheem, Nadeem alleged, only to spite the Delhi Special Cell for coming on to its "area" in Mumbai. The ATS were now attempting to illegally arrest Nadeem on some false charges—that too outside their jurisdiction. Mr. Khanna told me that the Mumbai ATS and Special Cell were "shooting" at each other, with innocent people like Nadeem and Faheem being caught in the "crossfire." He said that the Special Cell could not be trusted, even though they had given Nadeem correct advice about file a case. He asked me, rhetorically, "to consider the lawyer they had suggested," insinuating, in effect, that the lawyer Sheikh was corrupt and was too close to the Special Cell.

To be sure, despite the seeming extraordinariness of two rival police forces jostling against each other, it was not an unheard of occurrence.[5] Nevertheless, as I heard various iterations of this narrative, I was perplexed by its complexity. What was the relationship between the Delhi police and the Mumbai ATS? Was Faheem a "terrorist" as alleged by the Mumbai police or an informer for the Special Cell? Was Faheem merely a convenient scapegoat for the Mumbai ATS? Was the lawyer Sheikh colluding with the Special Cell? One police force uses Faheem as an informer; the other accuses him of masterminding some of the worst bomb explosions in Mumbai's recent history. One police force attempts to arrest Nadeem and is thwarted by another police force. One police force goes to the extent of advising Nadeem to file a habeas corpus case in the Supreme Court and even finds him a lawyer. The police here appear, not as institutionally coherent, but—to use the language of Nadeem's petition—as two rival gangs in a turf war. At times, the rivalry between the police forces seemed to drag Nadeem into the crossfire, as it did Faheem. At other times, it is this rivalry that allows Nadeem to escape. The police here are not conceived as a totalizing and all-powerful presence—as some theorists such as Derrida (1992) or Benjamin (1978) might claim—but as a power that is unpredictable: at times overwhelming, at times seemingly friendly, at times incompetent, but all the while, very intimate.

The concept of custodial intimacy that I propose aims to capture this unpredictability. Just as the nature of police power is uncertain, so is the relationship between Nadeem and Faheem and the police. As seen in this case, the relationship between the terror-accused and the police is not one of stable hostility. Far from being fixed characters, the police appear to have a shifting subjectivity, and their relationship with the terror-accused is a changing one. In their dealings with Nadeem and Faheem, the ATS comes across as comical and blundering but at the same time vengeful and underhanded, to say the least. The Special Cell officers come across as instrumental and manipulative, sometimes friendly, sometimes threatening, sometimes callous and heedless of the consequences of their actions. Think back to how the Special Cell tried to help Nadeem file a habeas corpus case against the ATS only to turn on him when he involved them officially. How would one describe the relationship between the two brothers and the Special Cell?

This particular narrative also shows that the police are not a distant power, but rather an intimate one. At the meeting on anti-terror laws organized in Delhi, where I met Nadeem for the first time, Lalu Prasad Yadav, a prominent politician from Bihar, compared anti-terror police to "hawks high up in the sky that suddenly swoop down and pick up our children." Ordinary, innocent people are getting on with their lives, while the police—represented as a violent, uncontrollable power—attack from above, without warning. As attractive as this metaphor is, the sense I am trying to build here is different: It is the idea of the police as a presence that is close at hand. It is because of a sense of intimacy between Nadeem and the Special Cell that he could feel a sense of betrayal when he thought the Special Cell had arrested Faheem, and the Special Cell officers could similarly feel that Nadeem had turned against them when he filed a habeas corpus petition that named them.

At the same time, it was precisely because of his intimate knowledge of the Special Cell that Nadeem was suspicious of the lawyer whom they suggested. Did the Special Cell's suggestion indicate that they were trying to help him and his brother or that they were just trying to get back at the Mumbai ATS? The confusion arose for Nadeem not because he had too little knowledge about the Special Cell, but because to have an intimate engagement with the police is to be confronted with "epistemic murk" (Taussig 1987). Having spent a substantial amount of time in close contact with the Special Cell, Nadeem felt that he had personal knowledge of the Special Cell. This knowledge, however, did not lead to clarity about the police's motives; rather, it occluded Nadeem's understanding of the role played by the police in his and his brothers' lives. To engage with the police is to be faced with the fundamental uncertainty inherent in custodial intimacy. Are they to be approached as friends? Or will they take on more monstrous forms?

In the next two parts, I delve deeper into two aspects of custodial intimacy. In the first, the police and the terror-accused have a relationship that approaches something like friendship, although the terror-accused cannot name the relationship as such. In the second, I look at an example of the police made present in monstrous forms, through rumors that that circulated widely through courtrooms and jails. Both sections seek to understand the fundamental instability and unpredictability that lies at the heart of any relationship with the police.

PART 1: TENDING TOWARD FRIENDSHIP

Through my time in Delhi's courts I often heard narratives of police violence. Accounts of physical torture, illegal detention, abduction, and verbal threats pepper my field notes. What initially surprised me, then, was to see people accused of terrorist crimes meet police officers as old friends, or to see parents of the terror-accused greet police officials in court rooms as if they were respected visitors. Recall that during the hearings before the tribunal concerning the Students Islamic Movement of India (SIMI) in 2008, I was perplexed to see Yaseen bhai hug police officers and officials who had not only arrested and prosecuted him, but also banned an organization he was a member of. To further add to my confusion, terror-accused individuals and their families would know and discuss intimate details about the personal lives of police officers, such as recent deaths, weddings, and other family events. The terror-accused would tell me how well they knew particular police officers, even as they cursed them.

So given this scenario, what vocabulary is available to describe these intimate relationships between police and terror-accused? For most legal scholars, there is very little difficulty in naming the relationship between terrorists and society. "Terrorists" are *hostis humanis generis*—or enemies of all mankind. (Greene 2008). Terrorism is seen as an existential threat to civilization, and therefore terrorists are seen as enemies of all states. Even as police violence is seen as a threat to civilization, the police are imagined as being at the forefront of guarding us against these enemies of civilization (Eckert 2005). On the other hand, for human rights activists, the police often emerge as the villains, acting with impunity and not held to account for the crimes that they commit on innocent civilians. Police are often described as *khatarnak* (an evil danger), and the general advice given is to *police se bachke rehna* (save yourself from the police). Violence at the hands of the police is described in terms of torture, abuse, and illegal detention. But whereas both sides give us vocabulary of enmity, an ethnographic sensibility yields a more complicated relationship between police and terror-accused.

Anthropologists have framed relationships with the police in terms of a fluctuating similarity and difference between the police and the community they police (Han 2013); a mutual fascination between police and terrorist (Aretxaga 2005); and an erotic attachment between police and criminal (Taussig 1988). While these are useful, they do not capture the intimacy that I witnessed in Delhi's courts. In attempting to describe this relationship, I was tempted to invoke Singh's (2011, 2015) agonistic intimacy or Hayden's antagonistic tolerance (2002), but these draw on the language of spirit possession and contested religious sites, respectively. Here, the moments of life I was attempting to describe seemed to be a friendship, albeit one that could not be named as such by my ethnographic interlocutors. The terror-accused

I came to know struggled to name the relationship that had developed, over time, with the police. I will try to further sketch out this idea of a friendship that could not be named as such, through an ethnographic vignette from the trial of a terror-accused who was alleged to have killed a police officer in a shoot-out in a Muslim neighborhood in south Delhi.

In the late 2000s, the Special Cell raided an apartment situated in a dense, Muslim neighborhood of south Delhi. The Special Cell claimed several terrorists who lived there had set off a series of explosions across Delhi several days prior to this raid. As is the case in many shootouts or "encounters,"[6] the police claimed that when they identified themselves as police officers, the "terrorists" fired at them. The police said that they then returned fire in self-defense and killed the occupants of the flat. In this case, unlike in the narratives of other encounters, one policeman also died. Further deviating from the encounter script, the police claimed that one of men in the apartment, whom I will call Shahid, managed to elude police officers stationed on the stairwell and surrounding the flat. Somehow—and the police never said how exactly—Shahid was able to avoid being caught by the many policemen who were part of the operation.

According to the police, he was arrested some months later in the neighboring state of Uttar Pradesh. He was subsequently brought to trial in Delhi for murder and attempted murder of officers of the Special Cell. Shahid was eventually convicted, and many commentators and legal scholars have questioned the soundness of the judgment. How could a person escape down narrow staircase when there were police officers *on that very* staircase? How did he then manage to avoid the police blockade imposed around the building? At one point during the trial, the judge excused the police from certain procedural requirements while collecting evidence, because they were working in a "hostile" Muslim locality. I leave those questions of soundness of the judgment aside for the moment, except to state that I too remain convinced that Shahid was framed and that I thought that the trial court's reasoning was shoddy, at best.

Shahid was eventually tried for two sets of crimes: he was tried along with others for the bomb blasts in Delhi (a trial that I discuss in Chapters 3 and 5) and then separately for the murder of the police officer. Officially, Shahid was a dreaded terrorist and involved in one of the most contentious, high-profile shootouts in recent Indian history. I would regularly see him being brought to court surrounded by ten uniformed, heavily armed guards. But at about five feet in height and of shy demeanor, he was barely visible behind the armed posse that escorted him to the courtroom. We often joked that with his personal security guards in tow, he might be mistaken for the prime minister, the president, or some other VIP.

Since Shahid was accused in two of the cases that I was following, I met him often. Over a period of time, I became quite friendly with him as we sat at the back of the courtrooms on each date of hearing, waiting for his cases to be called. One day we were sitting in the courtroom, watching the proceedings of another case labor on, as two lawyers haggled over what the stenographer had recorded, and a tall man in a white shirt and jeans came down and sat next to me. Shahid pointed to this man and mouthed "gavah," or "witness." I recognized him as a police official with the Special Cell—I will call him Dharamveer; he was there to depose against Shahid.

Shahid leaned behind me and tapped Dharamveer on the shoulder and offers him condolences for his son's death. I was shocked at this and could not help but ask, "Your son died? What happened?" Dharamveer replied, "Blood cancer. We found out eight months ago, and then he died one month ago."

As I offered my condolences, Dharamveer leaned across me and asked Shahid, "Who told you?"

Shahid: Muzzamil and Rizwan. They are with me in Jail no. 3.
Dharamveer: *Accha haan voh Bangladeshi hai. Do khaas dost hai na*? [Oh yes, those Bangladeshis. They are the best of friends, right?]
Shahid: Yes. Muzzamil and Rizwan.
Dharamveer: I arrested them. When I caught to the two of them and I was interrogating them, I told Muzzamil that out of the two of them, one of them had to die. "You choose." Then Muzzamil said to me, "Kill me," since Rizwan is still young. Then I told Rizwan the same thing, and Rizwan said, "Kill me." Look at their friendship! Another time, I caught two brothers and interrogated them. I told the younger brother that one of them had to die. He told me to kill him as his older brother had just gotten married. Then I asked the older brother the same question. Do you know what he told me? He told me, "I've just got married, so kill my younger brother!" What kind of world is this? Two brothers and two best friends. The friends say "kill me" and the brothers say "kill the other."

Dharamveer suddenly went quiet and turned away. I turned to Shahid.

Me: What's going on with you?

Shahid: My law course is still going on.

Me: That's great.

Shahid: Anyways, I was getting a practical training in law, so I thought I might as well study it properly. (laughs).

Me: Isn't Humam [another of the terror-accused] also studying law?

Shahid: No. He's studying BTS.

Me: BTS?

Shahid: Yes, Bachelor of Tourism studies. He was saying that for ten years we can't go anywhere, so we might as well see the world after we are acquitted and come out of jail (laughs).

Dharamveer rejoined the conversation.

Dharamveer: Yes, in these sorts of cases your entire youth gets wasted. Are you the only accused in this case? Do you have any other cases against you?

Shahid: I am alone in this case. I was accused in another bomb blast in [. . .] but they have not filed a chargesheet as yet. There's the other [Delhi] bomb blast case.

Dharamveer: What about Humam?

Shahid: He's only in that one Delhi bomb blast case.

Dharamveer: Anyways in this case there is no strong evidence against you. This case against you will probably be dismissed and you will be acquitted.

Shahid: *Pura umid hai* [I have full faith].

After some time, the reader called the case against Shahid, and Dharamveer went to the front of the courtroom. A police constable took Shahid by the hand to the front of the courtroom so that he could hear what was going on. The prosecutor reminded the judge that on the last date of hearing, the witness Dharamveer stated in his examination-in-chief (in response to questions asked by the prosecutor) that he was there at the scene of the encounter and had pointed out Shahid as the man involved in the shoot-out who had escaped. It was now time for Dharamveer's cross-examination by Shahid's lawyer, who questioned Dharamveer's memory of the events, going so far as to doubt his presence at the scene and accusing him of lying under oath and fabricating evidence against Shahid. Dharamveer stuck to his examination-in-chief and denied that he was lying. He reiterated that Shahid was involved in the shoot-out and that it was he who eventually escaped.

With his cross-examination over, the next witness was called. Dharamveer waited near the stenographer, so that he could sign a printout of his testimony, thus completing his deposition. Before leaving, he stopped in front of Shahid and said something quietly into his ear. Shahid bent to touch Dharamveer's feet. Dharamveer stopped him, held Shahid's face and blessed him by placing a hand on Shahid's forehead. A friend who was also present in court turned around and asked me, "Did he just bless him?" I shrugged, perplexed by what had just happened.

How could a person who—I was convinced—was being falsely accused bear such a close relationship with his accuser? Dharamveer had just accused him of murder, and yet Shahid had chosen to touch his feet. How could Shahid bow down to a person whose testimony could lead to his conviction? I tried to stop myself from pathologizing the event, as my mind reached out to phrases like "Stockholm syndrome." Further, this relationship that I saw earlier could not be seen as a strategic bid by Shahid to influence the outcome of his trial, as clearly there was no expectation that Dharamveer would testify in any other way.

As far as Shahid had told me, he had never faced torture at the hands of the police. Apart from the four days of illegal custody that Shahid says he spent with the police, he did not speak of violence at their hands. Of course, even if Shahid faced no overt violence, it could be argued that violence formed the structure of the relationship (Gupta 2012, 19). Shahid had spent several months in PC with the Special Cell and then three years in Tihar jail while his trial was going on. Through the conditions of incarceration Shahid could be said to be a "victim" of police violence—the very police that Dharamveer was certainly a part of. From this perspective, one could ask, how could Shahid, as a victim of systemic violence, touch the feet of his own oppressors?

Clearly the vocabulary of oppressor and victim is not adequate to understand relationships that emerge within trial courts. Shahid and Dharamveer appeared to have a place in each other's lives that was not one of enmity. They were able to identify with one another, but in ways that did not fit easy descriptions.

Observe how Dharamveer talked about love, death, and ideas of faithfulness in his discussion with Shahid. As he told us how he threatened two terror-accused with death and forced them choose between their lives and those of their brothers and friends, he framed the encounter as one of betrayal and the meaning of friendship. This encounter—situated amidst threats made by him—allowed him to reflect upon ethical questions about the responsibility that one bears for the life of another, in the face of one's own death. Later on, in the vignette, he told Shahid that he believed that Shahid will be acquitted. It was almost as if Dharamveer meant to tell Shahid that, despite his own testimony, Shahid should have faith that he would be exonerated—as though, while Dharamveer had a duty to testify against him, it was also his ethical responsibility to a person he had known for several years to provide comfort, even if for only a fleeting moment.

This is not the only occasion when I observed police officers raise ethical questions regarding the lives of the people they had prosecuted. In another instance, I joined a conversation that Bhandari was having with defense lawyers outside the courtroom. We had all just come out of a hearing for a case in which two men were accused of being members of a banned Maoist party (I discuss it further in Chapter 3). The defense lawyers, as they took long drags from their cigarettes, gently teased Bhandari about the flimsy nature of the evidence that the prosecution had brought to court on that date. Bhandari appeared to take these jokes to heart and became slightly defensive. "Look" he said,

> We know the evidence has no strength. But we all know Bharucha [one of the accused] is a Maoist. He is a *naxal*. You know it, I know it. If someone took my land to build a dam or my fields to dig a mine, *main bhi bandhook uthaoonga* [even I would pick up a gun]. Why not? If I was also dying of hunger like those people, I would also fight. I would also become [a Maoist]. [7]

It was almost as if he was sorry to bring a prosecution against these two people, but, as he explained to us later, he had no other choice as this was his job. Nevertheless, it was clear that Bhandari could understand why someone would join the banned Maoist party. Faced with an existential threat to his way of life, he too, like the "Maoists" he was prosecuting, would take up the gun.

Scholars have documented how state officials identify with the people they encounter. Rutherford (2009) deploys the notion of sympathy to describe the ways in which Dutch colonial officers sought out intimate moments with the residents of their Papuan colonies. For the Indian colonial state, Arnold (1986, 60–64) argues that there was an anxiety that the subordinate police might identify too closely with the populations they were meant to control and hence set up systems to distance the subordinate constabulary. Kelly (2012) maps another mode of identification through the ways in which immigration officials may be suspicious of asylum seeker's stories. This is not because of the immigration officials' lack of compassion, but because they closely identify with the asylum seekers' capacity to lie. There are modes of identification between people situated across hierarchies.

Far from inhabiting stable positions in the narratives I present here, the characters in them show changes in subjectivity. In Nadeem's case as in the scene described here, what is perhaps in play is not radical alterity, but rather a shifting of roles among protagonists. In Nadeem's story, the Special Cell appears first as threatening, then as collaborator, then as defender, and finally as a betrayed friend. Here, within the space of a little over an hour, Dharamveer appears first as a bereaved to whom Shahid offers his condolences, then as someone who gives words of hope and comfort to Shahid ("You'll definitely be acquitted"), and finally as an accuser, as he reaffirms that Shahid is the one who was present at the killing of his colleague.

These accounts paint a complex picture of the world in which the official roles of police and accused do not colonize relationships. While their initial encounters with each other may have been enmeshed in violence and framed by the official "roles" of police and terrorist, the relationship moves on, with time, into a space in which life and its challenges (friendship, death, trust, betrayal) forge a connection between them despite the ways in which they first encountered one another.

Still, I was curious to understand how Shahid himself understood his relationship with Dharamveer. Sometime later, after the courts' summer vacation, I had an opportunity to briefly speak with Shahid at the back of the courtroom in Tis Hazari, just after a hearing had concluded. I asked Shahid what he thought of Dharamveer. Rather answering directly, he described his acquaintance with Dharamveer. He told me that Dharamveer, along with two other police officials, had (illegally) arrested him and driven him away in the same jeep. Thereafter, he saw Dharamveer many times while he was in police custody. When he was finally officially arrested and proceedings before the magistrate commenced, Dharamveer was the police officer who was "in charge" of the case—though the responsibility had been transferred to another police officer since the case had been committed to the Sessions Court. Shahid told me that these regular encounters took place over two and three years. In reply, I said that it looked like he and Dharamveer had been very friendly with each other. Just before he was taken away by his guards, Shahid—as shy as he was—looked away and said, "Karna padta hai . . . hota hai" (It is necessary to do so . . . it happens). Suggesting that being friendly was something that he needed to do—perhaps for strategic reasons—Shahid was at the same time suggesting that these relationships simply happen. At the time, I felt that my statement had been careless, that perhaps my question came across as an insinuation that he was cavorting with an enemy. But it occurs to me now that perhaps Shahid also struggled to find a way to name this relationship.

In many accounts that terror-accused provided of their relationship with the police, "togetherness" was something that they emphasized. Like Shahid, other terror-accused also told me the amount of time that they had spent with certain police officials, from their first arrest, to their illegal detention, to their official custody, and then to their regular meetings in jails and courtrooms. They sought to avoid naming the relationship and instead explained that they had spent a long time together. I once asked Yaseen bhai how he could hug and be so friendly with bureaucrats and police officials who had banned his organization four times over, falsely prosecuted him as a terrorist, and imprisoned him and many of his friends and relatives. "We spent so much time together." he said. "Did you expect us to be enemies?"

This togetherness with the police was enforced because the terror-accused had been illegally detained, then kept in PC, and then put on trial for terror-offenses. This togetherness bred a form of relationship in which the terror-accused and the police could see themselves in the eyes of the other. Instead of togetherness being the object of friendship (Cavell 2004, 362), a friendship—albeit one that could not be named as such by terror-accused—emerged through this togetherness enforced by the investigative and trial court process. The time Bhandari spent with the "Maoist" terror-accused allowed him to identify with terror-accused, even to understand why he joined a Maoist revolutionary party. In the relationship between Shahid and Dharamveer, this enforced togetherness enabled the "sharing of conversation and thought" (Cavell 2004, 368) out of which the relationship emerged.

My sense is that the inability of my ethnographic interlocutors to name the relationship they had with the police, which went beyond the violence of their first encounter, was an acknowledgment that life during a terrorism trial still had to be lived and that living in the trial had produced unexpected bonds. By the time Dharamveer had deposed against Shahid, they had known each other for several years. It was almost as if the time they had spent together had somehow enabled a bond between police and terrorist to form. *Hota hai*, it happens, said Shahid—as if to say that such relationships organically emerge out of time. Similarly, Yaseen bhai—who knew his accusers for about nine years—disclaimed the idea of enmity toward them. Neither Yaseen bhai nor Shahid could explain this relationship—but time allowed for a complex one to emerge.

PART 2: POLICE, RUMORS, PARANOIA

Whereas in the previous section I looked at how the police and the terror-accused forged forms of intimacy that tended toward friendship (albeit one that terror-accused could name as such), here I look at another aspect of custodial intimacy. To many of my interlocutors, the police were not just an intimate physical presence, but were also constantly made present by the stories told about them. In this section, I want to think about another manifestation of the intimacy of the police, through rumors.

Such rumors circulated widely among lawyers and the accused. Recall that Nadeem "found out" that the lawyer recommended by the Special Cell was fighting the Special Cell in some cases. Similar stories of lawyers being paid off by the Special Cell or cutting deals with the police circulated among the terror-accused and their lawyers. Several stories also circulated about Dharamveer, the police officer we met in the last section. While Shahid said he never faced torture from Dharamveer, he had heard of narratives of Dharamveer's capacity for extreme violence and that he would often lace his verbal abuse of the terror-accused with expletives inspired by the Hindu right wing. One defense lawyer recalled that he himself had nearly gotten into a fist fight with Dharamveer. Dharamveer, the lawyer said, was physically preventing him from speaking to his client. "We were within a centimeter of each other's noses," the lawyer said. This experience buttressed the idea that Dharamveer was "one of the worst police of the Special Cell."

Often rumors about the police represented them as omnipresent. This affected the way that lawyers and the terror-accused went about their daily lives. For example, one terror-accused individual (who was out on bail) would refuse to say certain words—such as "money" or "medicine"—while speaking over his cellphone for fear that someone could be listening and would understand these as "code words." He also believed that his arrest, prosecution, and conviction were based on a conspiracy between India's Intelligence Bureau and (since he was a US citizen) the CIA. A defense lawyer I knew suspected that the police were tapping all his communications. Another lawyer I met told me that he thought all cell phones could be hacked into by the police and made into listening devices.

I do not deny that the police may indeed possess and use such technologies or that police agencies may conspire with others to falsely accuse innocent people of terrorist crimes. However, my point here is that stories about the powers of the police were disconnected from their actual capacities. Rumors suggested that they could be everywhere—in one's cell phone, in one's home, and as we will see, even in one's head.

During my fieldwork I was able to catch the end of a case against two Kashmiri men. The Special Cell alleged that the two men—one of whom I'll call Mohammed Irfan—were part of the Lashkar-e-Taiba[8] and were planning to commit terrorist acts in Delhi. The Special Cell claimed that they received a tip-off from a secret informer, who told the police of the duo's plans. At the end of one of the court hearings, I followed Mohammed Irfan's lawyer—whom I will call Mr. Chandolia—out of the courtroom. Chandolia signaled to me with a wide arm swing to follow him as he spoke to someone on his cell phone. Soon, we reached his chambers in the court compound: a small, bare room, with a steel desk and two chairs at one end and a rickety steel bench at the other. There was another man in the room who wore a crisp white kurta-pajama and had bright hair the color of henna. Later, he was introduced to me as Irfan's brother-in-law.

While he continued to speak on his cell phone, Chandolia plonked a thick volume of papers in front of me and signaled me to open it. It turned out to be the charge sheet in Irfan's case. I flipped through it and started noting down some the facts in my notebook, while another man came in to serve us tea.

Chandolia got off the phone and while still looking at it asked me for my name. "Mayur," I said. "Mayur" he repeated. "What kind of a name is this?"

> Me (hesitating, because I'm not sure what the question means): I think it's a Hindu name.
> Chandolia: Hindus have the name Mayur?
> Me (unsure because "Mayur" is readily identifiable as a Hindu name): Yes . . .
> Chandolia (shifting topics suddenly): Are you for or against terrorism?
> Me (awkwardly): I am against terrorism . . . but know that the government plants false cases.
> Chandolia: I only ask you that you write both sides of the story. All these journalists write only the government story and prejudice the accused. So, I am representing Mohammed Irfan.

I rushed to try to clarify that I was not a journalist, but he had already turned to Irfan's brother-in-law to ask: "Is Irfan a *maulvi* or an imam? What is the difference?"[9] he asked.

The brother-in-law began to answer, "An imam is one who leads the mosque in prayer, a *maulvi* is one who . . ." but then, Chandolia's gesticulating hand knocked over his cup of tea all over the other man. The next moment, Chandolia barked an order, and the man who was serving us tea came in to clean up the mess.

Chandolia turned to me and said, "Take down" and started dictating in English. I wrote down the following paragraph:

> Maulvi Irfan is a religious person, respectable person in his own area as well as in Muslim sect. He has a root in the society. He has no connection with terrorist organizations as well as he is not a political activist of any political party in India. He has a good, clean image of his family. His father is agriculturalist in village Lillon, Sanli, Muzzafarnagar [in Kashmir]. He was arrested on 21/3/2008 from Salimpur [Kashmir] when he was on the way to see relative at Seelampur. He was picked up/abducted by Special Cell from Salimpur, blindfolded and threw in the vehicle of the police. During the illegal custody/wrongful confinement he was tortured and through medical expert inserted microchip in his head that is visible from his head.

I looked up, trying not to betray my amusement, horror, and skepticism at the claim that a microchip had been inserted into Mohammed Irfan's head.

Chandolia (in response to my expression): I will tell you later. But a microchip has been inserted in his head.

Me: A microchip?

Chandolia: Yes, it is to relay thoughts. And it can also receive thoughts. It is a way of control by the government.

Me: You can see it in his head?

Brother-in-law: When he puts his head down, you can see it.

As I recalled that a balding Irfan had a visible vertical scar on the top of his head, Chandolia spread his finger two centimeters wide and said, "It is about this big. You can see the place where they cut and you can see the chip. As a result, he is in pain and can't sleep. He suddenly becomes very hot and very cold and starts shaking."

Brother-in-law: Sometimes he can hear people's voices.

Me: In his head?

Brother-in-law: Yes.

I was about to suggest that Irfan may have serious mental health issues, when Chandolia interjected.

Chandolia: It is called "Remote Neuro Brain System." You can get all these things on the internet these days. All the information is there. It was used by the United States government first time. It is a way for the government to listen to us and to control our thoughts. It is called "artificial intelligence."

Me: Artificial intelligence?

Chandolia: Yes. The thoughts that you have in your head is called "original intelligence." The intelligence that is planted in your head is artificial.

Stumped and not knowing how to respond, I just keep nodding and taking notes and tried to say something like "the government is very evil."

Chandolia continued:

You remember monkey man in Delhi? Maybe you were just a boy. That was also done by the government. You will not remember the Indo-Pak war. You were not born then. But the government sent tall gorillas to Kashmir to throw stones at people at night. They were so scared they could not sleep.[10]

He then showed me bail applications that he filed for Irfan and said that he needed medical help as the chip in his brain was causing him health problems. The appendices to this bail application had documents about the so-called Remote Neuro Brain System that were downloaded from the internet.

Over the next ten minutes, Chandolia produced a somewhat bewildering explanation of a wider conspiracy behind his client's arrest, which he told me to write down. For example,

> You will ask, "Who interrogated?" Write this: Military Intelligence and the Special Cell. Special Cell is a syndicate of Research and Analysis Wing [India's external intelligence agency], the Intelligence Bureau [India's internal intelligence agency], and military intelligence at that time. Now it is at par with National Investigation Authority. Special Cell [relies upon] the Mukhbir (secret informers). There is no investigation except secret information in order to justify the arrest.

At the end of this baffling session, Chandolia abruptly dismissed me and said he needed to get back to work.

I was not able to attend the next hearing of the case, but when I did get to the courtroom, the *naib* court told me that Mohammed Irfan had been acquitted, though his co-accused was convicted. I was not able to meet the brother-in-law again, and the lawyer Chandolia proved elusive. Apart from a brief look at the bail application, I could not get access to any of the court papers. However, I did find the trial court's judgment, which recorded the following in English:

> Accused Maulvi Irfan also pleaded that he was kidnapped / arrested by Delhi police on 21.03.2008 from Silampur, Delhi. A cloth was put on his eyes and he was pushed in a vehicle. Thereafter, he was beaten tortured mercilessly as a result of which he suffered unconsciousness and a microchip / magnet chip was inserted in his head.

I did not have the opportunity to ask why Irfan's lawyer or the brother-in-law thought a chip had been implanted in Irfan's brain. Did Irfan tell them? Was it something that they deduced? But notice that for Irfan's lawyer and brother-in-law, the fact that Irfan had a visible scar on his forehead that you could see "when he put his head down" lent credence to the chip theory. Also recall that the fact that articles about a "Remote Neuro Brain System" existed on the internet provided further evidence to Chandolia and Irfan's brother-in-law that the microchip theory was indeed plausible.

While this is the only story I heard involving the Special Cell implanting a chip into a person's brain, it was clear that the story had spread. Several weeks after Irfan had been acquitted, a journalist whom I knew and who covered the lower court beat telephoned me and asked me if I could tell him anything about the "chip-wallah" case. From his contacts in the courts, he had heard that the man had been convicted, and he thought that the story of a convicted terrorist who claimed to have had a chip implanted his brain would be newsworthy. I told him that as far as I knew, Irfan had been acquitted and that I had not been able to get in touch with him or his brother-in-law. On another occasion, when I was having tea with a lawyer in the court canteen, he asked me if I had heard about the man who claimed to have a chip inside his head. I told him that I had, and he then asked me if I believed the story. I said that I could not believe that even if such a technology did exist, that the Special Cell had the resources to go through with it. I doubted that he agreed with my opinion since he asserted that no one could possibly know the truth about what "technology the police had," and we left it at that. It was almost as if the story about the chip had taken hold and the lawyer and brother-in-law, at least, were convinced of its veracity. It was difficult to parse truth from rumor.

A very basic understanding of rumors would seem to imply that they are the opposite of constative utterances: that they describe something that does not exist in reality. However, this elides over the fact that rumors do not merely purvey (dis)information. Scholars have sketched out several aspects of rumor that I draw upon here: One treats rumor as a contagion that spreads, and the second sees rumor as destabilizing the boundary between fact and fantasy, which in turn gives rise to paranoia.

Stoler (1992) argues that rumor is a key form of "cultural knowledge . . . [and] shape[s] what people thought they knew, blurring the boundaries between events 'witnessed' and those envisioned" (154). Similarly, for Das (2007), rumors are utterances that bring into question the difference between reality and fantasy. In her study of rumors during the Delhi anti-Sikh riots, she argues that rumors gathered a perlocutionary force that brought into question the reality of what was happening. Rumors did not call into question the utterances' adequacy to reality (i.e., whether the rumor was true or not), but called into question reality itself.

Rumors dissimulate reality, feeding off things we may encounter in everyday life and reincarnating them in different forms. A scar becomes evidence of surgery to implant a chip; Irfan's alternating shivers and sweats come to indicate that he is receiving messages from the Special Cell. Fact and fiction merge into one another and render any knowledge of what is real tenuous. It made no sense whether to ask the microchip story was "true" or not, because the stories narrated about the chip rendered any distinctions between truth and falsity irrelevant. The lawyer Chandolia, Irfan, and his brother-in-law all proceeded as if the story of the chip were true. Indeed, for them, it was true.

What is also clear is that the story of the chip exercised a certain force and helped transform the police from a bureaucratic, if violent, form of state power, into an unnatural presence that was quite literally inside Irfan's head. Stories about the police's ability to tap all phones, influence lawyers, and pressure judges imbue the police with powers that they might not actually possess. It is through rumor that the police gain the power to implant a microchip into a person's brain and send him messages. It is through the medium of these stories circulated about the police that the police come to be reincarnated into everyday life in these awesome and terrifying forms.

Some scholars have read rumors as a form of resistance. In her discussion of rumors circulated about corporate trademarks[11] in the post-industrial United States, Coombe (1997) argues that where corporate symbols pervade cultural space, rumors about these trademarks are a way for people to reinsert themselves into a corporatized media space. She also argues that, even if not self-consciously done, circulation of these rumors directed against companies should be understood as "cultural guerrilla tactics" (270) and a form of "subaltern consumer counterculture" (256). Guha (1999) observes that rumor was central to popular peasant uprisings against the early colonial state in India, such that solidarity in a preliterate society was built by the uncontrollable force of the oral transmission of the rumor (257). Guha does not argue that these rumors were spread deliberately. In fact he argues that rumors are "immediate and unpremeditated utterance[s]" (262), but directed against the colonial state, they helped build a consciousness of a common enemy.[12] For both Guha and Coombe—the former a founder of the subaltern studies movement and the latter influenced by theorists of subaltern studies—rumor arises as a form of resistance to political and economic power.

The outline of rumor that I wish to sketch here treats rumor not so much as a mode of resistance to police power, but as a mode of how the power of the police is incarnated. Rumor's power to break down the fundamental boundary between fact and fiction is a key way that police power operates. Rumors cast reality into doubt. Is a cell phone merely a cell phone? Is a scar on one's head just a scar or does it mark the surgical implantation of a microchip? The fact that the police are incarnated in fantastical forms incites an anxiety over the actual limits of police power. What exactly can the police do? Who controls the police? Is the Special Cell acting on its own, or, as Chandolia would have it, on behalf of military intelligence?

Rumors do not merely negate the distinction between fact and fiction, but also extend the meaning of everyday objects and events (Guha 1999, 238–39). In the milieu of a terrorism trial, everyday objects and occurrences are seen then to conceal the *real* mechanisms of power (Boltanski 2014, 13). A scar is not just a scar. Behind the scar on Irfan's head, lies a microchip, which is connected to the Special Cell. Through the chip, Irfan's own mind is made to speak against him; he receives messages from the Special Cell, against his own will. Further, the cell phones and microchips are not just listening devices but are figured as extensions of the policeman's body. The police are not wholly organic beings, but are now monstrous combination of man and machine. One cannot trust one's phone or even one's thoughts since they may actually be machine-like extensions of the policeman's body.

This is precisely the form of intimacy that is conveyed through these stories: that the police can been seen to be potentially everywhere, under your skin and inside your head. According to the image of a spectral police constructed by rumor, one can never know where the police are, as they could be anywhere. And like the police, the rumors that circulate everywhere in courts seem to penetrate the very bodies of people who came in contact with them.

AN INTIMATE APPROACH TO THE LAW

In this chapter, I have outlined two aspects of what I have called custodial intimacy. In the first instance, I looked at relationships that grew out the time spent together—first during the period of illegal detention, then during the legal period of detention, then in the trial courts. These relationships do not lend themselves to easy description. The time that the police and the terror-accused spent together engendered a familiarity between them such that each could speak to the other about their hopes for the future, anxieties about the present, and tragedies that had befallen their families. Meanwhile, however, the time spent in courts also enabled the proliferation of rumors about the police. As we have seen, rumors call into question the boundaries of fact and fiction and fundamentally destabilize how one relates to the world. Through these rumors, the police came to be incarnated in monstrous, threatening forms.

By delineating two forms of custodial intimacy, I do not intend to argue that these two forms are separate from each other. Rather these two forms of intimacy are enmeshed in one another. Shahid's friendship with Dharamveer grew in a milieu of rumors about Dharamveer's capacity for violence. Recall that while Nadeem and Faheem were treated appallingly by the police, Nadeem still felt betrayed when the Special Cell refused to support his case in the Supreme Court. In their interactions with the police, the question that terror-accused individuals constantly had to navigate was whether the police would be friendly or monstrous. Most often, the two blended into each other.

This fundamental opacity of the police arose not from the distance of the police from the terror-accused, but from the intimate place that the police have in their lives. Although the terror-accused may feel that they have a personal knowledge of the police, the actions of the police are rarely transparent. This opacity then is not because of a lack of knowledge about the police, but from a seeming excess of it.

It is this intimate ambivalence that is also constitutive of the terror-accused's relationship to the law. For the terror-accused, the law is not distant; on the contrary, they are constantly immersed in it. This intimacy does not yield clarity; rather, it produces a deep uncertainty. In understanding and learning to use legal processes the terror-accused and their lawyers constantly face similar dilemmas, as legal technicalities could potentially help or harm them.

As we will see in the chapters ahead, all actors in the trial process—the terror-accused included—cultivated an intimate knowledge of legal processes. By constantly reading, writing, and speaking about them, they developed a knowledge of the legal processes that were close at hand. Nevertheless, they approached any engagement with legal technicalities tentatively, as they could only speculate on the outcomes. Legal technicalities were a source of threat, as it was through them that the prosecution tried to get a conviction. Simultaneously, legal technicalities were the only means by which terror-accused individuals and their lawyers could obtain an acquittal.

2

RECYCLED LEGALITY
Doing Things with Legal Language

When I asked the terror-accused to relate their memories of their first appearances in court, most of them described their utter confusion. When they were brought before magistrates, several did not even realize that they had been arrested by the police, let alone understand the charges that were being brought against them. They did not know if they were allowed to speak or what they were supposed to say. Their near universal experience of first appearances in the courtroom was that they could not follow what was being said about them—neither what the police and prosecutors told the judges, nor what the judges said in response. If they had lawyers in those early days, they rarely understood what the lawyers told the judges or what their lawyers told them. It was as if they had been plunged into an alien world in which the language was intelligible to everyone else but them. These initial experiences of hearing an alien language often mirrored my own during my first days in Delhi's courts.

In almost every case, the terror-accused did not merely accept the linguistic confusion. Instead, they took action to adjust to their new reality. As several of my ethnographic interlocutors put it, they had to learn the *naya bhasha*, or new language, of the law. As we will see in this chapter, a number of the terror-accused pooled their efforts and attempted to teach themselves this legal language. They borrowed legal textbooks from jail libraries, read and translated documents relating to their cases, asked other terror-accused individuals for advice, and shared legal strategies. They learned legal language by using it: They wrote out applications that they made to courts, they fully involved themselves in their trials, and some even conducted their own defense.

Learning legal language gave the terror accused a way of engaging with the world of courtrooms and jail cells. By using legal language, the terror accused were able to articulate their own arguments and questions in ways that were comprehensible to judges, lawyers, and the police. Learning, speaking, and writing legal language allowed terror-accused individuals to give meaning to their experiences and to establish relationships with other-terror accused persons and with the various players in courtrooms and jails. It alleviated the feeling of being lost in this "different" world and enabled them to find themselves within it.

Courtrooms and jail cells are not just spaces of judgment and confinement—they are also spaces of language. The great number of people who populate these spaces—judges, police officials, lawyers, defendants, clerks, stenographers, and so on—all constantly speak, read, write, and *do* things with legal language. This is a world that is defined by its use of legal language, with distinct modes of speech, argumentation, and thought. The urgent question before the terror-accused is how does one become part of this world and participate in it? How does one make the language of law one's own so that one can use it on one's behalf?

In asking how legal language enables the terror-accused to inhabit the space of the courtroom, I draw inspiration from theorists of language such as Wittgenstein and Cover, for whom language is inextricably linked to the creation of worlds and ways in which we inhabit them. For both, language has an openness and provides avenues for creativity. Wittgenstein (2009) describes language using the metaphor of an ancient city with "a maze of little streets and squares, of old and new houses, of houses with extensions from various periods and all this surrounded by a multitude of new suburbs with straight and regular streets and uniform houses" (§18). For Wittgenstein, language is constantly changing: New alleyways in the city of our words constantly emerge, giving us new ways to inhabit this city, while other routes may become blocked or be forgotten.

This similar openness is present in Cover's (1983) idea of a *nomos*, in which law is "not merely a system of rules to be observed, but a world in which we live" (5). Crucially for Cover, the *nomos*—or the normative universe that language provides us—not only describes the world that actually exists. It is also forward looking, a vision for alternative futures, a bridge toward future lifeworlds (9). The creation of legal meanings—what he calls *jurisgenesis*—enables communities to strive to create these alternate futures. This, for Cover is the potency of legal words: They give us the ability to imagine new futures and to create precepts and principles.

If language is intimately connected not only to how we inhabit this present city of words, but also to how new futures are forged, then there is much at stake legal language. Hence, instead of thinking of legal language as a closed system of orders or one that represents only state power, I want to persist with Cover's idea of law showing us the way to an alternate world and with Wittgenstein's image of language as a city that we inhabit and through which we find our way.

For both Wittgenstein and Cover, language is a lived experience. Rather than thinking about language as a closed system, Wittgenstein asks us to think about an endless series of "language-games." These language-games cannot be separated from the everyday activities into which they are woven. Similarly, for Cover (1983), in his *nomos* legal language not only has the capacity to signify actions such as resistance or disobedience, but allows us to "submit, rejoice, struggle, mock, disgrace, humiliate or dignify" (1983, 8). Language is an activity, and we constantly *do* things with language to find our place within it.

In this chapter, I look at legal language as a form of tekhne. That is, legal language as a form of knowledge that emerges through working with it. I provide an account of how the terror-accused came to inhabit the courtroom by constantly *doing* things with legal language and provided them with a way to imagine a future path to an acquittal. Through my time in the courts, I saw that the terror-accused came to understand the law by establishing a sensual familiarity with it. They copied out legal texts, translated them, shared legal knowledge, and strategies. As I hope to show in this chapter, the terror-accused did not seek to understand the law simply in order to follow it. Rather, they sought to understand the law in order to use it instrumentally, to obtain a certain result. In the short term, such a result may have been something like impeaching the credibility of a certain witness, while in the long term the desired result would have been an acquittal.

But, as I also argue in this chapter, there is more than the law's instrumentality that is at stake in understanding a rule—namely, the idea of feeling at home in legal language, not feeling lost in this city of words. Through the slow, repetitive process of engaging with the law, its language, its procedures, and modes of speech became more complete and more familiar to the terror-accused. The terror-accused were able to make the legal language their own, and thus they were able to make their way through the legal process.

In arguing that doings things with the law enabled terror-accused to inhabit legal language, I do not argue that the terror-accused obtained a mastery over it. An understanding of legal language as tekhne means that by using legal language, one develops an appreciation of what legal language can do and the futures it can open up. It also involves an understanding of the limits of language and the paths that it closes down. As we will see in this chapter and the next, part of inhabiting language involves making mistakes and understanding the boundaries of language. In this chapter we will see how learning legal language also involves making errors in understanding and deploying it. As Cavell (1976) notes more generally on inhabiting language, "We learn and teach words in certain contexts and then we are expected and expect others to be able to project them into further contexts. Nothing insures that this projection will take place" (52).

Inhabiting legal language in a trial is not about developing a mastery in using that language. Rather, it is about trying to maneuver through the trial and the courtroom. What is key to here is the ability to use legal language, not the success or failure of outcomes.

In focusing on legal language as a mode through which to inhabit the courtroom, I depart from existing approaches to legal language. For mainstream legal philosophers, legal language raises the question of interpretation: How do judges and other legal institutions impart meaning to or derive meaning from legal words.[1] From this perspective, legislatures produce legal rules, courts interpret the rules, and other institutions (the police, the bureaucracy) enforce the decision of the courts. The individual's importance to this institutional conception of law is relevant only insofar as that individual ought to know when and how to follow the rule and what will happen if the rule is broken. Institutions make, interpret, and enforce the rules, and we either follow them or are punished for breaking them.

The idea of legal language as something that constitutes a world in which we try to find our place is also fundamentally different from the idea of legal language articulated by many critical and sociolinguistic scholars of law. I depart from those who would describe legal discourse solely as a "language of power, as the pursuit or control over meaning and as an instrument and expression of domination" (Goodrich 1987, ix). For many critical legal scholars as well as anthropologists of law, the neutrality of legal language hides structural and social inequalities and injustices, and thus legal language perpetuates "powerful linguistic ideologies" (Mertz 2007, 3). By looking at modes of disputation and ways in which people speak in courtrooms, these scholars seek to understand how culture and social power emerge in courtrooms (Conley and O'Barr 2005; Mertz 1994, 2007). Even as legal language offers the semblance of equality and openness, these studies emphasize that legal speech is embedded in social divisions that frame the ways in which legal meaning is made (Merry 1990) and that ordinary legal language reveals much about power and social inequality (Conley and O'Barr 2005; Mertz, 2007). The picture of language here involves an elaborate linguistic bait-and-switch: While laws convince their addressees ("We the people") that they exist to guarantee equal protection to all citizens, they are actually aimed at concealing the power of capital, race, and gender and the displacement of politics from the public sphere. While legible on the surface, true meaning hides behind legal texts. Furthermore, in these theories, the highly technical form of legal language belies any form of democratic readership. Therefore, while the neutrality of legal language gives it the aura of being open and democratic, what the law actually does is to close off the sphere of politics from popular participation. It is a screen behind which real power lies (Sanín-Restrepo and Hincapíe 2018).

While questions regarding the interpretation of legal texts and how social power is constituted through legal language are important ones, this chapter looks at how learning how to speak, read, and write like a lawyer enabled terror-accused individuals to inhabit the courtroom. Some accounts of learning legal language have described a "jarring confrontation" (Mertz 2007, 22) that constitutes a rupture in one's world view when one first encounters legal language. While this is true of the terror-accused as well, it is not the end of the story. In this chapter, I look at how learning legal language allowed the terror-accused to find a footing in their trials.

DOING THINGS WITH LEGAL LANGUAGE

I offer the term "recycled legality" to describe the ways in which the terror-accused did things with legal language. I hope to flesh out the details of this idea through a narrative of a man I call Qayoom. Accused of being part of a conspiracy to commit bomb explosions in Delhi, Qayoom and his co-accused built knowledge about the cases against them—and in particular about the procedures that the police were required to follow during the course of their investigations. Eventually, Qayoom and his co-accused were acquitted, and the trial court ordered charges against the police officers for fabricating evidence. This remarkable judgment was made possible by the efforts of Qayoom and his co-accused to teach themselves, through trial and error, the granular details of legal procedure. Qayoom and his co-accused translated documents from English to Urdu and back again, filed their own applications before the trial court and higher courts, borrowed strategies from other terror-accused persons, and even cross-examined the prosecution's witnesses. Examples of such legal bricolage were commonplace in Delhi's courtrooms, with the terror accused—many of whom were housed together in a single block in the jail complex—sharing legal forms, strategy, case law, and background information on police officers.

By relating the trial records as well as conversations that I had with Qayoom, I trace how Qayoom and his co-defendants came to understand legal rules. As we will see in this chapter, Qayoom and his co-accused did several things. First, they sought to understand the nature of the charges against them and facts of their case as narrated by the police. Then they learned of the existence of certain rules that governed the way in which investigations were to proceed, and they sought to understand these rules. They also developed ways to construct a narrative to show that the police did not follow these rules and, importantly, also found ways in which these narratives could be presented to the court. In going through these various steps, I show how they put their knowledge of legal procedures to use in order think about ways to get acquitted. What Qayoom's narrative will show us is that learning the law is based on imitation and experimentation. It is fundamentally less about obeying the law than about being able to articulate one's own interpretation of a rule and thus inhabit the space of the courtroom.

I use the term "recycled legality" to describe this mode of legal bricolage. The term is itself gleaned and modified from media studies (Sundaram 1999, 2010). Recycled legality encapsulates the ways in which legal materials and information are shared—how they are copied, repurposed, and deployed. It seeks to forge its own space through shared knowledges of legal practice and procedure. It provides a concept of law that is derived not from learning the law in school, but from mimesis of legal forms and the cultivation of a tactile familiarity with legal texts. Unlike the idea of insurgent legality (Kannabiran 2004, 2014), which is premised on a resistance to the law, recycled legality feeds off of it and pirates it. Recycled legality involves gleaning bits of knowledge from here and copying other bits from there. While it is intimately connected to state power and feeds off its utterances, it claims a status equal to authoritative interpretations of legal language. Recycled legality provides a space for the terror-accused to participate in and influence the course of their trials and reveals that what is at stake in inhabiting the rule is nothing short of the ability to have a future in legal language. Recycled legality emerges out of a visceral experience of the law, as well as the effort to maintain a connection to life and to have hope in the future.

Recycled legality is an invitation to think about the law outside of the institutional settings through which law has been thus far understood. It is not about the enactment of statutes or about judgment. It is less about who made the rule and more about what the rule can do. It is less about understanding how courts have previously interpreted a rule, and more about how a rule can be interpreted in order to achieve certain ends. Recycling legality is not just about learning how to follow a rule; rather, it enables the production of new legal meaning. It is creative and contingent and does not respect the boundaries placed by institutions on the meaning of rules. Nor does recycled legality place violence or coercion at the center of its view of law. Rather, it sees the law as an environment, a world, which provides the means to move through it and the tools to inhabit it.

Recycled legality also draws into focus the fact that the law, as a form of tekhne, is fundamentally about processes that are creative. People can do things with legal language and can produce legal meaning. As it involves the production of legal meaning, recycled legality approaches what Cover (1983) calls "jurisgenesis." It is the production of legal meaning that is connected to, but independent, of "official" modes of producing meaning by the courts and the legislature. Recycled legality approaches the law less as a declaration of sovereign power or a means of social control and more as series of tools and resources that allow one to inhabit the world. The idea of recycling legality that I propose here points to the open nature of legal processes. Further, recycled legality shows that technicalities enable a variety of entry points through which parties in a legal dispute can intervene in their own cases (Liang 2005). Recycled legality describes the ways in which the terror-accused reprocessed legal language in order to create avenues for themselves to participate in their trials.

As we will see in Qayoom's narrative, he and his co-accused intervened in their trial by focusing on the procedural laws that the police had to adhere to while investigating a case. Procedural laws do not just describe how a trial is to be conducted or how the police should act. They also provide entry points. Qayoom and his co-accused were able to construct a narrative in which the policemen failed to comply with many small but essential procedural steps. This failure did not simply point to state lawlessness, but allowed Qayoom and his co-defendants to construct a narrative of the fabrication of evidence by the police. What was meant to be a trial of Qayoom and his co-accused became, in Qayoom's narrative, a trial of the state.[2]

A RECYCLED CONCEPT OF LAW

Before pursuing Qayoom's narrative, I want to briefly ask what recycling legality can add to our own concept of the law. How does an understanding of the lived experience of recycling legality—of a process that is imitative and derivative, productive and creative—change our understanding of the law? I contend that ethnographic attention to how people use legal language forces us to think of law less as an expression of a system of rules that demand obedience or as a gated entry into a linguistic system of social hierarchies and instead see it in terms of modes of inhabiting the legal process. Law is not just something that is handed down by the state. Rather, people creatively work with the law to create legal meaning in order to express their own demands.

Recycled legality helps us to see that people try to gain an understanding of the law in order to use it instrumentally. This idea of legal language as a strategic resource has been a trope in certain strands of legal anthropology. Scholars of the "dispute resolution" strand of legal anthropology often note the social and political malleability of rules and look at how disputants access rules as a strategic resource to win cases. For example, in their book about legal processes of two Tswana tribes in Botswana, Comaroff and Roberts (1981) provide an ethnography of how rules are employed as a strategic resource. They detail the "normative repertoires" (70) that are invoked by Tswana disputants before decision-making bodies and examine the ways in which arguments are constructed and rhetoric is formulated. According to them, the repertoires of norms afford the Tswana dispute settlement agencies room for maneuver, what Gluckman (1955) refers to as the flexibility and permeability of law.[3] Comaroff and Roberts (1981) argue that while rules are constantly negotiated and are negotiable, the behavior of individuals is, at times, rule governed. In the dispute settlement process, rules form a "strategic resource for disputants" (74), with disputants engaging in a series of rhetorical maneuvers that may simultaneously invoke, affirm, and negotiate specific rules.

As I will show in this chapter, knowledge of the law enabled the terror-accused to participate in court processes. In finding out what procedures the police were meant to follow, then by reading and rereading the charge sheets, in translating applications from Urdu to English and then filing them, Qayoom and his co-accused recycled legal forms in order deploy their legal knowledge tactically. They cultivated the ability to make arguments about the validity of claims made by the police, prosecution, and even those of their own lawyers, and these actions were made possible because they taught themselves the law.

But as I also hope to show in this chapter, there is another way in which recycled legality can alter our concept of law: Recycling legality has an ethical charge. It enables us to see how the terror-accused, in repurposing legal language, gave themselves the ability to articulate their demands and arguments. In other words, what is at stake in recycling legality is the ability for the terror-accused to have a future in legal language.

In trying to understand what it means to have a future in language, Das (1998) and Cavell (1990, 1995) look to rule-learning in Wittgenstein's *Philosophical Investigations* (2009). Their discussion centers on a reading of the open passages of Wittgenstein's text—in particular §1, where Wittgenstein considers Augustine's narrative of how a child acquires language,[4] and §2 where he provides the example of the builders' language, which the builders understand only as a series of directions.[5] Whereas, the child learns language in the context of moving through everyday life, and this learning enables the child to express his or her own desires, the builder learns language only to follow orders.

Contrasting these two paragraphs Cavell (1995), argues that the child in §1 has a future in language, whereas the "builders have, without luck, or the genius of invention, none—only their repetition" (146). Similarly, Das (1998) points out that there is no standing language game for imagining what Wittgenstein asks us to imagine with the builders' language. The builders' tribe, Das (1998) she suggests, seems to be bereft of a culture or forms of sociality (179).

Cavell argues that the child discussed in §1 forms a founding metaphor for the rest of the *Philosophical Investigations*. Instead of reading §1 as a scene in which a child learns how to correctly apply and follow a rule,[6] Cavell reads it as a scene in which a child moves unseen by his elders; the child is "the unobserved, observer of a culture" (1990, 98). In this picture, the child moves silently among his elders and language is portrayed as an "inheritance, but also as one that has . . . to be stolen" (99). Das (1998) argues that by juxtaposing the child with the builders, Wittgenstein appears to suggest that whatever else it may be, one's entry into language is not about inheriting a certain set of rules or a certain capacity to obey orders (179).

Understanding the law, then, is fundamentally tied to the ability to have a future in legal language. If one conceives of laws, not as rules to be learned only to be followed or applied, but as a type of language that is learned in order to participate in the world of the trial, then to follow a rule is not just to come up with the right answer or to apply a rule correctly. It is to make the law one's own—by recycling legal language. This is not only to deploy a rule strategically, but also to have a future in legal language and to learn its text as a child would—not to produce the same answer as the child's teacher, but to enable the child to say "and after I had trained my mouth to the form these signs, I used them to express my own desires" (Wittgenstein 2009, §1).[7]

Recycled legality therefore also draws our attention to the centrality of the perlocutionary to legal language. Recycled legality is not just about the creation of new legal meaning; it is also about claim-making, confrontation, and persuasion. To have a future in language is to be able to stake certain claims. As we will see in this chapter and the next (and later on in Chapter 6), the perlocutionary is essential to textures of everyday legality in the courtrooms. In looking at recycled legality through the idea of the perlocutionary utterance, we can understand the ethical stakes in inhabiting legal language, as legal language becomes a mode of expressiveness and a register of vulnerability (Laugier 2020, 2).

To inhabit legal language, then, does not mean that one is always successful in "express[ing one's] own desires." Rather, inhabiting a language is to learn, through trial and error, that language has boundaries and is replete with "misfires" (Austin 1962, 16). It is thus to learn that language has limits and that speech acts may be infelicitous, or that one's words may be taken out of context and be given a different meaning. As we will see in the next chapter, language is the site of vulnerability; speakers can have their utterances turned against them. Inhabiting language is therefore not about establishing a mastery over language. Rather, it is about cultivating the ability to maneuver within language.

In this chapter, I seek to understand the significance of rules—not just as words to be obeyed or as strategic resources—but also as engendering one's movement in the life of the trial. As I will show in this chapter, the terror-accused were not just meek observers of their own trials. Nor were they hapless victims of the legal system or the security state. Instead they actively participated in their trials: They read legal texts, pored over the charges and evidence against them, and intervened in the court processes. In doing so, they produced legal meaning. As I suggest in this chapter, in reading, writing and re-writing the various legal texts, the terror-accused created for themselves the ability to inhabit the law.

QAYOOM BHAT

In 2011, a trial court in Delhi acquitted Qayoom Bhat and six others of terrorism-related offenses, including possession of unlawful explosives, causing explosions, impersonating a public official, possession of arms and explosives, and the attempt to murder a police officer. The seven men were accused by the Delhi police's Special Cell of coming to Delhi with the intention of carrying out terrorist attacks.

According to the police version of events, the Special Cell received information in July 2006 about a planned terrorist attack in Delhi. Subsequently, the secret informer told the Special Cell the registration number of the car that some of the terrorists would arrive by and the highway they would take. On midnight on July 11, the police set up a checkpoint on this road and installed barricades. Soon after they saw the car approach and signaled for it to stop. Instead, the car sped away, forcing the police to give chase. According to the police, the car was finally stopped when it was boxed in by two police vehicles. At this point, the occupants of the car began to fire on the police and even made an abortive attempt to throw a hand grenade at the police. Eventually, by about 5 A.M., the terrorists were overpowered and arrested. These alleged terrorists then gave the police further information about four other terrorists who were staying at a nearby hotel and another terrorist (Qayoom) who was arriving by train at New Delhi Railway Station later that day. As a result of this information, according to the police, Qayoom was arrested outside a *gurudwara*[8] near New Delhi Railway Station. According to the Special Cell, a total of seven men were connected with the conspiracy to commit terrorist acts in Delhi, and the police recovered arms, grenades, and ammunition as well as vast sums of money and fake currency from the possession of these alleged terrorists. The Special Cell also claimed that all the accused confessed to being part of a terrorist conspiracy and were working at the behest of the Pakistani intelligence service, the ISI.

The defense of Qayoom and his co-accused was that the entire story related above was a complete falsehood. They argued that the car chase, the shootout, and even the report of the arrest of Qayoom and the other terrorists were completely concocted by the police. The seven men all testified that they had been kidnapped several days prior to the purported date of the incident; the entire investigative record had been fabricated. The trial court eventually found that the Special Cell of the Delhi Police had indeed manufactured evidence, which included falsifying the story of the shootouts and the arrests of Qayoom Bhat and his co-accused in this case. The trial court not only acquitted all of the accused, but also ordered a full investigation and prosecution of police officials for false incrimination and for the fabrication of evidence.[9]

This rare judgment was made possible, in part, by the efforts of Qayoom and his co-accused to understand the law and the cases against them. I spoke to Qayoom about how he and his co-accused built up their defense in their trials. Apart from just wanting to know the details of the police's case against them, Qayoom and his co-accused also felt that they had to learn the nuances of legal procedures for themselves because they did not trust their lawyers for several reasons. These include the suspicion that their lawyers were in collusion with the Special Cell and with prosecutors. This would enable the lawyers to delay their cases in order to extract more money from the terror-accused. Another suspicion was that defense lawyers would trade cases with the Special Cell—getting an acquittal in one case in exchange for allowing a conviction in another case. Qayoom himself hinted that his lawyer was "corrupt," but mounting legal fees were more of a concern for him.

> I got a lawyer. *Usne paise khaya, kuch kaam nahin kiya.* [He ate money, did not do any work.] He came [to court] only sometimes. He took so much money that my missus had to sell her gold. She has no gold now. She had to sell everything. I had a car—she sold the car. All that money went to him. I had no property, and I was a government employee. . . . I thought if we were going to give so much money to the lawyers and they did not do any work, we might as well do the work ourselves.

The trial court records show that many of the co-accused conducted their own cross-examination of the prosecution witnesses. At several instances in the court's record, the judge notes that the "accused has cross-examined the witness as his Counsel is not turning up." At one point at the beginning of the trial, one of the defense lawyers was dramatically fired by his client in the middle of a cross-examination of a prosecution witness, with the court dryly noting "at this stage, [Learned] Counsel for the defendant has been discharged and has withdrawn his *vakalatnama* [power of attorney]."

Qayoom and his co-accused did not eschew legal representation entirely. Qayoom describes how on occasion he went around his lawyer and filed applications through "legal aid," more formally known as Delhi Legal Services Authority in Tihar Jail. He even filed a petition in the High Court through legal aid asking for the case to be transferred to a fast-track court. The trial court record shows that accused who sometimes cross-examined witnesses themselves also sometimes asked for legal representation. Qayoom and his co-accused had a sense of when they thought it best to "do the work" themselves and when to approach a lawyer. In other words, they had a sense of how to go about intervening in the legal process.

Qayoom and his co-accused invested time and effort into learning the nuances of legal procedure not just because they did not trust their lawyers, but also because they felt that they had to take ownership of their case. As they were the accused, they had to know the case against them and decide how to respond. "Allah gave us this sadness only to show us the meaning of happiness. I knew that if I worked hard [on the case], Allah would reward me."

Their first hurdle in understanding the case against them was to overcome the linguistic barrier that they faced. As educated Kashmiris, they could read and write Urdu, but struggled to read and write Hindi or English, the two languages used in Delhi's courts. Qayoom described his efforts to read the charge sheet against him and his co-accused. They pooled resources and began the slow, collaborative process of reading; they translated legal texts from English and Hindi to Urdu and then from Urdu back to English and Hindi again. Qayoom described the process:

> I didn't understand English that much, but whatever I could, I read and tried to understand. Some of the guys couldn't read Hindi, so someone used to read it in Hindi, and I would write it down in Urdu. Then I would read it out to my friend, and he would write it down in English. Like this we translated it into English and Urdu, and Urdu to English because if people could not read the documents, then the case itself is bad. People should know what is written [in the file and in the law books].

As they translated the charge sheet, Qayoom and his co-accused realized that the case was built upon a variety of log books and diaries that the police had to maintain during an investigation. For example, when a police officer enters or leaves a police station, they must sign in and out of the station's Daily Diary Register. If the police officer uses an official vehicle, they must state the destination of that vehicle and the number of kilometers it traveled. There is a panoply of similar paperwork that must be completed for a number of police activities: use of arms and ammunition, arrests from a different jurisdiction, information given to and by other police stations, and so on.

Qayoom and his co-accused realized that the police had not submitted the original registers along with the charge sheet and then began a multi-year effort to gain access to these logbooks and registers. Crucial to their eventual success in the trial, was the strategy of filing applications under the Right to Information (RTI) Act. This legislation allows citizens to ask government departments for copies of their records. During the course of the trial, Qayoom and his co-defendants filed RTI applications asking for the log books of the vehicles that that the police said they used while pursuing and apprehending them; the daily diaries of various police stations that recorded the movements of the various police officials said to be involved in the case; and the arms and ammunition log books that documented the specific weapons that the police had requisitioned and used. These requests were premised on the knowledge of the rules that govern police activity. The replies to the RTI applications revealed that the vehicles that the police said they used to apprehend the "terrorists" never went to the place where the "terrorists" were allegedly arrested and that the police officers involved in the case lied about their whereabouts on the relevant days.

Qayoom told me about how he and his co-accused came up with the idea of filing RTI applications. He said that soon after he was arrested, the RTI Act came into force:

> One night we were watching the news—yes, there was a TV in jail. So then we saw the news, and heard that the RTI law had come into force. After that we asked our lawyer to bring us a book. We read it a bit, and it said that the RTI letter is like a *patthar ki lakeer* [a line in a stone— something impossible to change], no one can lie in it. We started in 2006, but we didn't get any response, and then in 2009–2010 maybe we started getting responses.

Qayoom told me that he was not "such an educated person" and that he did not "know much English but is fluent in Urdu." He began reading "little by little" and slowly came to know what power there was in the RTI. In repeating the phrase "voh patthar ki lakeer hai," Qayoom conveyed the idea that although the police might be lying in court, the log books and daily diaries could not be altered and would show in banal detail how the police had lied about their whereabouts on the day of the purported arrest. The strategy adopted by Qayoom and his co-accused was that the papers would "expose the truth." As we will see in Chapters 5 and 6, paperwork is essential to the fabrication of facts.

I asked Qayoom about the process of writing and sending the RTI applications. I asked him if his lawyer had filed the RTI applications on their behalf. He said that he and another of his co-accused first wrote out their applications out in Urdu and then slowly translated it English. He then gave it to his lawyer to file with the relevant police departments.

> My English is a bit bad, so my co-accused -he knew English - he wrote it out. But we sat together and decided what to write, what to ask for. We used to write it out first in Urdu and then he would make it in English. Then we gave it to our lawyer who submitted it.

Qayoom told me of how he filed RTI applications specifically regarding the case against him. He said that since the police narrative was that he was arrested from near the railway station, then police paperwork had to reflect this narrative. If the Special Cell received "secret information" that he was arriving at the New Delhi railway station, then the Special Cell's daily diary should have an entry stating that this information was given to the police. If the Special Cell then said that several policemen went to arrest Qayoom from close to the railway station, then the Daily Diary should mention the names of the police officers who went to arrest him, and the vehicle log books ought to mention the vehicle registration numbers and their purported destination. If the Special Cell were arresting someone from the jurisdiction of another police station—in this case the Paharganj police station—then the Special Cell should have informed the Paharganj police station and this information should have been recorded in the latter police station's daily diary. If a "terrorist" was coming to Delhi via the railway station, then the railway police should have been informed, and this information too should have been noted in the railway police's daily diary. He filed RTI applications asking for these various documents.

The first attempts made by Qayoom and his co-accused in 2006 were met with failure. Some RTI applications were met with silence, while others were returned with "irrelevant documents." According to Qayoom, they filed the RTI applications soon after the legislation was enacted and "maybe even they [the government officers] did not know how to follow the law." Qayoom also felt that they may have made mistakes in writing the applications, given that his "English is not so good." But he suspected that the police officers were deliberately avoiding submitting the correct documents in response to their RTI queries. That is why in 2006, according to Qayoom, "We didn't get any proper answer." But once they had "understood how to write *arjees* [applications] properly," they began to receive "correct answers."

After that, in 2009, when a lot of news [about RTI] started coming—it came on TV also—then we started in earnest. The police officer's statement [in the charge sheet] said that one a certain day, [he] received information from a secret informer that a terrorist is coming by rail and that he and other police men took certain cars to the railway station, that he reached the railway station and caught me near the gurudwara. That policeman's name and the vehicle number are written there. I filed an RTI, naming the relevant policemen, I said give me the DD [daily diary] entry [about these policemen]. The DD entry showed some [police officials] being on report duty [at the police station] and some of them being somewhere else. The vehicles were on thane [police station] detail; some of them had gone to Sangam Vihar [another neighborhood in Delhi]; none of them had gone to the railway station. I filed an RTI with the Paharganj police station, and they said, "We have no such record." We have no record of any such incident. If any militant is caught, then there is a red alert. Wouldn't the railway police force know? Wouldn't the Paharganj police station know if there was a terrorist who was caught? That answer also came. Then we put all the paper together and produced it before the judge. We completely destroyed the witnesses; we [cross-examined the witnesses] ourselves. [The reply to the RTI application] contained the log book which showed that the officer [who arrested Qayoom] was not on duty [on the day he said he arrested Qayoom]. You can't change a log book. They copied the log book, put a seal on it and sent it to us. The same DD entry, they copied it, put a seal on it and sent it to us.

While Qayoom sought to convey the idea that they "completely destroyed" the prosecution's witnesses, the court transcripts tell a slightly different story. There are many points when the judge disallowed certain questions or when the questions elicited irrelevant answers. At one point in the transcript, the defense lawyer of one of the terror-accused tried to undo the damage done to his client's case by an accused who chose to examine a witness on his own.

Apart from filing the RTI applications to show that the Special Cell had lied about the paper record of their case, Qayoom and his co-accused used the police's paper records against the prosecution. For instance, in their testimony to the court, the police told the court that the car that Qayoom's co-accused were traveling in was stopped by boxing this car in with police vehicles and that a distance of three to four feet separated the purported terrorists' vehicle from the police cars. At this point, according to the police, the "terrorists" began firing with automatic weapons. In their cross-examinations of these police witnesses, Qayoom's co-accused repeatedly asked the police officials if the police vehicles sustained any damage. The police had to answer in the negative—as they had provided no record of any damage to any of the vehicles. In pressing the point further, they were asked whether it was plausible for "highly trained terrorists"—as these defendants were alleged to be—to miss their targets at such short range. In reply to a question as to what they did after being fired on, one of the police witnesses said that instead of taking cover behind their vehicles, they ran toward the "terrorists" and "overpowered them." This led the judge to sardonically note in his final judgment that such "imaginary bravery is only seen in Bollywood movies and not in a real situation as is being projected by the prosecution in this case."

Another irregularity that the accused made use of was the timing of the arrest of several of the accused. Recall that according to the prosecution, after the "shootout" on the highway, the now captured terrorists "confessed" and told the police that several other accused people were staying at a hotel in Delhi. According to the prosecution, a police squad left the police station at 10:45 A.M., reached the hotel at noon, and arrested four of the accused in this case. From there, according to the police officer, they produced the defendants before a magistrate, had them medically examined, and then took them into custody at the police station at about 1:30 P.M. There were two issues with this narrative. First, the defendants obtained copies of the police station's daily diary, which stated that the policemen concerned left the police station at 6:30 A.M. and only returned at 6:30 P.M.; the daily diary made no mention of an arrest at the hotel—which it ought to have done. Second, and more damning, was the fact that the police held a press conference between 10:30 and 11:00 A.M. on that day, where they "produced all the accused persons before the media." So, while the police claimed in court records that the accused were arrested at noon, newspaper reports based on a press conference that occurred at 11:00 A.M. showed all the accused having already been arrested. The police officer who said he led the squad to arrest the defendants at noon is even seen with all the accused in a photograph that was taken at 11:30 A.M. and published in the next day's newspaper. The photograph and the newspaper article were entered into evidence for the defense.

These are just a few of the fabrications that the defendants and their lawyers managed to expose during the course of the trial. Other inconsistencies included the lack of documentation regarding forensic examinations of the arms and the fake currency allegedly recovered from the defendants and the absence of any documentation recording that the police had deposited the physical evidence into the evidence storeroom (indicating that the police had kept—and perhaps tampered with—the physical evidence in their custody).

Qayoom and his co-accused did not limit themselves to attempting to expose the factual contradictions in the prosecution's case. They also questioned the substantive charges that the prosecution made against them. For example, they queried why they had been charged under Sections 3 and 5 of the Explosive Substances Act, 1908, instead of just Section 5. As Qayoom explained to me,

> They put Section 3 on us. That is also wrong. According to the law, Section 3 was only relevant if blasts actually occurred. If blasts did not happen, then Section 5 is applicable. But where did the blast happen in our case? Where did we set off the bombs?

Here we see how through a slow, deliberative process of translation between Hindi, Urdu, and English, Qayoom and the other men accused along with him began to understand what was written against them in their charge sheets and also began to read the law. It was through these small steps, through trial and error, "little by little," that they came to understand legal rules. It was through this process of repetition, of copying the legal rule from one language into another, that they seem to have understood the law—and in particular the power of the RTI Act. Notice here how this was not only a collaborative process—there was sharing of information and they seemed to have worked together to come to an understanding of the law; it was also a repetitive process both in the act of copying and translation and in the repeated writing and filing of RTI applications. It is through this latter process of writing and filing applications that they were able to construct a convincing narrative of how the police had fabricated the case against them. Through this slow, granular process of working with legal texts, it is almost as if Qayoom and his co-accused developed a tactile familiarity with them, to recycle the laws that pertained to their case.

INHABITING LEGAL LANGUAGE

This is not the only example of defendants accused of terrorist crimes using the RTI to good effect (Indorewalla 2013; Khan 2016). Nor is this the only example of the terror-accused creatively understanding the law and mimicking its forms. During my time in Delhi's courts, I saw how the terror-accused collaborated with one another in trying to understand legal texts, shared strategies used in court, and offered their own interpretations of legal texts. They found different ways to come to an understanding of the cases against them and of the applicable rules that applied. Such creative practices around legal language, however, were not limited to terror-accused; other criminal defendants, civil litigants, and even lawyers did many of the same things that Qayoom and his co-accused did in their trial.

Recycled legality shows that legal knowledge must constantly be produced and that the production of legal knowledge is a contingent, creative process. Qayoom and his co-accused had to learn for themselves of the existence of the daily diaries and the vehicle and ammunition logbooks. Had they not filed the RTIs or had they not persisted in making their queries, they could not have produced the narrative of the police fabricating the evidence against them. If they had not asked questions in the cross-examination about lack of damage to the vehicles, they would not have been able to support the idea that the shootout had been entirely made up. Recycled legality shows that it is not just the police, lawyers, and courts who produce legal knowledge; defendants in the trial process can do so as well.

Qayoom's case also shows us that at one level, the ability to deploy legal language tactically is a strategic resource. To have legal language at hand is often the mark of one well-seasoned in the ways of the law. Legal language can be called upon and deployed in a number of different ways, and its repertoires and ways of speaking can be put to use in a calculated manner to outwit one's opponent or to press home an argument. Qayoom's story shows us how the terror-accused used the resources at their disposal to collaboratively intervene in their trial. At one level, they recycled their legal knowledge not to understand and obey the rules, but to deploy them tactically.

Moreover, as we can see from Qayoom's story, an ethical charge comes with this recycling of legal language. There was a certain confidence with which Qayoom spoke about his understanding of the procedures that the police had to comply with. He seemed comfortable talking about the meaning of legal words, and legal provisions flowed off his tongue with ease. It was almost as if he was a home in the "normative universe" (Cover 1983, 6) created by the law. He was comfortable with the rules, understanding them in his own way and projecting this understanding to the trial court. In doing so, Qayoom and his co-accused become co-creators of legal meaning.

Thinking back to Qayoom's account of his early interactions with the police, we might explain his initial sense of helplessness then in terms of his inability at that time to enter the world of legal language. He had not yet learned to navigate its roads. Compare this with how his story ends, when he appeared to know the law and seemed to be able to speak as fluently as a lawyer, or to express himself in the language game that operates in the courts. For the moment, he knew his way about the city of words. Legal language is not a prison house or a camp in which we must obey commands. Neither is it something whose true meaning is hidden and must be divined from above. Legal language opens up a world through which, like Qayoom, one must find one's way.

By comparing the beginning and ending of Qayoom's story, I do not want to suggest that there was a straightforward linear progression in which a person illiterate in the law gains legal knowledge and sets himself at liberty. As we will see in the next chapter, even those well versed in legal language—such as judges, prosecutors, and defense lawyers—can be caught unawares by sudden shifts in legal meaning. Nor do I intend to show that Qayoom became an expert in the law; many might disagree with his interpretation of the Explosive Substances Act. Instead, what I hoped to have demonstrated is that knowledge of a language-game enables maneuverability in a trial. In a world fraught with uncertainty, the understanding of legal texts allows for different modes of entering a courtroom. By recycling law, Qayoom and others showed that they were not mere spectators in the trial, but that they were active participants in it. They also showed that recycling legality is not merely about one's ability to understand and deploy law tactically, but also carries with it the tentative feeling of being at home in legal language. Knowledge of the law and the ability to use legal language allow the terror-accused to come to grips with their situation and to have the ability to express themselves in a language that is audible to the courts. This acquiring of language is not just about putting language to an instrumental use, but about having a future in language. To know legal language is to imagine a future lifeworld. Recycled legality describes the ways in which the terror-accused could play with legal language to make legal language they own.

Qayoom's narrative also calls attention to a complicated conception of the state and its relation to language. Qayoom and his co-accused come to use the state's own utterances—its rules and procedures—against it, and in the process, they understood the state as being vulnerable to the law. It is to this idea that I turn in the following chapter.

3

LAW AND THE VULNERABLE STATE

In the process of working with legal language, the terror-accused came to conceive of the law and its relationship to the state in several different ways. One was to think of the law as something that the state "said," as something that emanated from the state. They knew that the law signified state power—that the laws that had been used to arrest and prosecute them could also be used to convict them and to send them to prison for much of the rest of their lives. Another was to see the law as something that the state uttered into existence and to which it could be bound. This meant that the same laws that had been used to arrest and prosecute them could upend the prosecutions against them. Therefore, while at times the law was imagined as a "state's emissary" (Baxi 1992, 249), the law was also understood as a sign of the state's vulnerability. It is this idea—that the state could be vulnerable to its own utterances—that enabled the terror-accused to imagine a way to navigate the trial. They could shake the foundations of the prosecution by using the law against it.

In this chapter, I consider how the law may signify not the state's power, but its weakness. In pointing to an idea of the state that is present through its vulnerability, I join other anthropologists who have imagined the state through its incapacity (Scott 1998; Ferguson 1994; Gupta 2012).

This idea of the state's vulnerability is premised on a specific conceptualization of legal language in the trial process. Unlike other forms of discourse about the state, where the law is not expected to bind the state, the trial process reveals a form of language that binds all participants in the case (Constable 2014). For example, in narratives about corruption by state officials (Gupta 1995), there is a general expectation that state officials will not follow the law, despite the existence of laws against corruption. In a trial, where narratives of corruption circulate widely, there is nevertheless an expectation that all participants in the trial process should follow the law. This is not to say that the state—constituted by the judges, police, and prosecutors—always do follow the law. Rather, it is to say that there is an expectation that they ought to do so. It is this expectation that the participants in the trial process ought to follow the law that constitutes an imagination of the state's vulnerability to language.

I explore this idea—of the state's vulnerability to law—through a technicality found in the anti-terror law that threatened to upend many of the prosecutions during the period of my fieldwork. In 2008, an amendment was introduced into India's anti-terror law, the Unlawful Activities Prevention Act (UAPA), which mandated a two-step bureaucratic process before terrorism charges could be acted upon by the courts. Introduced as Section 45 of the statute, it stated that terrorism charges could be filed only after they were first approved by a designated government officer and then approved again by a second authority. This latter authority also had to review the charges before trial for the charges to commence. Nevertheless, after 2008, the police had been filing charges and the courts had been proceeding with trials based on these charges without the required bureaucratic approvals.

This oversight—deliberate or otherwise—provided a way for the terror-accused to challenge their prosecutions and in the process revealed one way in which they understood the relationship between the state and the law. I follow arguments related to Section 45 in two cases in which terror-accused argued that the state had failed to "follow its own laws." The charges against the state enabled the terror-accused to argue that their prosecutions were illegitimate and that their cases should be dismissed.

Crucially, the possibility that the state may be accountable for its words made hope possible for the terror accused. The idea that the law represents the vulnerability of the police and prosecution, rather than their power, enabled the terror-accused to imagine the possibility that their trials will eventually end in their acquittals.

LAW AS THE STATE'S UTTERANCE

This chapter asks what it means to think of the law *as* an utterance of the state and takes its cue from the frame provided by "law as . . ." studies

(Tomlins and Comaroff 2011; Mertz and Rajah 2014). As Mertz and Rajah (2014) note, the heuristic of "law as . . ." takes the shape of a metaphor, where "meaning is ascribed to law primarily via reference to the subject that occupies the space of the ellipsis" (174).

The main charge that the terror-accused leveled against the prosecution was that it did not follow the procedural process that was required to file terrorism charges. In the words of my ethnographic interlocutors, the prosecution "said" they would conduct their prosecutions in one way but did so in another. My ethnographic interlocutors imagined anti-terror legislations as something that the state "said." Even though these laws were written texts, for the terror-accused they were conceptualized as being uttered into existence by the state. The metaphor of the state speaking the law into existence allowed the terror-accused to pose the question of responsibility. The issue that they focused on is what accountability does the state bear to the laws it has spoken into existence? Having spoken a law into the world, can the state cast it aside? Or is the state bound by its word?

The question of what one's responsibility is to one's utterances has occupied philosophers of speech. In their readings of Austin's (1962) *How to Do Things with Words*, Cavell and Derrida have given us two different ideas of the relationship one bears to one's words. Derrida (1977) conceives of our utterances as being abandoned to the world and contends that once they are uttered, we no longer bear responsibility for them or authority over them. Having once spoken, Derrida would argue, we can no longer control our words and we lose our connection to them. In response, Cavell (1995) forcefully argues that our utterances are forever tethered to us. As a price of having spoken, we run the risk of having our words come back to haunt us. We do not abandon our words to the world, as Derrida might claim, but rather we are abandoned *to* them. Once I have uttered them, my words may be taken out of context, have their meanings altered, or be grafted on to other chains of signification, yet I still must account for them. Cavell asks us to image ourselves not as masters of our language but as vulnerable *to* our words. My words may come to be reinterpreted, and still I must account for them. As we will see in the following sections, the law that was uttered by the state was given a meaning through the trial process, and the prosecution was forced to account for this meaning. In this way, the conception of a state utterance allowed the terror-accused to think of the state as being made present in their lives through its vulnerability to the law.

The metaphor of the state's utterance allows for a reimagining of the relationship between the state, law, and violence in several ways. First, the metaphor allows us to think differently about the state: through the lens of vulnerability. The terror-accused experienced the state in various ways that could be conceptualized in terms of violence: they experienced kidnapping, duplicity, and violence at the hands of the police followed by years of incarceration while their trials wound through the court system. While the monopoly on legitimate violence is central to state formation (Weber 1991) and states have deployed violence, legality, and illegality to shore up their own legitimacy (Comaroff and Comaroff 2006; Nugent 2010; Chatterjee 2017), the metaphor of law as the state's utterance can help us understand how the state can also be constituted by its vulnerability. Thus, while terror-accused experienced the state as a source of violence, the state was simultaneously made present in their lives through its vulnerability to its own utterances: the law. Ethnographic attention to the metaphor used by terror-accused reveals an idea of the state that is constituted simultaneously by its force and by its vulnerability.[1]

Second, by drawing attention to how rules of procedure may signal the state's vulnerability to law, this chapter departs from accounts of how state domination and relations of power are enacted through courtroom processes. Instead, the metaphor of an utterance permits us to see rules of procedure in a different light. It allowed the terror-accused to imagine not only ways in which the state's authority was founded through legal language (Richland 2013), but also the ways that the state could be vulnerable to language. Instead of enacting state domination or translating social relations through the law, the rule of procedure here is imagined as a statement of how the state will do certain things. The charge leveled by the terror-accused at the police and prosecution was that the state promised to prosecute its cases in one way but conducted them in another. As we will see in the arguments around Section 45, the prosecution's actions were questioned by framing the issue as one of the prosecution's disregard for procedure, as failing to follow its own processes. This focus on procedures deflected attention away from the actions of the terror-accused and onto the legitimacy of the actions of the police and prosecution. This positioning allowed the terror-accused to imagine ways through which the state might be trapped by its own words.

Third, the metaphor adds to the ways in which we understand the relationship between the state and law. As I outlined in the introduction to this book, human rights and civil society organizations, as well as human rights activists, have argued that anti-terror laws entrench persecution against religious and caste minorities and are used to control people's movements. Thus, the aim of anti-terror laws is not to achieve a conviction, but to keep people in jail for as long as possible.

The argument made by civil liberties activists and scholars is that anti-terror laws entrench systems in which the police and prosecution can act without accountability. The police can kill and torture people on allegations of terrorism, without fear of any repercussions. The police and prosecution can arrest and prosecute people they know to be innocent. Terrorism trials can take years—sometimes even more than a decade—to complete. And they can do all of this with no consequences. The arguments made by activists and scholars alike is that anti-terror laws are an affront to the rule of law.

The metaphor employed by the terror-accused, however, differs slightly, yet significantly, from these rule-of-law arguments. While civil liberties activists argue that terrorism laws are an affront to the rule of law and that police officers who use terrorism laws to target ethnic, religious, or political minorities ought to face prosecution, the metaphor of an utterance creates another sense of responsibility. While the terror-accused would readily agree with rule-of-law arguments, the idea that they are conveying is that having once uttered the law into existence, the state is now bound to it. Through this metaphor, terror-accused are articulating a more fundamental point: that one has responsibility to one's utterances.

Further, the metaphor allows us to glimpse the ethical work (Das 2018) that must be performed to live in the milieu of courtrooms and jails. If the state was not vulnerable to its utterances, what future could terror-accused imagine? If the state was not bound by its word, how could the terror-accused inhabit courtrooms knowing that there was nothing to hope for? The metaphor used by the terror-accused shows the role of a seemingly insignificant rule of procedure in making courtrooms habitable. If the state said that it would prosecute cases in one way, surely the police and prosecution ought to do so. The idea that the state failed to "follow its own word" gave the terror-accused hope that they might be acquitted.

The idea of a state that is vulnerable to its words is not a straightforward one, as the words uttered by the state still need to be understood. In other words, when charging that the state did not "follow its own laws," the terror-accused and defense lawyers had to produce an image of what the rule meant and how the state's actions did not conform to this interpretation of the rule. In order to do so, the terror-accused and the defense lawyers had to produce legal meaning.

The question of how legal meaning is produced in a judgement has occupied some strands of legal philosophy. Influenced by Wittgenstein's theory of ordinary language philosophy (Bix 1991; Lefebvre 2011), Hart argues that legal rules have an "open texture"—that is, every rule will have a core area of meaning, and there will be "plain cases" (Hart 2012, 126) in which the rule will be "obviously applicable" (Hart 1958, 607). A corollary of this statement is that there will be cases in which the rule "obviously" has no applicability. Hart (1958) then turns his attention to those instances in the middle, where the rule is neither obviously applicable nor obviously ruled out—he calls these the "problems of the penumbra" (608). In the penumbral sphere of meaning, Hart argues that judges engage in "creative or legislative" (Hart 2012, 135) activity in deciding whether the rule applies to a given set of facts. Hart therefore rejects the position that judges merely apply the law to facts, but legislate law to apply to "penumbral" cases. Hart argues, as Wittgenstein does about language, that the law is incomplete and that judges, while interpreting rules, must creatively extend the rules and sometimes *create* law. While he rejects the idea that judges create legal rules in difficult cases, Dworkin (1982, 1986), like Hart, understands that there will be easy cases where a rule clearly applies and that there will be hard cases where the applicability of the rule is in doubt. He argues that when interpreting a rule, the ideal judge ensures that her judgment fits into the doctrinal history of the rule in the form of judicial precedent, while also having due regard to the social goals of the rule and principles of justice.[2] Dworkin therefore rejects the idea that law is incomplete and that judges create law and argues that the judge extends rules and principles that already form part of the totality of the legal system.

While there is much to separate Hart and Dworkin, they agree on the idea that legal words have a core meaning and that interpretation by a judge is required only when laws confront an ambiguous situation. While Hart and Dworkin focus on the judgment, anthropologists have confirmed what lawyers and parties to a legal dispute already know: that there are no such things as easy cases or cases in which the rule obviously applies. Anthropological attention to the processes of judging—which Hart and Dworkin regard as central to legal interpretation—shows that judges draw upon numerous sources to produce meaning for even the most "obvious" of rules (Bernstein 2018). All participants in the trial process know that a case is always arguable, and as language is never clear, every case is a hard case (to use Dworkin's language)[3] or in in the penumbra (to use Hart's). This "nontransparent approach to language" (Mertz 1994, 441) means that "even the most routine application of a law is a creative process" (Weissbourd and Mertz 1985, 639). While these anthropological approaches have been useful in understanding how legal meaning is produced, what is missing from them is how both "facts" of cases and law are simultaneously co-produced in the legal process.

Lefebvre (2005, 2008) provides an account through which fact and law produce each other in the legal process. According to Lefebvre, what is lost in most accounts of the legal process is the way in which the world and the law encounter one another. For him, interpretation should be seen as a creative moment when facts and rule produce each other. Law, or "the pure texts of statutes, of constitutions, and previous judgments, exists in a torpor and is aroused only by an encounter" (Lefebvre 2005, 113). Further, "facts" themselves cannot be understood in the absence of law. Facts and the law bring each other to light. Both the facts of a case and the meaning of the law emerge only through their encounter with each other. According to Lefebvre, the easy case "poisons" our understanding of interpretation because it purportedly shows how, in order to reach a decision, a judge need only apply a preexisting rule to a neat fact situation. What the "easy case" hides is that there is neither a pre-formed legal rule, nor a "fact" situation that can be apprehended outside of the rule.

I find certain aspects of Lefebvre's understanding of judgment as a form of encounter between "singular points of the case to singular points of law" attractive as it echoes my experiences in Delhi's courts, where fact and legal meaning were both constantly in flux. In Lefebvre's understanding, the moment of judgment is when the archive memory of the judiciary (the legislations, constitutions, judicial precedent) encounters the entirety of the facts of a case. He argues that the moment of judgment is when certain facts (derived from the entire matrix of a case) encounter certain points of law (derived from the entire archive memory of law).

As we will see in the following chapters, there was little that was certain about "facts." Similarly, none of the participants in the trial process understood the meaning of rules as being stable. In fact—given that no one can know the entire corpus of the law—judges and lawyers often did not know the *existence* of certain rules, let alone their meaning. The existence of rules and their interpretations come to light only when presented with certain facts. Conversely, "facts" can be produced to suit arguments about the meaning of a legal rule. As Lefebvre argues, legal facts and meaning emerge from their encounter with each other.

I would add to Lefebvre's account by noting that outside the moment of judgment, lawyers and the terror-accused created the meaning of rules in another way, by focusing on the potential of certain interpretations of the rule. The question that lawyers and the terror-accused asked of a legal rule is this: Which interpretations of a legal rule helps my case and which ones hurt the case of the prosecution? Once they tentatively established which meanings of the rule had the potential to help them and to harm the opposite party, they worked backward to produce facts and an archival memory to back up this interpretation of the law. The meanings of the rule emerged only through the push and pull of courtroom argumentation.

In order to flesh out this argument ethnographically, I describe how a seemingly innocuous and mundane section of the UAPA became the center of a flurry of activity for some weeks during my fieldwork period. The Special Cell had arrested two people—let's call them Bharucha and Kumar—who the police claimed were members of the Communist Party of India (Maoist), a banned terrorist organization. The police alleged that Bharucha was a member of the organization's highest decision-making body and that Kumar was a member of the organization's lower ranks.

The police arrested them and filed charges under the UAPA (membership of terrorist organization, material support to a terrorist organization, committing terrorist acts) and under the Indian Penal Code (IPC; conspiracy). After the pretrial paperwork was complete, the magistrate before whom the charges were filed took cognizance[4] of the case and committed[5] the case to the sessions court for trial.

As the police alleged that Bharucha was one of the top members of a banned communist organization, they escorted Bharucha from the jail to the court complex in a special van that was followed by another vehicle that carried armed guards. Once he reached the court complex, he was brought to the courtroom surrounded by armed guards. By contrast, although he was also accused of terrorist crimes, Kumar was brought to the court complex in an ordinary bus along with other defendants who had court hearings, and he was accompanied to the courtroom by a lone policeman. While cordons of security guards surrounded Bharucha, only one lone unarmed guard accompanied Kumar. What this meant was that I could not speak with Bharucha, but I could speak with Kumar quite easily while we sat at the back of the courtrooms.

Kumar was well aware of the differences between him and Bharucha. Kumar had grown up in a village in the hills of north India and graduated from high school. Bharucha had grown up in extremely privileged settings and gone to elite schools and universities in both India and the United Kingdom. While incarcerated, Kumar was employed to deliver newspapers to different parts of the jail; for his part, Bharucha gave talks on sociology and economics to jail inmates and even wrote an academic conference paper while in jail. In an attempt to get to "Bharucha's level," Kumar was taking a bachelor's degree in Human Rights through an open university. Kumar told me that Bharucha made extensive notes about the charges against them and regularly wrote to his lawyers pointing out what he saw as defects in the prosecution's case.

One of these "defects" was with the way in which the case had been filed. When the case was transferred to the Sessions Court, one of the first tasks for the court was to decide what charges, if any, to bring against the accused. Bharucha's and Kumar's lawyers' aim was to have all charges against the duo dismissed, and they set out to find different ways to have these charges dismissed or, at the very least, reduced. One of the ideas they hit upon was derived from Bharucha's close reading of the UAPA and the charge sheet against him.

Before arguments on the charges were set to commence, Bharucha wrote to his lawyers saying that he believed that the prosecution had not followed the procedure prescribed in the UAPA to file terrorism charges. According to Section 45, the police must obtain permission from the government to file charges under the UAPA—called a "sanction to prosecute"—before a magistrate could take cognizance of, or accept the registration of, UAPA charges. The defense lawyers examined the sanction to prosecute and realized that it could be argued that it did not conform to the UAPA.

According to Section 45, the sanction to prosecute is a two-step process.[6] The first requires an independent authority to review the evidence collected by the police and come to a decision on whether to recommend prosecution or not. The second requires an officer authorized by the government to review this recommendation and then to decide whether or not to give sanction to prosecute. According to the Bharucha and the defense lawyers, a magistrate could not take cognizance of the charge sheet without both of these steps being completed. The defense lawyers contended that the prosecutors and the government in Delhi, inadvertently or deliberately, had proceeded to step 2 without going through step 1. They believed that the government had not set up an independent authority to review the evidence and that a single official had granted the sanction to prosecute. They believed that the prosecution and the magistrate (and indeed, even they) had no knowledge of this provision when cognizance was taken and hence no attention was paid to it at that time. They wanted to argue that the magistrate had taken cognizance illegally and thus, as a result, the UAPA charges against the accused had to be dismissed.

Prior to making this argument in court, the defense lawyers discussed whether there was any point in doing so. One set of lawyers believed that they should bring up this point as it would lead to the dismissal of the UAPA charges against the duo. However, another defense lawyer said that this would be only a temporary reprieve; even if they won the argument, there was nothing to prevent the prosecution from refiling the charges, this time with a sanction to prosecute that conformed with the UAPA. Even so, the first set of lawyers seemed believed that if they were to pursue the argument, they would at least temporarily knock the prosecution of its feet. It would help build the idea that the police and prosecution were filing patently fabricated cases. Ultimately, the defense lawyers decided to present the argument to the judge, as the argument had the potential to force the judge to dismiss the prosecution's case against their clients—albeit temporarily.

The next day in the courtroom, the prosecutor opened the state's case against the two terror-accused men. He clearly did not have a clue of the potentially explosive preliminary point that the defense would make.

Instead, he opened the case as he normally would. He gave the judge a chronological narrative of how the case unfolded. He told the court how the Special Cell claimed to have first gotten wind of the presence of the two Maoists in Delhi and how they were arrested. He laid out all the evidence that the state would present to the court and gave details of the documentary and electronic evidence which would be presented by the police, and he also gave the court a summary of the witness testimony against them. He argued that there was enough material on record to charge the accused for offenses under the UAPA and the IPC.

After he finished his arguments, the defense lawyers commenced theirs. The basic position was that the "present proceedings are void" for the reason that "cognizance was taken without valid sanction to prosecute." In her opening arguments, one of the defense lawyers drew attention to the wording of Section 45 and noted that the two-step process needed to be followed and that the Special Cell had not followed the law. In written filings they filed, the defense lawyers argued that

> A perusal of the sanction filed along with the charge-sheet will indicate that it was granted *de hors* an independent review, by an independent authority, of the evidence gathered in the course of investigation, mandated by section 45(2) of the Unlawful Activities Prevention Act, 1967.[7]

The prosecutor was clearly caught off guard by this preliminary challenge. He immediately interrupted the defense lawyer to say that nothing was wrong with the sanction to prosecute. One of the other defense lawyers said sarcastically, "It is a recent amendment brought four years ago, in 2008. Perhaps you did not see it yet." The prosecutor, irritated by this, retorted that "this is not the stage to be questioning the sanction." If they wanted to question the validity of the sanction, the prosecutor contended, they should have raised this issue before the magistrate who took cognizance of the case and that it was now too late to raise this question.

In response, the defense lawyer argued that if the sanction to prosecute was invalid, then the UAPA charges had to be dismissed. As she observed, there was nothing preventing the defense from raising these issues before the Sessions Court. As these were arguments on the point of charge, the Sessions Court had to see if the charge sheet was properly filed. Section 45 was inserted into the UAPA via an amendment in 2008 in order to check prosecutorial and police abuse of power. This was an issue that went to the heart of whether the trial against Bharucha and Kumar should proceed.

In order to take the wind out of the defense lawyer's arguments, the prosecutor tried to paint this question around the sanction as a nonissue. He said that it was "not such a big thing" and that the defense was "making it bigger than it should be." Despite his efforts to downplay it, he became increasingly flustered by the defense's focus on a "minor issue" of the sanction. He told the judge that there was no infirmity in the sanction granted and that the procedure undertaken to give such sanction was in full conformity with Section 45. He argued that there is a general presumption that all governmental acts are in full conformity with the law. The burden was on the defense, he said, to show that the government had not set up an independent authority to review the evidence.

The defense lawyer was ready for this argument. As she could not directly answer the question of whether the independent authority had been set up or had produced a report, she sought to do so indirectly, by calling attention to the wording of the sanction order and thus demonstrating what a proper sanction to prosecute should be.

The defense lawyer read out the sanction order slowly to the judge. The sanction order stated that permission to prosecute was granted by government officer after a "perusal of the draft charge sheet and upon consideration of the allegations made in . . . [the first information report] registered at Police Station, Special Cell, Lodhi Colony, New Delhi and other material and evidence placed on record." There were three things that were mentioned in the sanctioning order, she said. "Firstly, the draft charge sheet. Second, the FIR. Third, other material and evidence." What was key, the defense lawyer argued, was what was *not* mentioned.

"Where is the report produced by the independent authority?" the lawyer asked. A proper sanction to prosecute would have mentioned the report produced by the independent authority. She argued that if the government officer who granted sanction had read the report produced by the independent authority, then he should have mentioned that. The fact that he did not would indicate that no independent authority was set up or, at the very least, that the sanctioning order was made without reading the report, which would be a violation of Section 45. In effect, she was painting for the court an image of what a proper sanctioning order should look like and also arguing that the sanctioning order that was filed did not match this image.

In response, the prosecutor said that merely because the report of the independent authority was not mentioned in the order granting sanction did not mean that the independent authority or its report did not exist. "Nowhere is it written in this section that the officer must mention every little thing that he has read," the prosecutor replied. In his opinion, there was nothing in Section 45 that mandated that the order granting sanction must state that the report of the independent authority was reviewed by the relevant officer. In effect, the prosecutor argued that the court must believe that the sanction was granted validly, until the defense could prove otherwise.

The judge seemed to be leaning toward the defense's arguments. He asked the prosecutor if "it could be believed that the report of the independent authority could have been relied upon by the sanctioning officer, if the sanctioning order did not mention it." Feeling that he had been backed into a corner, the prosecutor parlayed for, and obtained, an adjournment. At the end of the proceeding he made an off-hand comment, that was perhaps a strategic error. He said that on the next day that he would file a fresh sanction to prosecute, which should clear up what he continued to insist was a minor technicality. But this comment gave the defense a preview of the argument they had to meet on the next date of hearing.

On the next date of hearing, the defense lawyer got in the first word and needled the prosecutor by telling the court that "PP sahib" (Mr. Public Prosecutor) said he would tell us how the sanction order is valid." The prosecutor smiled and gamely took this reversal of burden of proof and proceeded with two arguments. First, just as he had earlier said he would, he had filed a fresh sanction to prosecute: This one mentioned the independent authority and stated that the sanctioning officer had read the independent authority's report. The prosecutor maintained that the first sanction was valid, but if there was any defect in it, it would be "cured" by the subsequent one. The second argument he made was that even if there was a defect in the original sanction and the subsequent one could not help "cure the defect," then the court was statutorily empowered to overlook any error or irregularity in the procedure followed by the trial court. To make these arguments, he relied upon certain provisions of the Code of Criminal Procedure and brought up three judgments delivered by superior courts that he claimed supported his position.

The defense lawyers, having been given a preview of his first point and anticipating his second, came armed with their own judicial archive. On the second point, they argued that on reading the law relating to criminal procedure, the trial court had no ability to correct irregularities in procedure (as this was a power reserved for appellate courts). In response to the prosecutor's first point they also relied upon judicial precedent, which, they claimed, established the position that there were extremely narrow circumstances when a fresh sanction could be taken cognizance of and that this case did not meet those criteria.

This hearing was not marked by the back-and-forth that characterized the previous one. Perhaps with battle lines drawn clearly, each side knew the arguments that they needed to make. Both the prosecutor and the defense lawyer led the judge through each of their arguments, reading key portions of judicial precedent and ensuring that the judge's attention was drawn to operative words in various legislations.

On the date listed for orders on charge, the judge read out the operative part of his judgment. He said, almost under his breath, "File be sent back to the Court of Learned Chief Metropolitan Magistrate." Later on, one of the defense lawyers and I had to clarify with the reader what the actual judgment was. The reader told us "MM ko bhej diya" (It is sent to the magistrate). The judge had dismissed the UAPA charges against Bharucha and Kumar and ordered the magistrate to conduct a trial for lesser offenses.

The actual judgment delivered by the court was more detailed and ran into sixty-five pages. The question for the court was a "conundrum," which concerned "whether the competent authority . . . had followed the procedure at the time of [approving the] sanction or not?" The question boiled down to this: What did a valid sanction look like? There were two potential answers to this question, based on the differing interpretations of the rule requiring a two-step process. On the one hand, the prosecutor argued that while the rule did require a two-step process, it did not require the document that accorded the sanction to prosecute to state that the rule was followed. On the other, the defense lawyers stated that Section 45 did require the sanctioning authority to state on what basis he had accorded sanction. As the sanction to prosecute mentioned that the documents relied on the sanctioning authority to come to his decision but did not mention the report of the independent authority, it was evident that the sanctioning authority did not follow the two-step process.

The judge ultimately held that the first sanction was invalid as the sanctioning officer had relied only on the evidence, the charge sheet, and the

FIR presented by the police and not upon the report of the independent authority. The court made no finding on whether the independent authority was actually set up. In effect, the court held not only that the two-step process must be followed, but also that this must be reflected in the order granting sanction to prosecute. It also decided that the trial court did not have the statutory power to correct any procedural irregularity and that therefore the second sanctioning order could not be taken into account. The court dismissed the UAPA charges against the two men and ordered that the trial before the minor IPC offenses be conducted by the magistrate.

I want to draw out several observations from this complex web of procedures. The first is to repeat the point made by anthropologists of courtrooms: that there is nothing obvious about legal meaning (Merry 1990, 94; Conley and O'Barr 1990). What this ethnography reiterates is that there was nothing inevitable about the conclusion that the judge eventually reached. While the judge presented his judgment as though the decision were an "easy" one and that his eventual decision was automatic, the "obviousness" of his eventual decision was more a function of the way in which the judgment was written, than of any self-evident meaning of the rule or the sanction to prosecute. In other words, the "obviousness" of meaning is produced by the legal process. Until the point of judgment, either of the two meanings attributed to Section 45 (one where the sanction order needed to state that the independent authority's report had been taken into account and the other where it did not) and the sanction to prosecute could have been possible. The meanings did not flow automatically, but rather emerged from the creativity of the courtroom process.

Second, the potential meanings resulted in the production of different archives. In making their arguments, the defense lawyers and the prosecutor harnessed both facts and legal rules to defend their respective positions and to assail that of their opposites. The prosecutor first said that there is nothing to indicate from the reading of the sanction to prosecute that would indicate that the two-step process was not followed. In response, the defense lawyers argued that the fact that the sanctioning authority did not list the report produced by the independent authority, while he had listed other documents that he had relied upon, would indicate at best that the report was never read or at worst that the independent authority had never been set up. In response to the prosecutor's second line of argument—that the sanction could be "cured" by a second sanction and that the court could correct such irregularities—the defense lawyers produced their own archive of precedent and statutory provisions. In both these cases the rival interpretations of the rule enabled the creation of competing archives.

Third, "fact," along with rule and its potential meanings all combined to make particular interpretations of the rule possible. While scholars have argued that it is only in disputes that the rule is brought into existence (Comaroff and Roberts 1981) and that it emerges in the course of the legal process (White 1984, 1985), observe here how both rule and fact are produced through the argumentative process. The "conundrum" before the court arose because, at the time that the magistrate took cognizance of the case, neither the magistrate, nor the prosecutor, nor the defense lawyers, nor ostensibly the central government, seemed to know about the two-step process in Section 45. Drawing from Bharucha's reading of the UAPA, the defense lawyers came to know about the two-step process only because they were looking for a way to argue that the charges ought to be dismissed. Once they realized the potential of the argument—that it could result in the charges being dismissed—they then brought the rule into focus. In doing so, they had to produce an image of what a valid sanction looked like and then argue that sanction in this particular case did not meet those criteria. In this way rule and facts mold each other.

It is difficult to overstate the importance of the ability to produce legal meaning, as it has consequences for whether cases end in acquittal or conviction. The immediate effect in Bharucha's and Kumar's case was that the judge dismissed terrorism charges and sent the case down to the magistrate for trial for the lesser offenses. Recall, however, that in discussions prior to the hearings about the application Section 45, one set of lawyers said it even if the argument succeeded, there was nothing to prevent the prosecution from re-filing the terrorism charges. And that is precisely what happened. Several weeks after the charges were dismissed, the prosecution filed another charge sheet, this time with a proper sanction to prosecute. But even at this stage, the defense lawyers argued—unsuccessfully this time—that the new sanction could not be taken on record. This argument that was eventually dismissed and the duo faced trial for UAPA and IPC offenses. Bharucha and Kumar were eventually acquitted of terrorism charges after a four-year trial.

Beyond the question of acquittal or conviction, the ability to produce meaning allowed the terror-accused to bind the state to the law. All participants in the trial knew that the state was bound by its words, even though meaning for those words came from elsewhere. This idea allowed the terror-accused to imagine a state whose law symbolized, not its power, but rather its vulnerability. It is to this issue that I turn in the next section.

BINDING THE STATE TO ITS WORD

The news of the dismissal of charges against two "high-profile terrorists" spread quickly through the jail. Days after the trial court delivered its judgment in Bharucha's and Kumar's case, several other terror-accused told me that the judgment showed the illegitimacy of terrorism cases and that UAPA prosecutions were going on "gair kanun" (outside the law). Of the police and prosecution, they said, "Unhone apne kanun mein phas gaya" (They became trapped in their own laws).

The Session Court's judgment in Bharucha and Kumar's case had material repercussions on other terrorism cases. Of the eighteen UAPA trials taking place during the period of my fieldwork, applications for discharge from UAPA offenses were filed in at least five different cases on the grounds that sanction to prosecute was defective. Several terror-accused individuals told me that they had asked their lawyers to file applications for discharge on the grounds that permission to prosecute was not properly given. In some cases, they even asked Bharucha and Kumar for copies of their written submissions, so that they could file similar ones in their own cases. One terror-accused person told me that when he went into the "sanction issue," he realized that not only was the sanction for UAPA-offenses against him improperly given, but also that the sanction to prosecute him under another statute was also defective.

One of the cases in which Bharucha's and Kumar's discharge judgment had an effect was against a couple whom I call Keshav and Sonia Shukla. They were also accused of being members of the banned Communist Party of India (Maoist). The Special Cell did not accuse the couple of committing any acts of violence or preparing to commit acts of violence. Instead, according to the police, theirs were crimes of membership. The police said that the couple were in possession of literature of a banned communist party and had been organizing meetings and "influencing people to join the party."[8] Early in 2010, the couple were arrested on charges of membership of a banned organization, membership of a terrorist organization, and conspiracy to commit terrorist acts. If they were convicted of being members of a terrorist organization, the couple could be imprisoned for life.

Keshav and Kumar knew each other. At the time, all terror-accused persons were housed in the same "high-security ward" of the jail complex, where Keshav delivered newspapers. The day after the judge dismissed his terrorism charges, while Kumar was still in jail, Kumar met Keshav on one of his delivery rounds of the jail and told him about the news of his discharge. Soon after, Kumar gave Keshav a copy of the judgment, and, after reading it, Keshav gave it to his lawyer and asked him to pursue a similar argument. As we sat at the back of the courtroom, Keshav explained the argument to me:

In the UAPA there's a Section 45(2). I saw the Unlawful [Activities Prevention] Act but I didn't see it entirely, I missed out on some stuff. What happened was that the judge dismissed the case against them [Bharucha and Kumar], and other UAPA cases have also been dismissed. In that case what happened was that when arguments on charge were going on, on one point, their lawyer said the sanction got by the prosecution was an invalid sanction. In that judgment, it was written that "I know that Bharucha was a Maoist leader and he is guilty under. S. 39, but since they have not got sanction, I am dismissing the case." For Kumar, also same thing. So, I got that judgment from Kumar, and I read it. So, I thought, I will tell my lawyer about this. I should get some benefit from this.

Keshav, having read the judgment, concluded that all UAPA cases that had been filed—and not just theirs—were, in his words, "null and void." The failure to go through the proper procedure for obtaining sanction in his case meant, he believed, that he and his wife were entitled to be discharged from the terrorism offenses. As he told me after he was released on bail,

The problem is that in the written submissions [the prosecution] filed in our case they themselves are saying that till 2010 October—when charges were filed against us—they said that there was no independent authority. When there's no independent authority, you're still proceeding with cases against other people.

They were saying that there was no authority, which is why we didn't get approval. Now we have a review committee so now we have brought [the new sanction]. This means that all the cases that you've put till October 2010, according to your own law, it is null and void. Which is why I thought I should fight it.[9]

And then, as if addressing the state directly, he said:

All the cases under unlawful [Activities Prevention Act], are null and void. You yourself are saying you didn't have an authority. You yourself are saying that the sanction is mandatory, there's no question of the cases proceeding. It's not just a technical matter. All the unlawful cases that you're prosecuting are invalid cases.

The problem faced by Keshav and Sonia was that their trial had already commenced when the terrorism-charges against Bharucha and Kumar were dismissed. At the time of framing of charges in Keshav and Sonia's case, neither their lawyers, nor the judge had realized that the sanction to prosecute might have been defective. By the time this defect came to light, they were about a year into the trial with twelve of twenty-nine witnesses having already been examined. Nevertheless, Keshav wanted to the court to dismiss the terrorism charges against them. Keshav described to me the arguments made on the next date of hearing:

My lawyer raised this point saying there's no proper sanction. "You have to dismiss this case." [The judge] told my lawyer that he should have raised the point at the proper stage, not in the middle [of the trial]. Out of a total of twenty-nine witnesses, twelve witnesses were done.

The judge kept the application pending and did not rule on this point. I attended the next date of hearing, when, in order to preempt the judge from possibly dismissing the terrorism charges against Keshav and Sonia, the prosecutor—who was the same prosecutor from Bharucha's and Kumar's case—rehashed the strategy he used in Bharucha's and Kumar's case and filed a "fresh sanction" to prosecute the Keshav and Sonia. According to the prosecutor, "Though there was nothing wrong with the first sanction, this sanction has been brought to clarify any doubts the court may have." The judge was livid. He asked, "What kind of prosecution is conducted in such a manner, where a case has gone on halfway and you [the prosecution] bring a proper sanction to prosecute?" The prosecutor tried to clarify that nothing was wrong with the first sanction to prosecute. This angered the judge even more, who asked, "If nothing was wrong, then why are you bringing another one?" Keshav and Sonia's lawyer, sensing an opening here, again asked that the charges against them be dismissed. In response, the prosecutor repeated himself and said that since a fresh sanction had been produced, there was no need to dismiss the charges.

Unlike in Bharucha's and Kumar's case, the prosecutor was in a stronger bargaining position. He stated that if the charges were dismissed, then the prosecution would file the charge sheet again, this time with the proper sanction. In doing so he issued a veiled threat to Keshav and Sonia—namely, that they would face the prospect of having to spend time and money going through the same trial all over again if the charges were refiled. This also served as a warning to the judge, who was particularly interested in making sure his trials moved quickly: that if the prosecutor was forced to refile the charges, then the judge would be forced to redo the entire trial from the beginning.

The question of whether the charges should be dismissed went back and forth for several hearings that spread over several weeks, with each side repeating its arguments and with the judge seemingly finding it impossible to rule either way. Keshav described the judge as *bechara*, or "helpless," as he found himself unable to decide. The judge seemed frustrated and unable or unwilling to decide, as these hearings during these weeks lasted barely a couple of minutes. Both the prosecutor and defense lawyers briefly appeared and tried to restate their arguments, but the judge adjourned the case. The judge seemed to want to have nothing to do with this particular issue.

If he ruled with the defense, he knew that the prosecution would refile the charges. This would mean, as the judge put it during one hearing, that the previous "two years were a waste." According to Keshav, if the judge sided with the prosecution, he knew that he would be "agreeing to all the illegal acts done by them." After several weeks of adjournments where the judge struggled to decide on the application for discharge, the judge sought to cut the issue both ways. Keshav told me that the judge told him, "You can tell your lawyer to apply for bail" (thereby hinting that he would grant bail, if such an application were made), and he told the prosecutor that he would accept the fresh sanction and proceed with the trial. Unfortunately, I missed that date of hearing, but Keshav told me what happened, after he was let out on bail.

[The judge] told me to take bail. I said I'm not taking it. I said you dismiss the case. I said what's the point of bail, when you have to dismiss the case.

Although Keshav thought that he did have a point to make, he also realized that if he pressed it, then the police would not just refile charges in this case, but file other charges as well.

I thought, and I'm probably right about this—that I couldn't push the point much. The judge was also trapped, he couldn't reject what I was saying and there was no ground for him to proceed with the case. So, he tried to take the middle path. I thought if I pushed the point, what's stopping [the police and prosecution] from putting five more cases on me— they have no difficulty to do so. That is the way they operate.

Keshav applied for bail that day and was released pending the completion of his trial. Meanwhile, the judge quietly accepted the prosecutor's refiled sanction to prosecute, and the trial proceeded as if there was nothing amiss.

Observe here how all the parties in the trial seem to be stuck. Given that he lost the same argument in Bharucha and Kumar's case, the prosecutor knew that his case against dismissing the charges against Keshav and Sonia was weak and hence resorted to muted threats of prolonged incarceration and a repeat of half the trial. The judge was caught between two positions as well—of dismissing the charges and having half the case retried or proceeding with a trial that was based on a significant flaw. And Keshav felt trapped, too: He believed, based on a reading of the judgment in Bharucha's and Kumar's case, that he was right to ask for the charges against him and his wife to be dismissed. But he feared that there would be nothing preventing the prosecution from refiling the charges or "putting five more cases" on him. Keshav experienced the state's words as a threat. The utterance of the state had trapped Keshav, the judge, and even the prosecutor.

Even so, Keshav's idea that the state is trapped by its own words is notable. Keshav's narrative reveals that he saw words as a threat to the state itself and as a source of hope for himself and his wife. Keshav's statement about the state failing to follow its own laws had a certain intensity. There is nothing new in saying that the state fails to follow the law; state acts, from the mundane to the extraordinary, are often marked by illegality. Yet, there is a certain charge that this accusation brings—notice the repetition the phrases of "null and void" and "invalid" in Keshav's narrative. In his eyes, the failure of the state to follow Section 45 was not merely illegal and hence *gair kanun*, or outside the law. Nor was it simply a failure to follow a law that rendered the trial "null and void." The sense conveyed is that in its failure to follow its *own laws*, the state had failed to abide by its word: The state is seen here as having uttered the law and therefore ought to be bound to it. The attempt here is to tie the state to its word. The phrase *gair kanun* implies a movement, a turning away or a breaking away from the law. The image that Keshav employed attempted to turn the state back to its law, to return the law to its author, as if to point out the duplicity of the state in uttering one thing and doing another. The attempt was not to cut the state off from its utterances, but to bind it to its word.

WHAT IS AT STAKE IN THINKING OF THE LAW AS AN UTTERANCE OF THE STATE?

The terror-accused whom I met during my fieldwork in Delhi's courts knew that the law could trap them. They were all too aware of the power of the state's words. They knew that the rules of procedure and evidence could ensnare them, regardless of the defense they and their lawyers mounted. But as we have seen, when the terror-accused conceived of the law as the state's utterances, the law acquired a dual nature. While the state's words could trap them, the terror-accused could equally trap the state in its own words.

This idea of trapping the state in its own words depended on the idea that the state was responsible for its own words: Having once spoken, the state is then accountable to its own utterances. Even if the meaning of the words may have been twisted and the law may have been given another meaning, the state was nevertheless bound to honor them. As we saw in this chapter, the law that was uttered by the state was given a meaning through the arguments in Bharucha and Kumar's case. The state (in the person of the prosecutor) then bore responsibility to this meaning. For his part, Keshav repeatedly invoked the idea that the law was something said by the state: "your own law," "you yourself are saying." At play here is the idea that the law was something that the state uttered into existence. And having spoken the law into existence, it was now bound by its word.

The idea that the state is bound by its words allowed the state itself to be put on trial by terror-accused. The focus on how the prosecution and police went about the case deflected attention away from terror-accused and onto the legitimacy of actions by the state. As we saw in the arguments around Section 45, the state's actions were questioned by framing the issue as one of the state's disregard for its own procedures, and in the process, it was the state that was cast as failing to follow its own word.

Undoubtedly this metaphor of law as the state's utterance is a "deeply personal" and "intrinsically partial" one (Mertz and Rajah 2014, 175). It does not represent the totality of how terror-accused generally viewed the state. At the same time, however, the metaphor reveals itself to be crucial for inhabiting the courtroom. It allows the terror-accused to maintain a hope that they will ensnare the state in its own laws, allowing them to be acquitted.

This metaphor does not just have implications at the time of a judgment of whether a terror-accused is guilty or innocent. It is what sustains the terror-accused for the duration of their trials. The phrase used by Keshav—"null and void," or *gair kanun*—indicate his understanding that the state is not simply conducting trials outside the law. What is a trap for the state does more than ask the state to own up to its utterances: It is a condition that makes life in a terrorism trial possible. That legal procedures may signal, not state domination but rather its vulnerability to its own words, is what allows the terror-accused to maintain hope, while their trials slowly grind through the courts.

4

HYPERTEXT

Files and the Fabrication of the World

During my time in Delhi's courts, I witnessed a trial relating to bombings and attempted bombings in Delhi and a city in Gujarat. The defendants faced two separate trials for these events in both Gujarat and Delhi. Mohammed Hanif—one of the terror-accused—and most of his co-accused were held in a jail in Gujarat and were "present" for his trial in Delhi via a videoconferencing link.

According to the charge sheet, the Special Cell claimed that Hanif had visited a southern city, Manipal, where he had met a "handler," who had provided him with the explosives that were later used in the explosions. The police claim that in order to contact this handler, Hanif had used a public telephone operated by a witness—Anthony. The Special Cell claimed that during the course of the investigation, they had taken Mohammed Hanif to Manipal, where he had pointed out the public telephone booth (called a "public call office," or PCO in official parlance) from where he had telephoned his handler. The police had then prepared a *fard nishandehi*, or "pointing-out memo,"[1] stating that Mohammed Hanif had pointed out the public phone. This memo was signed by the police officers who had purportedly witnessed his doing so. The police stated that they had then asked Anthony whether he recognized Mohammed Hanif, who then stated that he recognized the Hanif as having made a telephone call from his phone booth. The police then prepared an "identification memo" in which they stated that Anthony had identified Mohammed Hanif. This, too, was signed by the police officers who had witnessed Anthony identifying Mohammed Hanif.

These two documents came into play some years later during Hanif's trial. The prosecution needed to establish that Hanif had visited Manipal, had made a phone call from Anthony's telephone booth, and had then met his "handler," who gave him the explosives. Anthony was summoned to the court to identify the person who had made the call from his telephone booth. When Anthony appeared before the Delhi trial court, it was clear that he barely understood or spoke Hindi or Urdu and had only a rudimentary knowledge of English. The examination was conducted in a mixture of English and Hindi, which Anthony struggled to understand and speak. The prosecutor and the judge dictated such answers that he was able to give to the court stenographer in English, who transcribed the information into the court's file in the form of a narrative. As we will see in the next chapter, the deposition that was eventually inserted into the court file was not a verbatim transcript of the day's events; it is a record of what had been dictated to the stenographer by the judge or the lawyers.

Anthony was "helped" through his deposition by an officer from the Special Cell, Inspector Bhandari (whom we briefly encountered in Chapter 1). Bhandari stood close behind Anthony, and it was evident to the defense counsel that the officer was whispering the answers to him. Some of the defense lawyers repeatedly told the officer to stand away from Anthony, but Bhandari backed away only to step back several moments later.

Soon, it was time for Anthony to identify the man who the police said had come to his telephone booth that day. This was a crucial moment, as it was vital in proving that Hanif had procured the explosives used in the bomb blasts. One by one, each of the accused appeared on the videoconferencing screen. When Hanif came on screen, I saw Bhandari swiftly kick the back of Anthony's leg. Anthony let out a muffled, yet startled, whimper, and began nodding vigorously.

The defense counsel, who also noticed the kick, began to shout that the police officer was prompting the witness and asked that the judge to record that the witness was being prompted by Bhandari. The judge put aside these objections, saying that he had not seen any prompting by the police officer. He merely dictated the following passage to the stenographer, who typed it out on his computer:

At this stage, Ld. Addl. PP [the Learned Additional Public Prosecutor] has asked the witness to point out from the screen of the video conferencing as to who out of the six persons visible on the screen was accompanying the police on the aforesaid date, in the year 2008. Thereupon the witness has correctly identified Mohd. Hanif, accused present at No. 4 from the left as visible on the screen of the video conferencing (objected to by learned defence counsel on the mode of identification).[2]

The public prosecutor then dictated the rest of Anthony's deposition to the stenographer. While the excerpt below shows Anthony having made a detailed statement about the events that day in 2008, he barely spoke and only nodded when asked if the signatures on the memos were his. In the following excerpt from Anthony's testimony recorded in the court file, Anthony is portrayed as having stated that the police had prepared an identification memo that, in turn, stated that Anthony had previously identified the accused person during the investigation. The court records then show that Anthony authenticated that identification memo:

> On [date], police prepared memo when I identified the identity of Mohd. Hanif as the person who had come to my PCO on [date] and made phone call. I identified my signatures on the memo prepared in this regard. Same appear at Point C. The memo is **ExPW** [Exhibit Prosecution Witness] **128/F**.

With this, the prosecutor wrote a "C" on the relevant part of the memo with a red pen to mark where the signature was and wrote "ExPW128/F" at the top of the document.

Next came the turn of the defense counsel to cross-examine Anthony. During the cross-examination, the defense lawyer attempted to build the case that Anthony was lying. He questioned the witness on his ability to read and write English (the language in which the identification memo was written). Given that the phone call that Hanif allegedly made lasted for under a minute and occurred five years prior to that day in court, the defense lawyer questioned Anthony's memory. I could barely hear Anthony's answers, even though I was standing at the front of the courtroom. Evidently, the defense lawyer could, though, as he relayed Anthony's replies to the stenographer who typed out the deposition on his computer.

Anthony, who by this time was sweating nervously, kept looking down at his palms. I saw the defense lawyer suddenly reach over and take hold of Anthony's hand. He held up Anthony's hand for all to see, shouting that his answers had not been from memory, but had been scribbled on his palm. One of the defense lawyers started shouting that he should be immediately taken to the photocopy machine so that his hand could be photocopied and that the photocopy of his palm should be placed in the court file. Another defense lawyer, simultaneously joking and perhaps intending to intimidate the witness, referred to a rule that requires parties to tender only original documents in evidence: "No photocopy," he said, "we need the original. Just cut off his hand and put it on the file." Behind me the terror-accused who were physically present in court began to laugh loudly, while the court staff looked on with amusement.

The judge tried to calm down the courtroom but kept saying that he could not see anything written on Anthony's palm. The defense lawyer, who was still holding the witness's hand, dragged the witness toward the judge's platform. The prosecutor shouted at the defense lawyers, telling them not to manhandle his witness. Other defense lawyers told the prosecutor that the witness was clearly reciting the testimony that he was told to give. The witness was taken by the hand behind the judge's desk, where his sweaty palms were held up for the judge to see. The judge merely said, "I can't see anything written here." The defense lawyers pointed to the hand and argued that Anthony had the answers written down and demanded that the judge document in the record of that day's proceedings the fact that the witness was not deposing from memory, but was referring to information written on his palm.

Perhaps because the writing had been sweated away, or because the judge did not want his court file to be marked by such farcical events, the judge merely replied that whatever was written on his palm was illegible, and hence he could not record that the witness was reading from answers written on his palm. Things calmed down after the judge remained firm in his resolve not to record what actually happened that day into the court file. The defense lawyers backed down, and the cross-examination was completed. Once the stenographer printed the witness's statement, it was signed by both Anthony and the judge, thereby securing its place as the only authoritative account of the day's proceedings. And a very relieved Anthony hurried out of the courtroom.

Based on this dark, comic vignette, I would like to outline some points regarding the centrality of the file to the legal process. First, observe the importance of the file and paperwork to both the investigation and the trial.

Observe here how the police produced one memo to document that Mohammed Hanif had pointed to a particular telephone booth and another to document that the witness Anthony had identified Hanif as the man who had made a phone call on that particular day in 2008. Similarly, in the courtroom, the file must refer back to the memos produced during the investigation, and the existence of these memos must be validated by testimony in court. Therefore, the court file must not only contain the memos themselves, but also the narrative of how these memos came to be produced. Both the content of the files and documents and the way that they were produced are important.[3] The file is therefore crucial to both the investigation and the trial. Without it, legal truth could not be produced.

Second, we can see how the file constantly refers to events outside of it. This has to do with the file's essential role in producing juridical truth: If an event is not written down, and if that writing is not certified through signatures and other means of authentication, then that event never occurred. Observe how the police, through the two memos, stitched together a narrative of Hanif having made a phone call to his handler from Anthony's phone booth. If the police had not produced those memos, their narrative of the investigation could have been called into doubt. For an event to be recorded as having happened (the witness having information written on his palm, or Bhandari prompting the witness, for example), it has to be recorded on paper. To have juridical value, it is not enough that it be recorded; it must be recorded in the file in accordance with certification protocols prescribed by the law ("No photocopy, we need the original [hand]."). Since the judge refused to provide a record of the events in his courtroom, those events—officially at least—never happened. The file has fabricated a version of reality in which the events narrated above, which took place in the courtroom that day, never occurred.

In this part of the book, I turn to the centrality of technicalities surrounding the file and paperwork in producing legal truth. The centrality of the file to the investigative and trial process is the historical legacy of ideologies that see writing as ensuring accountability across time, space, and bureaucratic hierarchies (Moir 1996; Raman 2012; Hull 2012). A strong connection between writing and accountability continues to the present day. The written record maintained by the police ostensibly protects the integrity of the investigative process and ensures police accountability to trial courts. In turn, the written record maintained by the lower courts is thought to ensure the legibility of the actions of the lower courts to appellate courts. Further, because trials can take years to complete—at times more than a decade—and because judges are transferred so regularly, the written record also allows one judge to pass judgment on testimony recorded by another.

Paperwork is also thought to ensure epistemological certainty (Smith 1985; Raman 2012; Hull 2012). As Hull (2012) notes, the history of paper-based certification practices in South Asia was premised on a thoroughgoing rejection of trust in people (8), as all official acts had to backed up by a paper record. Raman (2012) shows how, in judicial settings in early colonial South India, the move to paper was believed to enable the production of juridical truth that was amenable to modes of proof known to the common law. It allowed for the investigative process to be tested in court and for the facts produced by such a process to be legible at various levels of the colonial judiciary (151). It is through paper and the practices that surround paper that juridical "reality" is produced.

My ethnographic interlocutors experienced the file as an object that produced different versions of reality. Defendants accused of terrorist crimes often came to know the full extent of the case against them only when the police entered a file, known as the "charge sheet," into the court records. They described the horror of reading how the story of their lives had been interpreted and narrated in the police file. "When I read I was accused of planting twenty-two bombs, my head started spinning," one said to me. Another told me of his shock upon learning that his work as a trade union activist had been interpreted as evidence that he had links to Maoist guerrillas. According to another, "The police can even say that you squeezed water from a stone." For many accused of terror, these files plunged them into alien worlds—worlds that were incommensurate with their own sense of reality. As other ethnographies of courtroom processes in India have shown (Baxi 2014; Chatterjee 2017), the trial process has the power to narrate one's life away. It is as if the file can take one's world as one knows it and replace it with another (Yngvesson and Coutin 2006; Sadiq 2008).

Even though recent scholarship has shown how the file is embedded in modes of governmentality and knowledge production in South Asia (Smith 1985; Moir 1996; Raman 2012; Hull 2012; Gupta 2012; Mathur 2016), scholars have not fully interrogated this capacity of files to produce a regime of truths. Some (Dery 1998; Tarlo 2003; Vismann 2008) have argued that while the bureaucratic practices around the file seek to ensure epistemological certainty, they actually produce their own regime of truths—what Tarlo (2003) has called "paper truths."[4] In other words, while "reality" might be one thing, the files that document it may depict another. Those accounts of paperwork that acknowledge the reality-altering capacities of the file concentrated on how people navigate the perceived gap between the version of reality that is produced by their eyes and the version that is contained in the file (Tarlo 2003; Hull 2012). In these chapters, I document how paper truths are contested, based not on their lack of alignment with "reality," but on other paper truths.

This part of the book attempts to show how the technicalities of the file enable the fabrication of alternative versions of the truth. The word "fabricate" helps us understand the capacity of the file both to "make" and to "fake." The capacity of the file to fabricate different truths can throw light on two issues that I brought up in the introduction. First, activists and academics have highlighted how the police mount "false cases" against minorities, activists, and dissenters. The following two chapters show us how this is done in granular detail—that is, how the police use the technical practices around the file to fabricate terrorism cases. Technicalities emerge here as the mode through which the state can use anti-terror laws to persecute Muslims, Dalits, and democratic rights activists. In this chapter, I argue that the technicalities that surround the production and maintenance of files enable the fabrication of a certain narrative by the state.

The second pertains to the argument about the "relative autonomy" of technicalities. As I argued earlier on, while technicalities are used by the police and prosecution to mount anti-terror cases, legal technicalities are not entirely colonized by the politics behind these prosecutions. In these two chapters I show how even though the police and prosecution make use of files to construct their truths about cases, legal technicalities enable the fabrication of not just one, but multiple versions of reality. As I show in the next chapter, this capacity of technical practices related to the file to produce multiple versions of reality, enables the terror-accused and their lawyers to fabricate their version of the truth.

In these two chapters, therefore, I think about how the state can use file-related technicalities to fabricate cases against minorities and activists, as well as the ability of terror-accused and their lawyers to use these same technicalities to produce their own versions of reality. In this chapter, I offer the term "hypertext" to describe the capacity of the file to fabricate, alter, and destroy "realities."

FABRICATING THE WORLD THROUGH FILES

"Hypertext" describes two aspects of the file. In one sense, it gestures toward the experience of many terror-accused who feel that police officers and lawyers are excessively obsessed with paperwork. Sonia Shukla (whose husband, Keshav, we encountered in Chapter 3)—the only woman accused of terror whom I came across in Delhi—described the police's obsession with paper. She recounted how, soon after she was arrested, the police tricked her into signing some papers "that were filled with lies." They replied that she could complain to the judge about the documents when she was produced for her first post-arrest hearing. But according to her, the "hearing" before the judge lasted barely a few minutes, after which she was whisked back into the police vehicle.

> So, then I said to [the police officer], "What happened? I had no time to say anything to the judge!" He told me, "How do you think the court works? It doesn't happen like it happens in the movies. When your turn comes, you can put all your complaints into writing."

She told me that she then realized that she would get her say before the judge only after the charge sheet was filed for her case, so she waited for that day for the evidence that they had concocted against her to be revealed. When she finally received the charge sheet, instead of the police's evidence, all she found was *kagaz pe kagaz* (paper on paper). According to her, the "police drove [her] mad with their paper, that was written in that dirty language of theirs." In one sense, therefore, the term "hypertext" conveys the idea of a state that cannot function without paper and, at the same time, a state that overwhelms anyone who comes in contact with it, with paper.

One aspect of this obsession with paper has to do with paper's epistemological role and its capacity to produce versions of reality. Realities can only exist if they are contained in the file. I use "hypertextual" in a second sense—to describe the power of the state to fabricate different versions of reality through the file. The word *hyper*text implies that there is something that is outside or beyond the text that is, nevertheless, connected to it. The outside world constantly enters into the file, and the file constantly produces things, people, places, and events outside of it. Through this process of in-flow and production, it claims to have authoritative knowledge of the world. In this chapter, I show how the file does not just *refer* to objects, people, places, and events outside of it, but actively fabricates them. I show that the file can conjure up not just one, but multiple versions of reality. And in this Borgesian sense, the term "hypertext" can be used—as it is by theorists of the internet (Montfort 2003, 29)—to describe a theory of the universe in which everything that is possible exists in some branch of reality.

The file's capacity to fabricate different versions of reality means that it has the power to destroy versions of reality as well. As I hope to show in this chapter, the experience of the file requires those who come in contact with it to understand that the file is a hypertextual universe that can destroy one version of reality while also holding different, mutually contradictory versions of the universe within it at the same time.

In the section that follows, I look at how the file can contain not just one, but multiple versions, of reality. By following the case from the State of Jammu and Kashmir filed by the wife of a "terrorist" killed by the army, I look at how the file can fabricate multiple and mutually contradictory "paper truths."

THE FILE PRODUCES MULTIPLE VERSIONS OF REALITY

I describe the file as hypertextual because can produce not just one version of reality, but multiple versions of it. These different realities are individually plausible, while being mutually contradictory. I detail these aspects of the hypertextual file through a Supreme Court case that originated in the erstwhile state of Jammu and Kashmir. The petitioner, Masooda Parveen, filed a case against the Indian Army and the state police, asking the court to order them to pay compensation and damages for their role in the killing of her husband, Ghulam Mohi-ud-din Regoo. While she claimed that her husband had been a victim of state brutality, both the army and the police claimed that he had been a terrorist who had been killed by his own booby trap. In response to her petition, the army produced documents to buttress their version of the events surrounding Regoo's death and also claimed that the police had conducted an inquest which exonerated the army. The police, for their part, submitted documents that supported the army's general narrative, but contradicted the time of Regoo's arrest, the time of his death, and other key details leading up to and following his death. Most notably, the police said that they had "lost" the inquest file and that the findings could not be traced.

Parveen lost the case. Drawing on the file in this case—comprising of documents filed by Parveen, the army, and the police, as well as orders issued by the Supreme Court—I show that the decision fundamentally had to do with the power of the file to fabricate and destroy different versions of reality. That is the file's hypertexual potential. First, I show that files can produce juridical "truth" and that Parveen lost her case (unlike, say, Qayoom in Chapter 2) because she had no files that could produce her version of reality. Both the army and the police used mundane technical documents to fabricate their version of the facts that lead to Regoo's death. Though the army and the police narratives were contradictory in certain details, both had the documents that produced "reality." Parveen, in contrast, did not have the power to produce such documents, and hence could not produce a narrative that demonstrated the army's culpability in her husband's death.

Second, I argue that in addition to their capacity to produce alternate versions of reality, files also have the ability to destroy and replace realities. In their attempt to locate the original inquest file, the police produced a "shadow file" that reproduced a selection of the "lost" original file—essentially, copies of some of the documents that had made up the original file. In conflict zones such as Kashmir, the government often "loses" files pertaining to human rights violations—for if there is no file, the juridical truth recorded therein is also lost. In the following section, I will examine the shadow file pertaining to Masooda Parveen's case. I show how the Indian government manipulated the technicalities of the file to construct alternative histories of the events leading up to Regoo's death, thereby evading responsibility for the killing.

Parveen's and the Army's Version of Reality

Parveen's case, officially titled *Masooda Parveen v Union of India*,[5] was heard against the backdrop of the Kashmiri struggle for independence. The long-standing separatist movement in Kashmir has been met with overwhelming force by India's security forces. Indian, Kashmiri, and international human rights organizations have documented widespread and systematic extrajudicial executions, enforced disappearances, torture, and rape of civilians by the Indian Army and paramilitary forces.

Parveen alleged that the army had murdered her husband, Ghulam Mohi-ud-din Regoo, in February 2008, at the army's Lathepora camp in Kashmir. She wrote numerous petitions to several state authorities, including the chief minister of Jammu and Kashmir and the prime minister of India, asking for an investigation into her husband's death and compensation from the state and national governments. One of these letters was addressed to the Supreme Court of India, which referred her letter to the Supreme Court's legal aid committee. The committee wrote to Parveen, asking her to file a case before the High Court of Jammu and Kashmir. Parveen declined to do so, stating that the High Court was unable to give her justice and implying that the High Court was under the thumb of the Indian government. She therefore wrote back to the Supreme Court's legal aid committee stating that she wanted the Supreme Court to rule on her case.

Ultimately, her case was referred to a lawyer who filed a petition on her behalf. The petition named the Union of India, the Indian Army, the State of Jammu and Kashmir, and the district administration as respondents. According to Parveen, a pro-government militia had been harassing her husband—a lawyer and saffron merchant in rural Kashmir—for protection money for some time. She said that in 1994, this pro-government militia informed the army that Regoo was a terrorist and that the army had illegally detained him for three months. Regoo, after being put through a "detailed interrogation,"[6] was found to be innocent of the accusations leveled against him.

According to Parveen's petition, which was backed by an affidavit, on February 1, 1998, a patrol party of the 17th Jat Regiment, along with pro-government militants, arrived at their residence. The house was searched, and nothing incriminating was found, but the patrol party nevertheless took Regoo away to the army's Lathepora base camp. There, he was tortured to death. Bombs were then strapped to his body and detonated, after which the remains of the body were handed over to the Pampore police station. According to the army, an entry had been made in the daily diary of the police station stating the army's version of Regoo's death.

As the name suggests, this daily diary (or DD in police parlance) records certain events that happen in the jurisdiction of a given police station, including the coming and going of police officials, the evidence that is brought into the police station, and information about the commission of serious offenses. The DD is recorded on carbon paper (so that there are duplicates of every entry) by the designated station house officer.

DD No. 24, dated February 3, 1998, was ostensibly prepared by the Pampore police station upon receiving information from the army regarding Regoo's death. The DD reflects the information that the army says it gave the police. According to the diary entry, when Regoo was taken into the army's custody, and he confessed that he was a Pakistan-trained militant and a former "divisional commander of the Al Barq militant outfit." According to the diary entry, Regoo had told the army officers present at the interrogation that he could lead them to a militant hideout. Several army officials had taken Regoo to the "hideout." According to the army, the entrance of the hideout had been rigged with explosives that had detonated when Regoo had tried to enter, causing his death.[7]

This narrative of Regoo's death as produced by the army in DD No. 24 is important, because the army was aware that the bureaucratic logic of the state requires everything to be documented and that, in particular, the death and its reasons must be recorded somewhere. They were also aware that documentation *fabricates* juridical truth. Hence, they used official paperwork to create a narrative that both explained Regoo's death and exonerated the security personnel from blame for it.

After narrating her version of the events leading up to her husband's death, Parveen's petition notes that after her husband's body was handed to her, a public funeral was held in Pampore town. This funeral procession quickly became a protest against Regoo's murder, and the protestors demanded that the local police immediately open an investigation into his death.

The army, in its response to Parveen's petition, repeated the story of Regoo's death that was narrated in DD No. 24. It also sought to dispute Parveen's narrative by stating that the Pampore police had undertaken an inquiry after the army had handed over Regoo's body to the police and found that Regoo had died in the manner stated by the army. The army also submitted the documents produced during this inquiry by the police, which included:

1. Seizure memos from Regoo's "hideout": "Seizure memos" are documents written by the police that record the physical objects taken

into custody by them while investigating an offense. In this case, the seizure memos list the arms allegedly seized from the "hideout."

2. A letter written by an army officer to the Pampore police station requesting that a First Information Report (FIR) be registered: An FIR is the first complaint that a police station receives regarding an offense. In this case, the FIR replicated the army's narrative of events, and in this way sought to justify ending the investigation.

3. The daily diary entry of the Pampore police station, which acknowledged receipt of the army's letter and stated that the FIR had been registered.

The DD entry recorded by the Pampore police station that was filed by the Army before the Supreme Court was different from the DD that Parveen said the Pampore police had recorded. The one submitted by the Army bore the following notation at the end:

> It is worthy to mention that matter abovementioned does not require any further action by the police. Even then this matter will be investigation [sic] will be conducted as per conditions on the spot and departmental actions will be conducted and *the proceeding u/s 174 Cr.P.C. will be conducted*, and SI Tahir Kaiser is hereby directed to conduct proceedings u/s 174 CrPC. (Emphasis added)[8]

This last document became the subject of hearings over the next few months. The army provided a DD entry that the army states was produced by the police, which stated that the police were going to commence "proceedings u/s 174 [under Section 174] CrPC[of the Code of Criminal Procedure, 1973]." Section 174 prescribes the mode and purpose of conducting an inquest into the cause of a person's death. In making this notation, army claimed that the police had ordered an inquest proceeding and that this proceeding was underway. Even though this notation showed that the police had prejudged the matter as not requiring "any further action by the police," because of the specific averment that the police had ordered inquest proceedings under Section 174 of the Code of Criminal Procedure, the army committed the police to showing that they—the police—had conducted an inquest to determine Regoo's cause of death.

In response to this statement (that inquest proceedings had been conducted by the police), Parveen, in her rejoinder affidavit stated:

No such investigation as contemplated under S. 174 appears to have been conducted by the police. On the other hand it is now learnt that the police have since closed the investigation and submitted the case to the . . . Magistrate 1st Class Pampore for closing the case. The case is now reported as a case of accidental death.[9]

At the hearing before the Supreme Court, the lawyer appearing for the army stated that the police had conducted an inquest and that it had found that the "allegations made by the petitioner were not true."[10] Despite their denial of Parveen's allegations, the police were now committed to showing that they had conducted a proper inquiry into Regoo's death because the documents that the army had submitted to the court stated that they had done so. The court directed the lawyer for the Jammu and Kashmir police to place the "inquest report and other connected documents" on the court's record.

The immediate question before the Supreme Court was whether the inquest was conducted and what the outcome of the inquest was. Perhaps to avoid answering questions regarding the inquest, the lawyers for the state police did not appear in court for the next couple of hearings. At one of these hearings, the Supreme Court's frustration was evident as its order noted that the lawyer for the State of Jammu and Kashmir seemed to have "disappeared from the scene,"[11] and that the court was "in the dark as to what investigation was done pursuant to the first information report lodged in connection with the incident in question."[12] As the state was not represented in court, the Supreme Court issued an order directly to the chief secretary (the highest bureaucrat of the state government) to produce all the documents connected with the inquest.

At the next hearing, on May 10, 2006, a new lawyer for the state finally appeared in court and filed a reply to Parveen's allegations. There were two noteworthy aspects to the police's reply. First, while it had submitted documents that produced a narrative that broadly aligned with the army's, it differed in terms of details. Second, with regard to the inquest report, the state's counter-affidavit contained an averment that only a "shadow file" was available—indicating that the original inquest report had been "lost." I will now focus on each of these points in turn.

The state government's response on behalf of the police meant that the file did not contain just two competing narratives—that of the petitioner and of the government—but rather *three*: the petitioner's version, the army's, and that of the police. We can see a comparison of these in Table 1.[13]

According to the petitioner and the police, Regoo was arrested by the army at 8:30 P.M. on February 1, 1998. According to the army, he was arrested at 8:30 P.M. on February 2, 1998. According to the police, Regoo died at 3 A.M. on February 2, 1998, while the army states that he died a full twenty-four hours later. In effect the army says that Regoo died in their custody *after* the police said his body was handed over to them. There is also a discrepancy as to which DD entry first documented Regoo's death: According to the police, it was DD No. 23, dated February 2, 1998, but according to the army, it was DD No. 24, dated February 3, 1998. The army and the police even produce two different post-mortem reports, though they both state that only one post-mortem examination was ever performed.

Thus, both the army and the police generated narratives through documents that agreed on the point that Regoo was a terrorist who had been killed by his own explosives, but they differed on the important details surrounding the death. They not only produced different times of Regoo's death, but they also differed substantially in describing both the events surrounding the death—the number and identity of the witnesses, the number of injured soldiers—and the events subsequent to Regoo's death—location of the body, post-mortem, and so on. The army's own documents regarding the time the post-mortem was conducted and when the body was handed over to the police also contradict their own narrative. Further, the police produced affidavits allegedly signed by Regoo's brother and his neighbor, which confirmed the narratives of the police and army (though the testimonies confirmed the time stated by the police). The petitioner, in response, produced an affidavit signed by Regoo's brother stating that he had never been examined by the police and had never signed an affidavit at the behest of the police, thereby implying that the testimony submitted by the police was fabricated.

By pointing out the differences in the narratives of the army and the police, the petitioner's lawyer argued that as the records of the police and the army did not corroborate each other, neither narrative could be believed and

TABLE 1. Comparison of different narratives provided in Masooda Parveen's case

Event	Parveen's version	Police version	Army version
Date of arrest	February 1, 1998	February 1, 1998	February 2, 1998
Time of arrest	8:30 P.M.	8:30 P.M.	8:30 P.M.
Time of death	Sometime on February 3, the date the body was handed over to the family	3:00 A.M. on February 2	2:30 A.M. on February 3
DD/FIR details	DD No. 24, dated February 3, 1998	DD No. 23, dated February 2, 1998	DD No 24, dated February 3, 1998
Number of hours of detention before death	At least 30 hours	6½ hours	6½ hours (but 24 hours later than the police version)
Number of soldiers injured in the "recovery"	No statement	One	Three
Civilian witnesses to the death	The witnesses' testimony produced by the police was false. The petitioner submitted affidavits from the police "witnesses" stating they had never been examined by the police.	Two witnesses—Regoo's brother and his neighbor.	There were no witnesses to the death.

Events after the death	The death occurred at Lathepora camp. The body was sent to Pampore camp. A unit of Pampore camp handed body over to Pampore police.	After receiving information about the death, the police proceeded to the spot and began investigations. They took the body to the subdistrict hospital for the post-mortem.	The post-mortem was conducted at Civil Hospital, Pampore, and then the body was handed over to Pampore police. However, the documents provided by the army indicate that the post-mortem was conducted after handing over the body.
Date and time of post-mortem	No statement.	10:00 A.M. on February 3, 1998; conducted by the police at the subdistrict hospital, Pampore.	1:30 P.M. on February 3, 1998; conducted by the army at Civil Hospital, Pampore.
Post-mortem documentation	No statement.	No cause of death; conducted by the assistant surgeon, Pampore.	No cause of death; no signature; no details of examining doctor. Report incomplete.

that hence her version of the events must be true. But her lawyer could not produce any documents that could corroborate her version of events. In dismissing the petition, the court held that each of the differing versions of reality created by the army and the police was plausible. But because Parveen's lawyer could not produce documentation to back up his version of reality, there was no document to suggest that the events as suggested by the petitioner could have occurred.

Parveen's lawyer needed documentation to buttress her version of events. As Parveen herself could not produce documents that authenticated her version of events, her case had to rely on the files produced by the state. In order to convince the court of Parveen's narrative, her lawyer hitched his arguments to the lost inquest file, to which we will now turn.

The "Lost" File and the Destruction of the Petitioner's World

The second point of interest in the police's response was their claim that the original inquest file had been lost. Hidden in the text of the counter-affidavit, in which the police had produced an alternate timeline of events regarding Regoo's death, is the following averment:

> v) That so far as the original file was summoned by Tehsildar [the district administrator] Pampore and was accordingly sent from P.S. [Police Station] Pampore to Sub-Division Office Awantipora, however a *shadow file* of the inquest proceedings conducted by P.S. Pampore is available. (Emphasis added)[14]

Implicit in the averment that only a shadow file was available was that the original file could no longer be found and that only a shadow file could be submitted to the court. This file contained a selection of documents from the proceedings conducted by the Pampore police. It contained a summary of the inquest proceedings and the statements of the army officials involved in Regoo's arrest, which concurred with the police's version of events. However—and this is critical—this shadow file did not contain any documents concerning the proceedings that were conducted by the magistrate who supervised the inquest. The examinations and the cross-examinations of the witnesses, the evidence collected by the magistrate, and, most importantly, the magistrate's conclusions about the cause of death were unavailable. The entire judicial record of the inquest proceedings had been "lost."

Frustrated by the absence of the entire file, the Supreme Court directed the State of Jammu and Kashmir, and in particular the relevant district magistrate, to locate the entire and original file pertaining to the inquest proceedings.

The "Lost" File Creates Another File

In his affidavit dated November 25, 2006, the district magistrate of Pulwama stated that the entire inquest file could not be found, and he detailed the efforts made to locate the file, which in turn, created another file. The district magistrate deputed a senior prosecuting officer to conduct an inquiry into whether the relevant file had been lost due to "sheer negligence, mismanagement of the records or due to mischief."[15] The officer's inquiry report (which was annexed to the district magistrate's affidavit) stated that the file had been sent from the Pampore police station to the *tahsildar*'s office and was returned "against an appropriate receipt,"[16] but nevertheless could not be located.

The need for a separate report on the missing file highlights the paperwork needed to maintain files—that is, the work required to produce files that organize files. In order to track the "movement of the file," the inquiry officer stated that he examined daily diary registers at police stations, the dispatch registers of different offices (documenting what files had been sent out from them), and the receipt registers of these offices (documenting what files had been received there). The inquiry officer examined various officials who deal with paperwork at the lower levels of the police bureaucracy: a reader, a *dak* (post) runner, various *moharirs* (file keepers), and *munshis* (clerks).[17] The report pointed out lapses in how the files were transported and the mistakes that had occurred in how the files were recorded in various registers. The senior prosecuting officer recommended departmental action against several lower-level officials and instructed the officials to keep looking for the missing file. What is also revealing about this account is that producing and maintaining files is a collective endeavor, and not the sole responsibility of one or two officials. The elaborate bureaucratic infrastructure to keep account of files, instead of fixing responsibility for the "loss" of the file, had managed to dissipate responsibility. As the production and maintenance of files was the result of a network of officials and other files (Hull 2003), no one officer could be held responsible for the file's "loss."

Human rights groups have argued that the use of shadow files "seems suspiciously common in cases involving human rights abuses by armed forces in Jammu and Kashmir" (Jammu and Kashmir Coalition of Civil Society 2014, 4), with files being regularly "lost" during fires or civil unrest. As we have seen, a shadow file is a fragmentary reconstruction of the original lost file. And what is particularly galling is that while it is known that only parts of the original file are available, no one knows what exactly has been lost. While the shadow file points to gaps, no one knows what had previously existed in those gaps. Did the original documents point to the army's culpability? Or did they bolster the army's version of events? What did the lost papers say? Parveen's lawyer was asked this very question by the Supreme Court judges:

> We put it to Mr. Ganesh [Parveen's lawyer] repeatedly as to whether he could identify the information that could be obtained from the [original] police record. He could give no categorical answer to this query except to state that the reluctance of the civil authority to produce the file betrayed a guilty mind and the possibility existed that there was something in the file which needed to be hidden.

According to the Supreme Court, Parveen's lawyers had "been at pains to emphasise that had the original file been produced the true story of the circumstances leading to Regoo's death would have been revealed and it is for this reason that the file had been withheld."[18] According to the Supreme Court, because the petitioner had tied her arguments to the inquest file and could not prove her narrative of events without the "lost" file, her version of reality could not exist. Yet, at the same time, even though the accounts provided by the army and the police were inconsistent vis-à-vis each other, both the army and the police had provided documentation to back their respective versions of reality.

Parveen's lawyer had no choice but to rely upon the documentation produced by the state, given the "loss" of the file that might have buttressed Parveen's version of reality. The version of reality that Parveen wished to present could not be produced, as she had no documents to produce it with. With this, the court found that there was no evidence to support the petitioner's version of events except her own allegations, and they dismissed the petition.

One may ask why the district magistrate who supervised the inquest and prepared the inquest report was not called to testify as to the contents of the lost inquest file. Unfortunately, the Supreme Court's records do not tell us whether this request was made. Or if it was made, this request was not put in writing. Perhaps this was because Parveen and her lawyer did not trust the magistrate to back up her version of events. Or maybe the request was not made because of the underlying assumption that juridical truth is produced by documents and files, and not by people. Indeed, as Hull (2012) notes, the prominence given to files and paper in South Asia is premised on a thoroughgoing rejection of trust in people. Judicial truth is produced by files, and not by people.

It is difficult to understand why the police and army produced different versions of Regoo's death. According to one of the lawyers for Parveen, the reason for these different versions was a mixture of impunity and incompetence. The police and army knew that they would not face any repercussions for killing Regoo and therefore did not even bother to properly fill out the paperwork required. The knowledge that they would never be held accountable for their crimes had made them exceedingly lazy about filling out the necessary paperwork.

Nevertheless, as this chapter has revealed, documents have consequences. As we saw in the last chapter how one may become vulnerable to legal utterances, one must also account for what is written into legal files. While the army probably produced the document stating that an inquest had been conducted in order to evade their own responsibility, doing so meant that the police were now committed not only to responding to Parveen's allegations, but also to buttressing the army's averment. While eventually both the police and army produce documents that fabricated a narrative of Regoo's "accidental" death, the fact that they contradicted each other on the minor details leads to a near-unraveling of this narrative.

The tussle over the smaller details of the files shows what is at stake in dealing with technicalities. In particular it draws attention to the hypertextual capacity of the file. Control over the file is vital because the file has the power to not just to determine the outcome of this case, but to determine what reality is. While the state used these technicalities to fabricate its own narrative of events, Parveen attempted to intervene in the state's production of documents to create her own narrative of events. In tracking the movement of the "lost" inquest file and the shadow file that emerged to replace it, we can see how various actors jostled to control the truth fabricated by the files—the district magistrate, the Supreme Court, the army, the police, the defense lawyers, the senior prosecuting officer, and the file about the lost file. The attempts to produce the original inquest file in themselves show why the file is so important. Its hypertextual capacity means that it can determine the outcome of a case. Or, to put it more starkly, the hypertextual nature of the file means that without the file, the world that Parveen sought to construct could not exist.

What the narrative of Masooda Parveen's case also reveals is how politics emerges through legal technicalities. This is apparent not only from the ways in which the army and the police attempted to excuse themselves of responsibility for Regoo's death. It is also apparent from the Supreme Court's eventual judgment, which Court located Regoo's killing in a specific construction of the Kashmiri independence movement such that Indian citizens "who have gone astray" are met with the "force of arms." The court ignored the systematic, brutal, and everyday violence of the Indian administration in Kashmir and framed the situation as one in which "some unfortunate incidents do occur" in the course of the "nation's fight."[19] But the political framing of the case also emerged in subtler ways through legal technicalities.

Implicit in the judgment is the technical idea that the burden of proof is on the petitioner. It places the burden on her to prove her allegations, despite the fact that she cannot produce documents to buttress her narrative of events. The army and the police are able to fabricate different versions of events because they have documents to do so. By framing its judgment through the idea of the burden of proof, the Supreme Court essentially states that Parveen has to produce documents to back up her allegations; since she could not, the court could dismiss her petition, while allowing the mutually contradictory versions fabricated by the police and army to stand. In this way we can see what is at stake in a legal technicality. Here, "minor" technicalities enable the murder of a lawyer and small-time trader at the hands of security forces to be narrated as the accidental death of a terrorist.

5

CERTIFICATION AND THE FABRICATION OF TRUTHS

In the previous chapter, I looked at the capacity of the file to fabricate different versions of reality and how the capacity to produce paperwork is implicated in the ability to produce certain versions of the truth. In this chapter, I examine technical practices of certification and their relation to the production of truth. Certifications are the granular processes through which realities come to be simultaneously produced and contested by the case file. I argue that the process of producing different versions of reality depends on a series of seemingly insignificant technical and certificatory practices—the maintenance of log books, signatures, countersignatures, stamps, seals, and so on. Think back to the case of Qayoom in Chapter 2: After learning that the police had to maintain log books to monitor their own movements and their use of arms, he taught himself on how to file right-to-information (RTI) applications. Qayoom did not contest the prosecution's version of his case by summoning witnesses who could testify to his actual whereabouts on the day or to his kidnapping by the army. Rather, by obtaining certified copies of daily diary entries and vehicle and arms log books, he and his co-accused adopted a strategy based on their knowledge that at the heart of any case are these humble sheets of paper and the certificatory practices that surround them. They knew that they could contest the version of reality produced by the police's file only through the protocols of handling the file. They had to fight paper truths with paper truths. In this chapter, I think more carefully about the role of these documents and certificatory practices in the production of different versions of reality.

I do so by following the investigation and trial that followed a series of bombings in Delhi in 2008. This is the same trial that Mohammed Hanif was a part of, the case I briefly discussed in the last chapter. In this chapter, I focus on the investigative and trial processes in the case against another accused person, Fahad, as I call him, whom the Delhi police accused of planting a bomb in Delhi and of being part of a conspiracy behind another series of bombings in the state of Gujarat. The Special Cell alleged that Fahad had placed a small bomb in a bag and then hired an autorickshaw to take him to a crowded market. Upon reaching the market, Fahad allegedly got out, leaving the bag behind, and asked the driver to wait. The police claim that the bomb exploded several minutes after Fahad left the market. Several people were killed, and the rickshaw driver and several others were injured. In the days following the explosion, the police arrested Fahad along with others who the police claimed were part of the conspiracy. In this chapter, I show how this narrative was built up through documents produced during the investigation and how, during the trial, the defense challenged this narrative by questioning the validity of these documents.

I discuss the place of documentary practices in constructing narratives during evidentiary processes.[1] While some authors have argued that scholars ought to be more concerned with the place of rhetoric and argument in understanding the idea of evidence (Hastrup 2004; Twining 2006, Engelke 2009), I focus in this chapter on the documentary processes that go into producing legal knowledge.

ACCOUNTABILITY AND EPISTEMOLOGICAL CERTAINTY THROUGH CERTIFICATION

While courts in India and England have historically attempted different methods of ensuring the probity of the facts "found" during the evidentiary process,[2] files and the accompanying certificatory processes are currently the primary way of producing facts in a trial. Raman (2012) argues that the move to paper during the early establishment of the early colonial state in south India was intended to ensure that the juridical truth that was produced could be subject to certain certification processes, which was not possible under previous practices.

The centrality of scribal practices in producing scientific truth has been drawn attention to by science and technology studies scholars. In highlighting the prominence of paper processes in the production of scientific truth, Latour (1999) argues that objects from the world are converted into writing by the gradual transcription of the material world into language. Latour shows the process by which a scientific "fact" is not discovered, but rather produced through a chain of inscriptions and practices that depend on paper.

In contrast to his work on science, Latour's (2010) seminal ethnography of France's Conseil d'Etat gives little space to understand how the law produces facts (van Oorschot and Schinkel 2015; Pottage 2012). As he tracks the file's movement through the court's bureaucracy, Latour is concerned with the "processes of enunciation" (Pottage 2012, 169) and the movement between different types of writing (Latour 2010, 86). Latour (2010) does not engage with how "facts" are constituted by the file and seems to assume that they are simply brought on record by the various parties to a case (79) and that the various iterations of the file are meant to "constitute a domain of unquestionable fact" (229) that will allow for an "unquestionable decision" (230). While he is correct to focus on the procedures that make the file "ripe for use" (70)—that is, that enable the transformation of "facts" into issues of law—Latour does not see that these "facts" themselves are brought into being by the step-by-step procedure that he details in his work on science.[3]

In bringing attention to the processes by which legal facts are brought into existence, this chapter makes two contributions to the scholarship on documentary practices and their relation to the production of legal truth.[4] The first is to show how juridical truth is simultaneously produced and undermined by the official practices that create and certify documents. There is a rich sphere of scholarship that has shown how the truth claims made by government papers are undermined when official documents circulate through bureaucratic networks and the communities that come in contact with these documents (Tarlo 2003; Das 2004; Hull 2012; Kafka 2012; Raman 2012). This chapter, however, analyzes not only how official papers gradually enact juridical truth, but also how truth claims can be undermined by the same official practices through which these documents have been created.

Second, while scholars have shown how bureaucratic documentary practices have produced objects and people, I show how files also produce time and narrative. This ethnography shows how documentary practices enact different objects and place them in a certain narrative chain of past events.

The evidentiary process is an attempt not just to prove that the referents of the file—the objects—exist, but also to weave a story around these objects, connecting them to each other. The file, therefore, does not just enact objects, but in weaving a narrative around the objects, also enacts time.

THE ACCRETION OF NARRATIVES THROUGH DOCUMENTARY RECORDS

Sociolegal scholars have pointed to the centrality of narratives to the working of the law (Ewick and Silbey 1995; Twining 2006, 286–92; Mertz 2007, 79–82; Scheffer 2010, 1). Some have noted that narrative is essential to rhetorical forms of claim-making and persuasion (White 1985; Constable 2014). Mertz (2007) notes that the stories told by courts—especially appellate courts—in their judgments are structured by the legal issues at stake in a particular conflict (61, 146). She argues that the narratives that are presented in cases are made to fit certain conceptual categories, which are in turn generated by statutes and precedents.

These ways of thinking about narrative imagine a story being told at a single moment—say, in final arguments or a judge's decision. This chapter shows that while linked to both claim-making and legal categories, the narratives in a case are the sum of smaller narratives dispersed through documentary records. I argue that the "facts" that are eventually relied upon by courts to produce their judgments are themselves produced by the creation and reading of more humble texts—such as the memos, certificates, and the like. The totality of the "facts of a case" is produced by the slow accretion and contestation of these minor documents. In order to understand how these facts are produced, we need to look not just *through* documents (to their content) but also *at* documents to understand how they are produced and how they circulate (Hull 2012; Lowenkron and Ferreira 2014).

In his ethnography of English criminal trials, Scheffer (2004, 2010) draws attention to how the stories that defense lawyers built into their legal arguments were presented in court orally, and also how they were distributed through their files. His approach to "case-making" (Scheffer 2010) sees the narratives of defense lawyers as being dispersed in time and across the various documents that comprise the defense lawyers' case file. He shows that the defense lawyers' stories have been put together gradually over time and through several documentary iterations (Scheffer 2004, 384).

While Scheffer concentrates on the dispersed production of the narrative of a case through the file, the file also contains another narrative—of itself. As Hull (2003) points out, a file is a "chronicle of its own production," and "signs of its own history are continuously and deliberately inscribed upon the artifact itself" (296).[5] Thus, a file contains (at least) two narratives: its own history and that of objects and people referred to outside of itself.

By examining the evolution of the file in Fahad's case, I show how these two narratives are intertwined in the materiality of the file. I show how the police's file reveals its own birth and history and, in doing so, gives us a narrative of the investigation. In telling us of its own history—the history of the investigation—the file in the Fahad case also reveals a narrative of the events leading up to the bomb blast. I show that since the narrative of the bomb blast is so dependent on the narrative of the investigation, the defense lawyers' aim was to discredit the papers documenting the investigation. To do so, they inserted their own counternarrative into the court record.

Here, I look at several key documents in the case against Fahad. These documents pertain to the seizure of the autorickshaw after the explosion and the medical treatment provided to the driver. To present a coherent narrative, each sheet of paper produced during the investigative process needs to be enmeshed with others. But writing is not sufficient to produce juridical truth, and I describe the variety of certificatory practices—signatures, countersignatures, stamps, seals, identification—that shore up the truth produced by these documents. What emerges in my account is that the production of juridical truth depends upon evidential processes that consist of a series of smaller certificatory practices related to documents. For the defense, this meant that questioning these certificatory procedures could displace and change the narrative that the prosecution had tried to build. Further, the defense inserted a counternarrative into the court's record by challenging the validity of these certificatory procedures. I therefore show that documentary practices are implicated in the production of juridical truth and that juridical truth is vulnerable because of the very documentary practices upon which it depends.

To do so, I follow the examinations-in-chief (direct examinations) and cross-examinations of the witnesses in Fahad's case. By looking at the examinations-in-chief, I detail the prosecution's attempts to inscribe its narrative of the investigation and the bomb blast into the court record. Because the prosecution's narrative of the bomb blast is so tied to the narrative of the investigation—which is in turn dependent upon the investigative documents—if the prosecution can prove that the police investigated the offense in the way that the documents say that they did, it can also prove its narrative of the bomb blast. In order to prove that the investigation proceeded exactly as the police claimed, the prosecution needs to prove that the documents created during the investigation were prepared in the proper manner.

The defense strategy then is not to directly question the narrative that the prosecution has proposed, but to impugn the validity of the investigative documents. It is by questioning the validity of the investigative documents that the defense can insert a counternarrative into the court's record.

According to the defense lawyers, it was not enough to challenge the prosecution's version of events. What was essential to get an acquittal was, in the words of one lawyer, "to put forward our own story." This contrasts with some ideas of trial advocacy, which that while the prosecution must present a coherent narrative of a particular case, all the defense must do is to poke holes into this narrative. In contrast, what Fahad's lawyers believed was that they needed to weave together a coherent narrative to challenge the prosecution's narrative. As one of them said to me, they had to keep this narrative in mind and build it slowly over time to insert it into the court's documentary record.

In this case, the defense lawyer constructed a simple narrative to the effect that (a) Fahad did not place the bomb in the autorickshaw and (b) the police concluded that he was guilty prior to beginning the investigation. She argued that rather than do a proper investigation and allow the evidence to lead them to a suspect, the police first zeroed in on Fahad and fabricated evidence to support their starting assumption. Therefore, the defense's aim was twofold: to show that the prosecution's narrative of the investigation was false and to insert into the court record the allegation that Fahad was a convenient suspect. If the defense could show that the narrative of the investigation was false, then the police's version of the events surrounding the bomb blast would lose credibility. In order to do this, the defense had to attack the validity of the documents produced during the investigation. The defense's strategy was premised on the "ideology [that] the validity of records (or more precisely, their referential correctness) is ensured by following the procedures established for their production" (Hull 2012, 203).

This highlights the importance of certificatory practices in ensuring the referential correctness of documents, such as whether the objects, people, and places referred to in the document actually exist. I show how the defense's line of questioning built up the case that the police did not properly create and certify the investigatory documents, which meant that the documents they produced in the investigative process were not valid, which in turn meant that the narrative of the investigation produced by the police was not valid. If the narrative of the investigation was not valid, then the official narrative of the bomb explosion was not valid either.

THE BOMB BLAST CREATES A FILE

Recall that Fahad was accused of planting a bomb in Delhi and being part of a conspiracy to bomb a city in Gujarat. He and most of the others accused in Delhi were subsequently arrested and charged with coordinating the bomb blasts in both cities. Because he and his co-accused were being tried in two trials in two different cities, Fahad and most of his co-accused (including Hanif, from the last chapter) were "present" for their trial in Delhi via a videoconferencing link. As we will see in the last section, this becomes pertinent when we discuss how the prosecution's main witness attempted to identify Fahad.

To recap the police's case against Fahad: Fahad hired an autorickshaw (with registration number 1438) to go to a market in central Delhi—let's say, Gole Market—and left behind a bomb in the vehicle, while he had walked away, asking the driver to wait for a couple of minutes. After Fahad left, the driver—Dhyan Chand—parked the rickshaw and walked several feet away. Several moments later, the bomb that had been placed in the autorickshaw exploded, leaving several dead and many more injured, although the autorickshaw driver himself survived the blast. Both the autorickshaw and its driver play a crucial part in the evidence against Fahad, so let's follow them carefully through the various documentary iterations of the case. As we will see, this narrative is not told in a single document, but rather is slowly built up through various papers.

During the investigation, there were two sets of files: the court's file and the police's file. After registering the first complaint, or first information report (FIR), the police sent it to a magistrate to be authenticated. A copy of the complaint was kept in the magistrate's file, and the original—which was stamped and certified by the magistrate—was returned to the police (this process is to ensure that the police make no alterations to the FIR). At this point, the court file consisted of only a few pages—the FIR. When the police made arrests, they filed arrest memos and applications for remand, which were added to the court file. This file also contained orders by the magistrate, allowing or refusing remand. Over the course of the following weeks, the police made written applications to the court for permission to take voice, handwriting, and body tissue samples and for further time to interrogate the accused. These applications were made in writing and kept in the court file. If the accused had a lawyer, the court asked counsel for their replies to these applications, which were placed in the file as well, along with the magistrate's decisions on them.

In parallel, the police compiled their own records documenting the progress of their investigation. This file was periodically presented to the magistrate so that they could monitor the investigation. In the next section, we will see how the police file came into being—or, more precisely, how the police file says it came into being.

THE FILE NARRATES ITS OWN BIRTH: THE AUTORICKSHAW AT THE SCENE OF THE EXPLOSION

One of the first documentary iterations of the explosion was the FIR registered by the jurisdictional police station. This is the beginning of the police's narrative of the investigation. In this case, the FIR was registered as "FIR No. 176/2008 Police Station Gole Market." All the paperwork that resulted from this FIR was supposed to bear this number.

According to the FIR, Sub-inspector Rajinder Singh was the complainant, and in the FIR, he stated that the police station had received information about the bomb blast and that he was sent to the site. According to the FIR, when he reached the spot, he found a number of people "in injured condition," who were shifted to hospitals with help from the public. He said he saw an autorickshaw with license plate number 1438 that was badly damaged. A part of it was hanging from a nearby *peepal* (sacred fig) tree. He said he also saw the damaged fuel cylinder of this autorickshaw. In addition, he said that he also saw several damaged vehicles and listed their license plate numbers. He then stated that the area was cordoned off to "preserve" the scene and that he handed the investigation over to a senior officer, Inspector Akash Thakur. The FIR concluded with the statement that the investigation should proceed for offenses under several criminal provisions.

We get a sense of what the police did next from a series of documents called "seizure memos," which were prepared by the police. These documents record the taking of certain objects from the blast site and describe them and the manner in which they were preserved for future analysis. They are one step in establishing a chain of custody of evidence collected during the investigation. Let's look at one of them. Recall that Sub-inspector Rajinder Singh had seen the badly damaged autorickshaw and recorded this in the FIR. The fact that he recorded this justified what he did next: He seized it. This act of seizing the autorickshaw (three-seater rickshaw, or TSR in police parlance) was documented in the seizure memo that I have translated (and edited for clarity) in the box below.

Case FIR No 176/08 dt. 14/10/2008 u/s 307, 323,121 IPC, 3, 4, 5 Explosive Substances Act 1908 & 10, 12, 13, Unlawful Activities (Prevention) Act, 1967, Police Station Gole Market New Delhi

Seizure Memo Badly Damaged T.S.R Different parts of T.S.R. No DL IGH 1438—Suspected I.E.D Exploded in the T.S.R.

The below mentioned witness states that at Lakshmi Road near numbers 42 and 43, Gole market, west side, New Delhi some expert teams came there to suggest what exhibits to seize, and after that they saw the Badly Damaged T.S.R. No. DL 1GH 1438, upon which the bomb (IED) was probably exploded. Badly damaged pieces of it were thrown in different directions and different parts of it were taken from the below-written places to one spot <illegible>

1. Iron piece which was the lower part upon which the tire would fit [i.e., the axle], which was taken from the site and was on the peepal tree that was in between shop no. 42 and 43.
2. Back seat along with piece of metal which was stuck at about 15 feet up in the peepal tree.
3. The back portion upon which was written the name of the owner which was hanging from some cables near shop no. 43, at about 8–9 feet above the ground.
4. The front side portion upon which the number was written [. . .] This piece was fallen about 20 meters away, near an electronic transformer, behind the WagonR Car No [registration number]

5. CNG [compressed natural gas] cylinder which belonged to the TSR on whose side there were many marks made by pellets (made of iron). This was found fallen near shop no. 43 on the road.
6. Three tires of the TSR, were taken from about 5–7 feet away, in the direction of <illegible>
7. <Illegible> portion of the front mud-guard part, found in front of shop no. 42, below the peepal tree.
8. Apart from this, several smaller and bigger pieces, which were thrown in different directions, which were about 15–16 in number, were collected together in one place.

The witness, from carefully looking, found that the TSR number was DL 1GH 1438. In the upper pieces of the TSR there are holes and it is badly broken. By looking at its state it seems as if the blast happened in this TSR. All above pieces <illegible> were seized by memo in the above named case and has been written up by the police
Memo is complete.

Signed: Witnessed by:

Rajinder Kumar Singh   Akash Thakur

The seizure memo contains a brief description of the objects taken into custody by the police and the reasons for doing so. It was signed by Sub-inspector Rajinder Singh and another officer, Akash Thakur, who signed as a witness to the seizure. These two signatures seek to certify that the objects were seized and that the memo is an accurate account of the seizure. Similar memos were prepared for other items seized from the scene of the blast. Each item was packaged in a cloth bag called a *pulanda* and was then sealed with wax and with a seal bearing the initials of the investigating officer, in this instance, "A.T." The same process was followed for the seizure of a burned plastic bag containing the autorickshaw driver's license and other registration documents. Each of these seizure memos maintains a link to the original FIR through its heading, in which it states the FIR number and the jurisdictional police station, and each of these memos documents its own certification, that is, the signature of Inspector Akash Thakur, the officer who witnessed the seizure by Sub-inspector Rajinder Singh. The signatures certify that the document accurately reflects the actions of Sub-inspector Rajinder Singh. As we will see in the next section, when these memos were presented to the court, it was the accuracy of these papers that was called into account in order to question the seizure itself.

As in Latour's (1999) idea of the "circulating reference," every step that the seized articles subsequently took was turned into a document. This, again, was done to ensure the chain of custody of the material. After their seizure, the articles were deposited in an evidence storeroom, called the *malkhana*, or the MHC(M)—the Malkhana Head Constable (Moharir)—and the details of the seized articles were entered into a register. When the materials, including the remains of the autorickshaw, were taken to the Central Forensic Science Laboratory for analysis, they were entered into the laboratory's register.

From this brief description of how a part of an autorickshaw became evidence of a bomb blast, we can discern three points. First, the eventual truth-value of the objects seized by the police depends on the links between documents that mediate their seizure and attest to their movement from the blast site to the evidence storeroom. For the truth-value of these objects to be maintained later, and through to the end of the trial, the links of mediations must remain unbroken, like "electricity through a circuit" (Latour 1999, 69). Each of these documents must link with the others. If the FIR number was not written at the top of the seizure memo, this might indicate that the material was seized in another case or that it was prepared prior to the FIR being registered (indicating that it had been fabricated). If the Central Forensic Science Laboratory failed to enter an object into its register, it would be uncertain whether an analysis had been conducted. Thus, these documents were prepared so as to form a continuous chain.

Second, the truth-value of these objects is maintained not just by documentary linkages, but also by elaborate certification procedures. Akash Thakur countersigned the seizure memo that had been prepared by Rajinder Kumar Singh. Akash Thakur then sealed the evidence and affixed his personal seal—a seal that should remain in his custody alone. This was aimed at ensuring that he alone was responsible for any objects in the *pulanda*. The entries in the registers and the signatures and countersignatures all aimed to certify that the objects were collected and preserved in a proper manner and in the manner stated in the documents. Thus, the referential correctness of the documents was built up by following smaller certification practices (Hull 2012, 162–209; Power 1997, 12, 69–90).

Third, we see how the police file started to document its own time and begins to build a narrative of the investigation and of the bomb blast. The first mention of the narrative of the autorickshaw was in the FIR, where the sub-inspector reported seeing the badly damaged autorickshaw; this narrative was built upon in the seizure memo, where he stated, "By looking at its state it seems as if the blast happened in this TSR." Another memo on seizing the license and registration of the driver gave a first documentary glimpse of the autorickshaw driver, Dhyan Chand. The narrative around the autorickshaw was therefore built up by the slow accretion of different documents, so that by the end of the investigative process two complete narratives emerged: the investigation around the autorickshaw, and of the bomb being placed in the autorickshaw. The narratives built up around the autorickshaw brought in other objects and people—notably the driver, Dhyan Chand, to whom we now turn.

DHYAN CHAND: THE SECOND DOCUMENTARY LAYER

Recall that the autorickshaw driver, Dhyan Chand, survived the blast. In FIR No. 176/08, Sub-inspector Rajinder stated that when he arrived at the scene, he saw several people lying on the ground in an injured condition and that with assistance from unnamed members of the public, these people were taken to a nearby hospital. Though the documents do not reveal how he got there, Dhyan Chand was one of the patients who were seen in the emergency ward of this hospital on that day.

There, a doctor—let us call him Dr. Pasha—examined him. Dhyan Chand was one of fourteen patients that Dr. Pasha examined that evening. For each of these patients, he filled out a medico-legal certificate (MLC), which detailed the injuries of each patient, their blood pressure, and the preliminary treatment they were given before they were moved to specialist wards. In Dhyan Chand's MLC, Dr. Pasha noted that he had suffered "grievous injury," including several "lacerated wounds" and "moderate bleeding," and that he was put on a drip. According to the MLC, Chand's blood pressure was 110/70, and he had an elevated heart rate. Crucially, the MLC also noted that Dhyan Chand was fit enough to give a statement to the police. In the next section, we will see the relevance of this statement. This document was signed by Dr. Pasha and sent to the police.

According to other documents filed by the police, after Dhyan Chand was discharged from the hospital, he stayed with family as he convalesced. Several weeks after the bomb explosion, an interview with Fahad was published in a popular news magazine. (Fahad told me that he never gave an interview to the magazine.) According to the police, Dhyan Chand saw this magazine cover, which pictured Fahad's face, and realized that this was the person whom he took to Gole Market. Dhyan Chand then approached the police, who then had his sworn testimony recorded before a magistrate. A copy of this magazine cover as well as Dhyan Chand's testimony were filed along with the charge sheet.

So far, dispersed through the documentary record, we find the following narrative: the bomb was placed in an autorickshaw (from the FIR and the seizure memo discussed above); the autorickshaw was seized (from the seizure memo); Dhyan Chand was the driver of the autorickshaw (from another seizure memo); and he survived the blast (from the MLC); Dhyan Chand recognized Fahad as the person who had traveled in his autorickshaw immediately prior to the explosion (from his sworn testimony before the magistrate). Thus, these documents (together with other documents not discussed in this chapter[6]) weave a narrative of the bomb blast. This narrative was not created in a single instant, but through the slow accretion of documents. Without these different documents, this narrative of the case could not exist.

In the next section, I look at how various other documents were produced and entered the court file. Let us move forward by four years and revisit these documents and the people in the courtroom.

THE FILE GOES ON TRIAL: NARRATIVES AND COUNTERNARRATIVES THROUGH CERTIFICATORY PROCEDURES

After a prescribed period, the police filed the final report, more commonly known as the charge sheet, before the magistrate's court. This charge sheet established the chronological narrative of the investigation, through which a narrative of the events surrounding the bomb blast was proposed. It was here that the defense officially reads the full narrative of the investigation and the case against Fahad. The charge sheet also listed the offenses against the accused, the witnesses, their testimony as told to the police, and all the documentary evidence relied upon by the police, including memos that documented the seizure of certain evidence, forensic reports, and many other papers that documented the police's actions. The charge sheet listed the documents that we encountered in the previous section and scores of others. At this stage, the police file was submitted to the court and merged with the court's file. The court file dramatically expanded in girth and weight, now running into multiple volumes of hundreds of pages each.

After the magistrate's proceedings concluded, the trial commenced before a sessions court, where a single judge (not a jury) is the trier of facts. As we saw in the last chapter, the judge could not simply rely on the police file, because systems of verification are essential to Indian evidentiary practices due to historic suspicion of police investigations, and because the adversarial trial demands that the defense is allowed to confront the witnesses. The prosecution had to prove that the investigation took place as the police claimed. Through courtroom testimony, the prosecution had to prove that the police prepared the investigative documents in accordance with proper procedures—that is, that they were properly certified. As stated earlier, trials in India—especially terrorism trials—take years to complete. This means that courtroom testimony about the documents most often takes place years after the documents have been created. There was a gap of about four years, between when the documents discussed here were (purportedly) produced and when they were testified to in the courtroom.

The rest of this chapter looks at how the narrative presented in the police's documents was mediated by the court file. Another documentary layer was added, enabling objects collected from the blast site to become part of the court record. The testimonies of police officers and witnesses, and the documents pertaining to them, were also inserted into the court file. Thus, both the narrative of the investigation and the narrative of the bomb blast were entered into the court's record.

The rest of this chapter also highlights the place of certificatory procedures in producing narratives. The police aimed to prove the referential correctness of the documents by highlighting that the documents were properly certified. Conversely, if the defense could call the certifications on the documents into question, then the referential correctness of the documents could also be questioned. The defense would ask whether the certifying procedures were adhered to during the investigation, and through these questions, the defense would introduce its own narrative into the court file: that the certification procedures were not adhered to properly and that, as a result, the file falsely implicated Fahad. This draws our attention to the process of a courtroom deposition. Therefore, before discussing the testimony of the subinspector, the doctor, and Dhyan Chand, I want to briefly look at the deposition as a certifying process.

TRANSCRIPTION AS A CERTIFYING PROCESS

The transcripts of witness depositions are not verbatim records of what was said in the courtroom. The statute that covers witness depositions (Section 276 of the Code of Criminal Procedure) states that evidence of each witness will be taken down in writing by the judge, or by dictation by the judge, and may be taken down as a narrative, instead of in a question and answer format. During examinations-in-chief (sometimes known as direct examinations), the lawyer or judge asks the witness a question, and the witness replies. The lawyers and the judge then dictate the witness's answer to the stenographer. A similar process takes place during the cross-examination of the witness.

As an example of how this process works, we can look at the cross-examination of Rajinder Singh, the policeman who seized the autorickshaw. We will go through the content of his testimony in greater detail in a later section, but for the moment I would like to focus on the way in which the testimony was recorded. The following box is a what a page of Sub-inspector Rajinder Singh's testimony in the court file looks like. (Note the series of Xs, which denote the start of the cross-examination.)

XXXXXX by Ms. [Defence lawyer], defence council for Mohd. Fahad (Accused No. 1).

The scene of the crime which I inspected about which I have referred in my examination in chief, was an area of 50 meters in length and 20/25 meters in width. I left the spot on 12/09/2008, at about 12 noon. From the spot we reached PS Gole Market. Regarding our arrival at the police station, DD entry was made at the police station. At this stage, witness has shown to learned defence counsel DD Entry No. 9A dated 12/09/2008. As requested copy of the relevant page containing DD entry no. 9 is being taken on record. Same is **ExPW133/DA**.

At that time I was accompanied by the staff of the police station. Inspector Akash Thakur remained with me during the investigation conducted by me at the spot.

It is correct that the area where the occurrence took place is a public case [sic] where there are many shops. It is correct that I did not join anyone from the public during the investigation conducted by me at the spot. At the time, I left the police station for the spot, I was empty handed.

The material used in preparing the parcels at the spot was

My own notes of this page of the Sub-inspector's cross-examination look something like this:

Defense lawyer: How big was the scene of the crime?
Witness: 50 m in length
Judge (dictating): The scene of the crime which I inspected was spread over 50 meters in length.
Judge to witness: Breadth?
Witness: 25 meters
Judge (dictating): and 20–25 meters in width
Defense lawyer: *Kitne der ruke the?* (How long did you stay?)
Witness: (inaudible)
Judge (dictating): I left the spot on *bara-nau-do hazaar aath* (twelve-nine-two thousand and eight) at noon.
Defense lawyer: *Jab spot ko choda tha, kaun tha?* (Who was there when you left for the spot?)
Witness: *Kaafi log the.* (There were many people.)
Judge (dictating): At the time I was accompanied by staff of the police station.
Defense lawyer: *IO aapke saat the?* (Was the IO [Investigating Officer] with you?)
Judge to witness: *IO kaun tha?* (Who was the IO?)
Witness: Thakur sahib
Judge (dictating): Inspector Akash Thakur remained with me during the time of investigation.
Defense lawyer: *Vahaan se, kahan?* (From there, where did you go?)
Witness: PS (police station).

Judge (dictating): We reached PS Gole Market.

Defense lawyer: Did you make an entry in DD?

Witness: *Ji.* (Yes.)

Judge (dictating): DD entry was made at PS.

Defense lawyer: *DD entry la sakte hain?* (Can you provide the DD entry?)

Witness shows the DD entry.

Judge (dictating): At this stage, witness has shown DD entry no. 9A.

Judge to Defense lawyer: They are careful [in making sure they record a DD entry].

Defense lawyer to Judge: *Hamara kaam hain, poonchna ka* (It's our job to ask).

Judge (dictating): As requested copy of DD entry <inaudible> and same is exhibited as ExPW 133 <inaudible>

Defense lawyer: <inaudible>

Judge (dictating): It is correct that the place where the blast took place is a public place. There are many shops there.

Defense lawyer: Did you join anyone from the public during the investigation conducted by you?

Witness: No.

Judge (dictating): It is correct that I did not join . . .

Defense lawyer: *Jab spot pahuncha, kuch samaan leke aye the?* (Were you carrying anything with you when reached the spot?)

Witness: *Nahin.* (No.)

Judge (dictating): It is correct that I was not . . .

Defense lawyer: *Transparent jars kahan se leke aya?* (Where did you get the transparent jars from?)

Witness: *Staff se mangvaya.* (I asked my staff to get them).

Judge (dictating): . . . was requisitioned through staff . . .

By comparing my notes with the deposition that was recorded, we can see that the testimony is not a verbatim transcript of what was said in the courtroom. Rather, the testimony is what has been dictated to the stenographer by the judge or by the lawyer with the approval of a judge. As we can see by comparing the two "transcripts" above, the stenographer altered some phrases in the recorded testimony (for instance, the stenographer has added details surrounding DD no. 9A). Often, if it is a pro forma witness—that is, a witness who needs to depose for a formal, rather than substantive reason—the lawyer or judge will dictate the testimony without actually questioning the witness.[7] When the testimony is completed, it is printed out in court and signed by both the witness and the judge, certifying that it accurately reflects what "happened" in court.

As we see in the example above, as in the narrative from Hanif's case in the last chapter, it was common for things that were said in courtroom testimony not to be recorded in the file. Conversely, pro forma witnesses often said nothing more than their names for the court, but nevertheless the court record—signed by the pro forma witness and the judge—shows them as having made extensive statements.

This seeming disregard for orality in the courtroom is a result of several factors. As Indian trial lawyers know, the judge who hears the evidence is most often *not* the one who pronounces the eventual judgment. This is because trials can take years to complete, and judges are transferred periodically. This means that the evidence that is recorded by one judge must be legible to another. When judges give final judgment, it is expected that they take into account what is written in the court file as they would not have seen or heard many, if not most, of the witnesses. Further, if an appeal is made after the judgment, then it is expected that the higher court can base its eventual judgment only on what the trial court has recorded in the court file. As with other bureaucratic documents in India, the courtroom testimony must also be legible across time and judicial hierarchies.

Furthermore, linguistic practices in Indian trial courts are not aimed at telling a coherent narrative to a jury, but rather are aimed building a narrative through the certificatory processes. As we will see in the following sections, the aim of the prosecution was to build a story of the bomb-blast by building a story of the investigation through the investigatory documents. The defense's aim was to question the narrative of the investigation and to build its own narrative by questioning the validity (and hence veracity) of the investigatory documents. Thus, the role of the direct examination was to establish the certificatory correctness and veracity of the investigatory documents, while the role of the cross-examination was to undermine them. This, perhaps, is why the transcription is not a "verbatim" reproduction of what was said in court, but rather is aimed at capturing the dynamics around establishing and questioning the certificatory correctness of the investigatory documents. Ethnographic attention to the process of transcribing oral testimony[8] draws our attention once again to the idea that Indian courts are built upon the ideology that documents and their certification produce the truth. The transcripts of courtroom testimony, and not the oral testimonies themselves, are an essential certificatory process in the Indian trial.

In the next sections we look at the examinations and cross-examinations of the three witnesses (Sub-inspector Rajinder, Dr. Pasha, and the driver of the autorickshaw, Dhyan Chand) we have come across so far. We start with Dr. Pasha's testimony in Fahad's trial.

THE DOCTOR'S TESTIMONY: THE DEFENSE NARRATIVE AND THE CREATION OF CERTIFICATORY MISSTEPS

As a first step, the prosecution had to prove that the bomb explosion actually occurred and that it resulted in deaths and injuries. After the eyewitnesses to the bomb blast were examined, the doctors who had tended to the injured and who had made declarations of death were summoned to court to testify to those injuries and deaths.

The prosecutor treated the doctors as pro forma witnesses, dictating their examinations-in-chief to the stenographer without questioning any of the witnesses themselves. Most of these witnesses were not cross-examined either. "We are not denying the bomb blast occurred," a defense lawyer told me, "so what is the point in cross[-examin]ing most of these witnesses?" The exception was Dr. Pasha—who was prosecution witness number 10 (PW10)—because he tended to the injuries of the only witness whom the prosecution could use to place Fahad in the autorickshaw: Dhyan Chand.

What follows is an excerpt from the examination-in-chief by the prosecutor of Dr. Pasha. From this excerpt, it is evident that the prosecutor dictated the deposition to the stenographer and that the doctor actually said very little. It was highly unlikely that the doctor had remembered all the patient details and the medico-legal certificate (MLC) numbers, three years after the event.

> **PW-10**. Dr. Miraz Pasha . . . On the intervening night of 13 and 14.07.2008 I was posted and working at . . . hospital . . . as a Casualty Medical Officer. At that time I examined 14 patients—Ram Singh, male, age 36 years MLC No. 6531; Arvind Kumar age 58 years, male, vide MLC No. 6352;

Radha Krishna aged 47 years, male, vide MLC No. 8631; Siddharth Kapur aged 21 years, male, vide MLC No. 3931; *Dhyan Chand, aged 40 years, male, vide MLC No. 3151* [emphasis added].

The deposition goes on to name the other people Dr. Pasha examined and their respective MLC numbers. After this, the prosecutor entered as evidence all the MLC's prepared by Dr. Pasha, in a list-like manner:

ExPW-10/[9]A; ExPW-10/B; ExPW-10/C; ExPW-10/D; ExPW-10/E . . . (14 in number) are prepared by me and all bear my signature at point X . . . I after examining the patient made a note about the injuries at point P to P-1 on all the MLCs [*sic*].

As he dictated this, the prosecutor took a red pen and wrote the exhibit number (for example, ExPW10/A) on each of the documents, placed an "X" next to each of Dr. Pasha's signatures, and wrote "P" and "P1" next to the injury notes on each MLC. In this way, the prosecutor certified in court that Dr. Pasha had prepared each of the MLCs and entered them into the court's file. Further, through the various red marks on the MLCs (EXPW10/A, X, P, P1), the court file now referred to specific points on the MLCs in the police file.

With this, the prosecutor indicated that his examination in chief was over. The judge, assuming that no one would be cross-examining this pro forma witness, was about to dismiss the doctor when Fahad's lawyers said they wished to cross-examine him. The prosecutor was clearly surprised by this. He turned to Inspector Bhandari (who was the "in-charge" of this case) and asked why the defense was cross-examining this one witness. Bhandari whispered something into the prosecutor's ear, and the prosecutor seemed to realize that this pro forma witness was actually a very material one.

As I stated earlier, the defense's counternarrative was that Fahad had not put the bomb in the autorickshaw and that the police had zeroed in on Fahad even before their investigations had begun. Thus, the aim of Fahad's lawyer was to insinuate that the doctor had falsified Dhyan Chand's MLC at the behest of the police.

With specific regard to Dhyan Chand, a defense lawyer told me that this would be their narrative arc: that it was Dhyan Chand who ought to have been the police's first suspect, since the bomb had been in his autorickshaw and he had survived.

If they believed that the bomb was placed in the autorickshaw, the first thing they should have done would be to find the driver. Instead the police did not even bother to go looking for him. They just sat there. By their own case [in the sworn testimony recorded by Dhyan Chand], it was the driver who came to them!

According to the lawyer, the fact that the police did not even question or bother to go looking for Dhyan Chand showed that even before the investigation had commenced in earnest, the police had already zeroed in on Fahad as a suspect. Consequently, she told me, their narrative would be that the police had massaged the evidence to take attention away from Dhyan Chand and place it on Fahad.

In order to build that bigger narrative, the defense had to create a smaller narrative around Dhyan Chand's MLC. They wanted to show that, on the instigation of the police, Dr. Pasha had made it look as though Dhyan Chand was *more* seriously injured than he actually was. The eventual point is that since he was not that seriously injured, the police could and should have questioned Dhyan Chand.

The defense's lawyer's cross-examination began with a contention that the notation that Dhyan Chand had sustained "grievous injuries" was not supported by the rest of the facts recorded by the MLC and placed into the court record. Through her questions, the lawyer built the narrative that Dhyan Chand had not been as injured as the MLC recorded—that is, they questioned its referential correctness. The defense lawyer asked about the notation on the MLC that stated that the "Patient is conscious, oriented and fit for Statement." The defense lawyer had, prior to this day's hearing, told her team that she would be drawing attention to the contradiction between the statement that Dhyan Chand was conscious and fit for statement and the statement that he had sustained grievous injuries. Her line of questioning would be that the doctor had first written the statement that Dhyan Chand was conscious and fit for statement. Then, under pressure from the Special Cell, the doctor had written that Dhyan Chand had sustained grievous injuries. The next and concluding part of the doctor's deposition concerns these two statements.

> Certification on the MLC . . . about fitness of the patient to give statement are not by me . . . I have not given any certification on the day of the examination of the patient about fitness of the patient to make statement

on 13.09.2008. . . . It is wrong to suggest that the injuries sustained by the injured Dhyan Chand were simple and I have deliberately shown [them] as grievous on the asking of the IO [Investigating Officer].[10]

In her attempt to suggest that Dhyan Chand was fit for statement and ought to have been the police's first suspect, the defense lawyer drew attention to this statement and asked if he had written it. To everyone's surprise Dr. Pasha denied ever having written the first statement on the MLC (about Dhyan Chand's being "fit for Statement"), thus calling into question the rest of the MLC as well. The fact that he did not know who wrote that Dhyan Chand was "fit for statement" would indicate that there was no way to certify the accuracy of the rest of the document. The fact that the author of this document did not write a key part of it meant that there was no way to certify that it had been correctly prepared. Thus, the narrative contained in that document could be seriously called into question.

We can see here how doubts over certificatory procedures can be created, even inadvertently. As we left the courtroom when the day's proceedings drew to a close, the defense lawyers chuckled among themselves that they had stumbled into a "little victory." They clearly knew that they could bring this point up at the time of closing arguments: that a key document in the prosecution's case against Fahad had been called into serious doubt. As a senior member of the team explained to his junior colleague, these cases "are built little by little." He meant to say their case would involve not only the slow chipping away at the prosecution's documents, but also the slow building of their own counternarrative.

What we will see in the next section is how the defense's narrative—that the documents were fabricated by the police only to falsely implicate Fahad—will be repeated in different forms in the cross-examination of the officer who seized Dhyan Chand's rickshaw. Again, this is done by questioning the preparation of documents and their certifying practices.

THE AUTORICKSHAW: BUILDING NARRATIVES

The prosecution had to prove that the bomb was placed in the autorickshaw. To do so, they first had to demonstrate that the objects collected at the scene of the blast were collected and stored according to the prescribed procedure. They could do this only through the documentary traces that these material objects left in different official records (the seizure memos and registers). They then had to bring the physical items to court in order to prove that these items actually existed and to prove the referential correctness of the seizure memo. The fact that they brought in the physical items, which were then identified as the same seized items, also had to be recorded in the court file.

To prove that the autorickshaw and other objects were seized by the police in the manner in which they were said to have been seized, Sub-inspector Rajinder Singh was summoned to court to depose to this effect. He was witness number 143.

He first repeated what he had stated in the FIR: the time and manner in which he had reached the blast site and the fact that he had seen a portion of the rickshaw hanging from a tree. He also stated, "On seeing the TSR, one could say that the bomb had been planted in the TSR." He then described seizing the pieces of the autorickshaw documented by the memos discussed in previous sections. Recall that, in his seizure memo, he had described the parts of the autorickshaw that were collected, made into parcels, and seized. The following excerpt from his deposition indicated that these memos were all entered into the court's record as exhibits:

> From the spot, we also collected eight different parts of above referred TSR. These were turned into separate parcels. These were seized vide memo **ExPW143/G**.
>
> I may mention that the large portion of the TSR referred to above, found hanging from the tree, was cut into pieces and then those pieces were seized after [being] turning into parcels and sealed with the aforesaid seal bearing impression AT vide memo **ExPW133/J**.

In Sub-inspector Singh's testimony, we can see how the pieces of the rickshaw were positioned in the narrative of the investigation: he proceeded to the bomb blast site, saw the blown-up autorickshaw, reasoned that the bomb had been placed in it, hence seized the pieces, prepared a memo documenting this seizure, and then packaged and sealed the pieces. The narrative justifying the seizure of the autorickshaw pieces had thus been inserted into the court file, as were the seizure memos themselves. At this point the meshwork of documents extended from the bomb site, to the evidence depository, to the police file, and into the court file.

But this was not enough. At this point, all that Sub-inspector Singh had managed to establish was that he prepared the seizure memos. The materials that he says he seized had to be presented in court to certify their physical existence. The fact that they physically existed then had to be recorded in the court file. Hence, at a later point, the sub-inspector stated that if the physical objects, such as the pieces of the autorickshaw, were brought to court, he could attest to the fact that those were the physical objects that he had seized.

On the next date of the hearing, a representative from the police evidence depository presented various articles associated with this case number. As the larger pieces of the rickshaw could not be brought into the courtroom, I went with several of the defense lawyers and some police officers to the parking area adjacent to the court complex. There, we saw several large rusted pieces of twisted metal heaped onto the back of a small open-backed truck, which were painted in the distinctive green and yellow of a Delhi autorickshaw. Some of the court staff hauled the metal pieces onto the ground, and one of the police officers explained that one piece was the chassis and the other was a part of the front frame of the autorickshaw. The police officer pointed to a part of the metallic frame where the registration number 1438 had been painted.

We all then went back to the courtroom where the prosecutor dictated the following paragraph to be added to the deposition:

> During investigation, at the aforesaid spot . . . I also picked up one iron piece, i.e., bottom portion of the above referred to TSR which is **ExPW143/20**, one metallic piece of the said TSR which is **ExPW143/21**, a metallic [part] of the said TSR bearing owner's name which is **Ex PW143/22**, front portion of TSR having its registration number which is **Ex PW 143/23.**

After the deposition was completed, an official from the evidence depository affixed labels stating the exhibit number on the relevant pieces of the autorickshaw. Again, this was done to definitively connect the court record to the items referred to outside of it.

We see how the autorickshaw was transported from the world into the court file. In one layer of inscription on top of another, it was rendered into documentary form first by the seizure memo and then by its registration in the evidence depository. Subsequently, it left a documentary trace when it was sent to the Central Forensic Science Laboratory, and then, when presented to the court, it was transformed into a document (as seen in the excerpt above).

Recall that each document was linked to the police file through the FIR number. By following the pieces of the autorickshaw, we can see how it was translated into the file and became evidence in the case against Fahad. By following documentation procedures and certification protocols, the police and prosecution managed to establish a continuous documentary record that mediates the autorickshaw from blast site to courtroom. Furthermore, we can see how, in following the various documentary iterations of the autorickshaw in the investigative process, the "bomb-in-the-autorickshaw" narrative was created.

We will now turn to the sub-inspector's cross-examination.

Again, since it was pointless to contest that a bomb blast had taken place, the cross-examination was aimed at questioning whether the objects were seized in the manner stated by the police officer, which it did by suggesting that procedures for seizing the objects were not followed. Take for example, the following from the sub-inspector's cross-examination:

> It is correct that the area where the occurrence took place is a public case [*sic*] where there are many shops. It is correct that I did not join anyone from the public during the investigation conducted by me at the spot.

These statements are made in response to the cross-examination by the defense lawyer. (Recall that under Indian criminal procedures, testimony is recorded in narrative form, and rarely in the form of question and answers.) Here, the defense asked if there were any non-police witnesses who could independently certify that the search and seizure actually took place. Did the bomb blast occur in a public place? If it did, did the police officer ask any member of the public to witness the seizure of objects? The underlying logic behind this line of questioning was that if there were independent public witnesses who were around the blast site, why were they not made to officially witness the seizure? The answer must be, because the seizure was not conducted in the manner stated by the police.

The defense then also tried to suggest that the memos could not have been written and the parcels could not have been prepared, because the police officer did not have any of the requisite materials with him:

> At the time I left the police station for the spot, I was empty handed. The material used in preparing parcels at the spot was requisition by me through my staff. But I do not know as to from where my staff had arranged the same.

This point is made more directly later on when the transcript states:

> It is wrong to suggest that the entire writing work was done at the police station and not at the spot.

In addition to alleging that the seizure memos were fabricated, the second aim of the defense was to show that the autorickshaw was seized only to construct the case against Fahad. If there were other vehicles that were severely damaged, why had the police not seized those? Why had they not taken steps to ascertain the owners of these other vehicles? Take, for example, the following excerpt from the cross-examination:

> In addition to the above referred TSR, one or two other vehicles had suffered severe damage while other vehicles were partially damaged. I did not taken [sic] any steps as to who were the owners of these other vehicles which suffered damages. I also did not collect any certificates of registrations of other vehicles which suffered damage.

By calling attention to the fact that the police did not seize any of the other vehicles "severely damaged" in the blast, the defense tried to create doubt as to which vehicle might have contained the explosive. The defense further attempted to suggest that the police had invented the "bomb-in-the-autorickshaw" theory as part of a preconceived plan to implicate Fahad. Recall in the previous section how the defense began to build the narrative that the police had deliberately ignored the most obvious suspect (Dhyan Chand) in order to implicate their client. This is reflected in the following excerpt from the cross-examination:

> It has come to my notice during investigation by me at the spot as to who the registered owner of the above TSR but I did not conduct further investigation regarding the registered owner, the reasons being that other senior police were there to investigate this part of the story.

Here, the defense asked if the police knew who the registered owner was (when they seized Dhyan Chand's license and registration from the blast site) and thought that the bomb had exploded in the autorickshaw, why did they not first find the driver? The fact that they did not could indicate that they zeroed in on Fahad without any reason. Pushing this further, the defense then questioned the police officer's expertise and his ability to state that the explosion had taken place in the autorickshaw. If he did not have the expertise to prove that the bomb had been placed in the rickshaw, then the "bomb-in-the-autorickshaw" theory would lose credibility. In other words, the defense was trying to question the referential correctness of the document. The sub-inspector replied:

> I am a graduate in Economics. However, during in service training, I have learnt to assess explosives. It is wrong to suggest that I have no such expertise even in service training. It is wrong to suggest that I had no expertise to say that "on seeing the TSR, one could say that bomb had been planted in the said TSR."

The defense here was trying to question whether the police officer had the training to have come to the conclusion that the bomb was placed in the autorickshaw. If they had challenged this statement in the memo, this assertion, that the bomb was placed in the autorickshaw, would have remained standing.

The last section of the cross examination contains responses to the defense lawyer's suggestion that the entire memo was fabricated. Here the defense lawyer is suggesting that each averment made in the seizure memo is false and, in response, the sub-inspector denies these suggestions.

> It is wrong to suggest that no part of the said TSR was found embedded in the tree as stated by me in chief examination. It is wrong to suggest that evidence was introduced falsely to show that bomb had been plated in the said TSR with a view to falsely implicated the accused persons.
>
> It is wrong to suggest that [the] front portion of TSR had not got severely damaged.

Thus, we see from this testimony that the defense was attempting to build on the narrative that it had begun by implying that the doctor may have fabricated the MLC at behest of the police. The defense attempted to undermine the referential correctness of the memo documenting the seizure of the autorickshaw by questioning whether the protocols that ought to have followed while producing the document (that is, the seizure memos) were actually followed. The defense lawyer repeatedly asked questions about the procedural steps that the police could have taken to certify the production of the document, focusing on the police officer's lack of questioning of public witnesses, lack of writing material or material to produce the parcels, lack of interest in other damaged cars, and lack of knowledge of explosives in order to bring his testimony into question. Recognizing that it was possible to call the police's version of the bomb blast into question by calling into question whether the certifying processes were followed, the defense lawyer introduced the defense's version of events through cross-examination and made sure that this version was also incorporated into the court file.

DHYAN CHAND'S DEPOSITION: NARRATIVE TRIPPED UP BY CERTIFYING PROCEDURES

To cement its case against Fahad, the prosecution summoned Dhyan Chand to corroborate their story that Fahad had planted the bomb in the autorickshaw. Chand was the prosecution's most important witness, as only he could tie Fahad to the bomb blast. Recall that Fahad and most of his co-accused were present for their trial in Delhi via a videoconferencing link, as they were being physically detained in Gujarat. Hence, Dhyan Chand was asked to identify Fahad on a video screen in the courtroom.

Chand was prosecution witness number 161. He was sworn in, and then, in response to the questions put forward by the prosecutor, he provided a narrative of the bomb blast that everyone had expected: a young man carrying a bag had hired his rickshaw and asked to be taken to Gole Market; they reached Gole Market where the man asked Chand to wait while he went to a shop; the man left the bag in the rickshaw; after about fifteen minutes, Chand stepped out of his rickshaw and walked some distance away from it; a blast occurred; the next thing he knew, he was in the hospital and had suffered injuries on his back.

Apart from providing a narrative of the case until the moment of the bomb blast, his deposition was also linked to previous testimony and to various documents that had been entered into the court's file: that he was the owner of the autorickshaw (corroborated by the seizure of his license, documented by a seizure memo); that the rickshaw had been parked under the peepal tree (referred to in the seizure memo); that he had suffered injuries as a result of the blast (referred to in the MLC). Thus, Dhyan Chand's testimony was built on previous statements made by other witnesses and on documents produced by the police.

After this, Dhyan Chand was asked to identify Fahad. Identification is a procedure by which a witness is asked to physically point to the accused to certify to the court that the witness is speaking about a particular person. This process is similar to the marking of the MLC and the pasting of labels on the autorickshaw, in that it ensures that the court record refers to something outside of it and that it does so correctly.

Unfortunately for the prosecution, Dhyan Chand's testimony dramatically collapsed. Chand was asked to pick out Fahad from among the different accused "present" on the video screen. The judge recorded the following excerpt in the court file:

> I can identify the said boy if shown to me.
>
> At this stage, [the prosecutor] has asked the witness to point out from the screen of the video conferencing as to who out of the six persons visible on the screen is the concerned boy whom he can identify.

Chand took his time. He asked that each of the accused come forward to the camera so that he could take a closer look at each of their faces, and then he asked the operator in Gujarat to take long shots of each of the accused so that he could look at their height and build. He was clearly struggling, and Inspector Bhandari—the same police officer who kicked the back of Anthony's leg in the last chapter—tried to signal to him which person to identify. The defense lawyers protested, and the judge ordered this police officer to leave the courtroom immediately. One of the lawyers asked the judge to record the fact that the police officer had tried to prompt the witness. The judge ignored this, and the official record makes no mention of the fact that the defense lawyers had accused a police officer of prompting the witness or that the judge told the officer to leave the courtroom.

After a tense forty-five minutes, Chand said that he was unable to identify the accused. The prosecutor then casually said, "He probably wants to see all of them in person." Dhyan Chand took up the not-so-subtle suggestion and said that he would be able to identify Fahad if he could see all the accused in person.

Fahad's lawyer made a tentative objection that gathered steam over the next few minutes. With increasing tempo, she argued that if another opportunity were given to the witness to identify Fahad, the police would use the time to coach the witness on whom to identify, and his testimony would undoubtedly be tainted. The judge agreed with the defense and temporarily discharged the witness, dictating the following order to be included in the court file:

In the given circumstances ... providing another opportunity to the prosecution may lead the concerned authorities to show the concerned accused to the witness in the meanwhile. Therefore, this court does not find any ground to allow the submission of the witness ... for identification of the concerned accused by way of another opportunity.

This document was printed and signed by Chand and the judge, securing its place as the authoritative account of what happened in court that day. The failure of the prosecution's main witness to identify the accused man was a massive relief for the defense. Had Dhyan Chand correctly identified Fahad, we can only speculate on the nature of the questions he may have been faced with. He would have been questioned about the chain of events after the bomb blast: How did he get to the hospital? Was he really grievously injured? Given that the defense's narrative was that the police had already decided to implicate Fahad prior to the investigation, Dhyan Chand would have probably been accused of fabricating his testimony at the behest of the police.

After that day's hearing, I joined some of the defense lawyers and Fahad's brother for a celebratory tea in the court canteen. There were smiles and laughs all around, as the prosecution's key witness had failed to identify the "main accused" in this case. As the lawyers spoke about the day's proceedings, they explained the victory to Fahad's brother. The defense lawyer's argument about giving Dhyan Chand another opportunity to identify Fahad was not just that Dhyan Chand would be coached to identify Fahad. If the prosecution had coached Dhyan Chand behind the scenes, and Dhyan Chand had correctly identified Fahad on the next occasion, the court record would then have documented a procedurally valid identification. For all intents and purposes, Dhyan Chand would have certified to the court that he had correctly remembered Fahad, even though this identification was built upon a procedural infirmity. This failure to perform the certificatory procedure in court had pulled the rug out from under the prosecution's narrative.

CERTIFICATION AND THE PRODUCTION OF DOUBT

In this chapter, I have shown the relationship between evidence, narrative, and files. I have shown how we can approach epistemological questions by understanding the material and narrative elements of investigative and courtroom practices. Further, I hope to have provided an understanding of how legal files come to represent and enact the outside world through slow and laborious material processes. In doing so, I have shown how the evidentiary process enacts not just people and things, but also produces narratives of the world.

In highlighting the contours of the cases built on certificatory procedures, I have argued that a trial's epistemological processes are fundamentally material and highly technical. In India, evidentiary questions are intimately bound up with paper. This is not to deny that there are other aspects of the materiality of the trial (Scheffer 2004), but to explore how epistemological questions are tied up with the referential correctness of paper and the certificatory practices that went into producing them. If there had been no seizure memo of the autorickshaw, then the police would not have been able to present it as evidence in the trial court. If another officer had not witnessed and affixed his signature to the seizure memo, then more doubt would have been cast upon the seizure itself. If Dhyan Chand's MLC had not been recorded, the court could not have been told of his injuries and even more doubt would have been cast on his "innocent" role in the bomb explosion. Indeed, if the trial court did not record testimony on paper, no judgment could have been given; if a witness's signature was missing from a particular deposition, it could not be relied upon at the time of judgment.

What is as important to the judicial process is not just inscription but also certification. Everything that the police do, all material they seize, all information they receive, and all testimony before the court, must be transcribed onto paper. But, as we have seen, for these documents to have a truth-value, they must be signed, countersigned, stamped, and registered—that is, certified. One of these certificatory processes includes ensuring that they are referentially correct—that is, that the objects and people they refer to exist. That is why the mangled parts of the autorickshaw had to be marked, and Dhyan Chand had to correctly identify Fahad. Because Dhyan Chand could not identify Fahad, the referential validity of his testimony could be called into question.

Juridical truth in a courtroom setting is contingent on both the police and the courts following set processes to certify the referential correctness of documents. Because the referential correctness of the police's papers was dependent on the evidentiary procedures that went into producing the papers in Fahad's case, the defense's strategy was to question whether these procedures were followed. As we have seen, the defense's aim was to undermine the documents by attacking the procedures that the police undertook to certify them. If the documents were not produced in a procedurally correct manner, then the objects, things, and events they refer to could not have existed.

Thus, during cross-examinations, certification becomes a way not of producing truth, but of producing doubt by multiplying narratives. In particular, the defense's strategy, as we have seen in this chapter, was to attack the layers of certificatory practices that mediated the transition of people and things from the world into the file. It aimed to show that the police did not collect the autorickshaw in the way the documents said they did. It aimed to show that the MLC about Dhyan Chand was falsified by Dr. Pasha or by someone else. If it could produce certificatory missteps, then it could change the narrative of the investigation, which in turn could change the narrative of the bomb blast. The defense's counternarrative was therefore built up by producing doubt by in the prosecution's story by repeatedly questioning the certificatory practices that went into producing these documents. As we have seen from the testimony of Dr. Pasha and Dhyan Chand, sometimes missteps in the certification process are more a consequence of accident, than of deliberate strategy on the part of the defense.

The production of papers and the certificatory practices that accompany them are instrumental in producing the narrative presented by the police and prosecution. As we have seen from Qayoom's narrative in Chapter 2 and again in this chapter on Fahad it is also through these very practices that one "truth" is undermined and another one is produced. The narratives produced by the prosecution and defense are not just of the case as told in final arguments but are dispersed through various documents. Through small steps, both the prosecution and the defense attempt to weave a story around things and people that enter the court's file. In Fahad's case, as in other trials, these stories are woven around the minutiae of the various documents the police have produced, with each document adding another layer of narrative. For the defense, as well, narrative matters, and I hope to have shown how the defense narrative is inserted by questioning certificatory practices. If we think of evidence as a process by which a narrative of events is stitched together by the careful linking of papers that document this process, then this narrative chain is vulnerable at every link—and the defense will try to exploit this link. Thus, juridical truth is less a matter of finding "what really happened" and more about the competition between narratives that depend on the certificatory correctness of mere sheets of paper.

6

PETITION WRITING

Desire, Ethics, Mourning

One of the abiding concerns of this book has been to bring human voice back into the law. It has sought to trace the ways in which the law is a lived experience in which legal technicalities enable voice—as an expression of human vulnerabilities, passions, pains and demands—to emerge. I have sought to think of technical legal rules as tekhne, as that which constitutes the texture of existence in the courtrooms where the law becomes the site of human expressiveness and vulnerability.

This chapter focuses on how we can attune ourselves to hear human voice in the legal process. It draws on the idea of the perlocutionary utterance, which, as I argued in the introduction to the book, obliges us to think of what speech does to us. Unlike the illocutionary (or performative), which is concerned with the conventions that make speech successful, the perlocutionary invites us to think of speech as the place of human expressiveness, creativity, desire, and vulnerability. Instead of drawing our attention to felicity conventions, in the way that a failure of illocutionary or performative utterances does, perlocutionary utterances draw our attention to finding the "right expression, pitch, the right tone of voice" (Laugier 2020, 19).

In this chapter, I attend to pitch and tone of voice in forms of writing that were ubiquitous in the trial court.[1] In previous chapters we saw that writing undertaken by court staff, judges, police officials, and lawyers is essential to the working of the investigative and judicial process. What is striking is that much of the writing produced in courtrooms and by terror-accused take the form of a letter. The right-to-information (RTI) applications that

Qayoom and his co-accused sent took the form of letters. Basic criminal documents, such as the first information report (FIR), were framed as letters to the heads of the police stations. The charge sheets that the police filed in courts were framed as letters to the jurisdictional magistrate. These charge sheets, in turn, included a number of other documents, many of which were written in the form of letters. As scholars have pointed out, the letter is a specific genre of bureaucratic writing, through which the state addresses and is addressed.[2] Unlike other forms of legal and bureaucratic writing though which claims or requests can be made,[3] the letter provides the space for narrative and a conception of the author and the addressee.

One of the legal documents that takes the form of the letter is the petition.[4] Take, for example, this petition on behalf of one terror-accused individual, challenging the magistrate's order allowing the police from Surat (in the State of Gujarat) to take custody of him. The petition begins, as shown in the box that follows, with a recital of the parties, and the nature of the dispute.

In the High Court of Delhi at New Delhi

[Criminal Miscellaneous] (Main) No. _____of 2008

In the Matter of:

A petition under Article 227 of the Constitution of India read with section 482 of the Criminal Procedure Code, 1973

And in the matter of:

A petition seeking setting aside/quashing of orders dated [. . .] of the Learned Shri [. . .] Duty Metropolitan Magistrate, Delhi allowing the application for the transit remand of the petitioner and rejecting the petitioner's application for a copy of the application for transit remand.

And in the matter of:

[Name of petitioner]

Son of . . . , Resident of . . . ,

Azamgarh City, Azamgarh, U.P . . .   . . . Petitioner

Versus

1. State (N.C.T. of Delhi)

Through P.S. Special Cell, Lodhi Colony,

Delhi . . .   . . . Respondent No. 1

2 State of Gujarat,
Through the Resident Commissioner,
Baba Kharak Singh Marg,
New Delhi . . .   . . . Respondent No. 2

The text then moves on, like many letters, to a salutation, as shown in the box:

To,
The Chief Justice,
And his Lordship's Companion Justices of the Hon'ble High
Court of Delhi
The Petitioner abovenamed most respectfully submits:

The body of the petition narrates the facts and circumstances that necessitated the petition and articulates the need for the court's intervention.
In this particular case, the petitioner sought to persuade the High Court
that the magistrate's order was invalid. The petition ends with a prayer, in
which the petitioner asks the court to perform or direct the performance of
a certain task, followed by the signature of the person making the petition,
the mark of its author.

PRAYER

In the facts and circumstances stated above it is most respectfully
prayed that this Hon'ble Court be pleased to:

   a) set aside/quash the orders dated [. . .] of the Learned Shri . . . ,
      Duty Metropolitan Magistrate, allowing the application for the
      transit remand of the petitioner and rejecting the petitioner's
      application for a copy of the application for transit remand

b) declare that the custody of the petitioner with either the Gujarat Police or the Special Cell, Lodhi Colony, from the [date] onward, to be illegal

c) pass any further orders as this Hon'ble Court may deem fit

[Signature]

Petitioner

[Name of Petitioner]

Through

[Signature]

Counsel

[Name and Registration of Counsel]

Notice how the petition is premised on the idea of a letter. It begins by identifying the recipient of the letter through a salutation, then narrates why this petition is necessary, and then moves to what the petitioner is asking of the court. The petition—like all letters—ends with the signature of the writer of the letter.

In Tis Hazari courts petitions were referred to as *arzis*. The word *arzi* is a form of the word *arzdasht*,[5] a type of letter that was extant from the founding of the Delhi Sultanate in the thirteenth century through the Mughal Empire and its successor kingdoms.[6] Crucial to the *arzdasht*, or petition, was the idea that it was a letter addressed from a social inferior to a superior. Verbose and replete with honorifics, it was framed in deferential, supplicatory tones to encapsulate a relationship of dependence and lordship between author and addressee (Zaidi 2005, 13) and sought to create an affective relationship of intimacy across hierarchy.[7]

Mohiuddin (1971) argues that the *arzdasht* sought to effect change in several ways. First, it aimed to open a case, or a *mudda'a*, wherein the author would narrate facts that necessitated the petition. But the petition was not meant only to convey the facts of the cause; its writer was supposed to weave a pattern of feeling, through words, epithets and metaphors. This in turn lead to the third purpose of the letter: to communicate a sense of the author. One object of the petition was to sketch parts of the author's character—temperament, emotional state, and personal qualities. The aim of the letter was also to create a specific affective bond between author and addressee, so that the addressee would be moved to respond or even accede to the request of the author. The response was claimed upon the specificity of the relationship that the author sought to build up in the letter. According to Raman (2012), examples of *arzdasht*s "suggest that they were written texts of praise and/or fealty that simultaneously and reciprocally . . . sought the grace of superiors" (165–66) and tapped into the "polyvalent hierarchical intimacy that associated petitioning with divine address" (166).[8]

If the precolonial *arzdasht* was premised upon the idea of intimacy across the hierarchy, the colonial petition was built around different affects: a dispassionate narrative of the self and an objective appeal based on rules.[9] Raman (2012) argues that while petitioners of the subcontinent viewed petitioning as a way to access a semi-divine sovereign power, the colonial state's view of petitions was grounded in Protestant ideologies of conscience and toleration. Petitioners were expected to be sincere and to frame their objective claims in terms of universal, normative rules. As a mode of bureaucratic writing, petitions were to be stripped of any social context and weighed in terms of their own rational contents. As a result, petitions during the colonial period spoke in multiple voices that could both appeal to the semi-divine nature of the colonial state and to the liberal ideology of rules and regulations.

The *arzi*s I encountered in Delhi's trial courts were written in these "polyvocal" terms (Dirks 2015, 152) as they both invoked both the graciousness and mercy of their addressees and appealed to rules, with authors' identities shifting between supplicant and citizen. These *arzi*s also contained the features that marked petitions more generally: They were written by an "inferior" to a "superior"; they contained a narrative of the *mudda'a*, or facts that necessitated the writing of the petition; and they stated the requests or demands of the addressee. And in the process, they narrated shifting conceptions of both author and addressee.[10]

While some of these petitions, such as the one above, were drafted by lawyers and bore a more formal appearance, many of the *arzi*s were handwritten by terror-accused individuals and were about both mundane and deeply troubling subjects. I came across a set of such letters to the National Human Rights Commission, which provided graphic descriptions of the torture that their authors aced at the hands of the Mumbai Anti-Terrorism Squad (ATS). I was also given and shown letters written by terror-accused persons to a number of different officials and authorities, including the president of India, the lieutenant governor of Delhi, the prime minister, chief ministers of Delhi and Jammu and Kashmir, and the International Committee of the Red Cross. These petitions spoke of the injustices that their authors had suffered and the long years they had spent in prison, and they pleaded with their addressees to intervene in their cases. Kumar, about whom I wrote in a previous chapter, gave me copies of several letters he wrote to the trial judge, in which he told the judge about the verbal abuse and threats that he faced from other jail inmates for "being a terrorist." In these letters he asked the judge to direct the jail authorities to transport him in a separate vehicle between the courts and the jail. Other petitions I came across were more mundane. One petitioned the trial court judge to direct the jail authorities to allow him to get his eyes tested. Another asked for permission for his parents to give him clothes from home.

What struck me about these letters was how repetitive they were. Kumar gave me copies of three different letters he wrote to the same judge on the same topic. His first two letters to the judge received no reply, and the third received only a rudimentary one. Recall from Chapter 2 that Qayoom's multiple RTI applications for copies of police logbooks and received replies only on the third or fourth attempt. The vast majority of petitions received no response.

In this chapter, I ask two interrelated questions. Why did the terror-accused write petitions? And why, in the face of overwhelming epistolary silence, did they continue to write? In order to answer these questions, this chapter focuses on writing by one terror-accused individual, whom I call Mohsin.

MOHSIN

While the Delhi trial courts were on their summer recess in 2012, I went to Srinagar (in the erstwhile state of Jammu and Kashmir) to meet several men who, like the majority of people accused of terrorist crimes in India, had been acquitted of the charges.[11] I visited one of them, Mohsin, with his two nephews, at his brother's home in Srinagar. He told me about how his life had been ruined by a trumped-up terrorism charge.

In January 1996, sixteen-year old Mohsin went to Delhi to help with his brother's handicrafts business. In May of that year, a bomb placed in a car exploded in a market in South Delhi. The Delhi police's Special Cell claimed that a Kashmiri terrorist group was behind these explosions. They alleged that the conspiracy was hatched in Pakistan, that explosives were sent across the border, and that a group of Kashmiri men, one of whom was Mohsin, executed the plan. The trial court acquitted Mohsin and his ten co-accused in 2010, by which time Mohsin had spent fourteen years in prison.

Mohsin began by telling me about the main charge against him: that he had harbored people who had been behind the bomb blast. The only evidence tying Mohsin to the conspiracy was that he was in possession of the "stepney" (spare tire) of the car that was used in the bomb blast. As he told me this, he sent his nephews to bring a document from the next room. After some back and forth, the nephew finally brought in the correct one. This was a police document upon which the entire prosecution of Mohsin rested: It was the "seizure memo," which stated that that he was arrested while in possession of the spare tire of the car that was used in the bombing. This apparently was the prosecution's chain of thought: Since Mohsin was in possession of the tire, the people in the conspiracy must have given it to him; hence he must have harbored the people accused of planting the bombs.

Mohsin also told me about how the prosecution's witness, who was supposed to attest to the allegation that Mohsin was in possession of this spare tire, had turned hostile in the trial—that is, this witness refused to corroborate the prosecution's narrative. As Mohsin told me this, he sent his nephews to the next room, asking them to bring the relevant witness statement to show me. They returned with the incorrect document, and Mohsin gave them instructions in Kashmiri on where to find the correct one.

Every time Mohsin referred to an event from his trial, he would ask his nephews to go into the next room to retrieve a document or file. When they brought the wrong document and were sent back to get the correct one, their rolled their eyes in frustration. Finally, exasperated with this documentary go-fetch, they both dragged a large, heavy metallic trunk into the room where we were sitting and said something to their uncle in Kashmiri, which I guessed meant "Find it yourself."

The trunk was filled with paper. I was astounded by the sheer volume of paper that Mohsin had collected. The top layer was lined with magazine and newspaper articles about Mohsin. Some had pictures of his face as an adolescent before he went to jail, juxtaposed with a more recent picture of him, showing the toll that time and the trial had taken. One article contained an open letter from politicians and human rights activists to the state's chief minister asking for compensation and a rehabilitation package. Another reported on a question asked in Parliament about Mohsin's case, and a third was headlined "Life in jail was hell, it is no better outside."

The next layer was comprised of documents from his trial. Digging through these documents seemed to recreate the trial process for Mohsin. Not only did the papers index something that happened during the trial, but it was also as if the trial could be relived by showing these documents. As he pointed to the memo that documented the date and manner of his arrest, he asserted that the document had concocted the story of how he was apprehended and then gave his version of the events that had led to his arrest. He spoke of the fear and frustration he felt while being held in (illegal) police custody for twenty-five days. As he looked at the magistrate's first order remanding him to judicial custody, he described how he was taken to court with a pistol at his back, remembered his crushing disappointment that the magistrate did not even look at him at the hearing, and hinted at the humiliation of being subject to a "full-body search" at the juvenile jail.

He also showed me petitions that he and his family had written to courts, officials and other authorities, the overwhelming majority of which were met with no reply. In one petition, which was sent to the High Court in 2000, he adopted a number of rhetorical strategies to convince the High Court to grant him bail pending trial. It was written in the third person, as if Mohsin were presenting an objective version of himself. He tried to evoke sympathy from the court: "The applicant was just a boy . . . when he was sent to jail, [the] accused suffered all kinds of hardships during this period, his entire youth has been ruined due to prolonged delay." He drew attention to his "exemplary conduct" and the fact that "he did many courses in jail like computer courses . . . and also did his graduation in jail." He then shifted from a claim premised on his own individual suffering, to a claim based on the violation of rights that should have been inherent to him as a citizen: "[The] applicant's right to life and liberty enshrined under [Article] 21 [of the Constitution] and his right to have fair trial stand violated." He pointed out that the main prosecution witness against him had exonerated him: "The sole witness of the prosecution on the basis of whose statement the applicant was implicated in the case. . . . [He] has not supported the prosecution story." Finally, he ended his petition with a Gandhi-like appeal: "That if trial is not concluded expeditiously alternatively applicant is not granted bail he shall be compelled to go on hunger strike till his death."

This petition was significant for Mohsin as it was one of the two that he sent that had actually received a reply from the High Court. He showed me the High Court's order, directing that the case be heard on a day-to-day basis and be completed within six months. Instead, the trial took nine more years. "After that, I had lost all hope," he told me. "Twenty-six judges had changed in my trial. They would never to let me go."

The trunk that his nephews brought in from the neighboring room contained several spiral binders and files, all of which contained a staggering volume of petitions that Mohsin had sent. Some of these were handwritten, and some typed out. Sometimes the same petition was copied out and sent to different authorities. What was even more astonishing was that Mohsin continued to write petitions after his release. These petitions, which were also in files, were sent to the Jammu and Kashmir state government, the government of Delhi, the Indian government, the Jammu and Kashmir High Court, and the Supreme Court, asked for compensation for being falsely accused and imprisoned, a job, and free educational training. All of these later letters followed a similar structure: They narrated all that had happened to him and asked the addressees to provide him what he had asked for. He showed me petitions he had sent to president of India, the deputy prime minister, the chief minister of Jammu and Kashmir, the state's law minister, the National Human Rights Commission, the State Human Rights Commission, but "no one listened." None of them received a response.

While he was in jail, both his father and his sister passed away. He petitioned the High Court to grant him temporary bail so that he could attend the funerals. In both of these instances, the High Court did not respond:

Though the High Court would do nothing, I sent them an application. I wrote it out by hand. I had my father's death certificate, my sister's death certificate. I thought that at least they would listen to this. It is the duty of a Muslim to do the last rites of his father and sister. It is my duty to do these last rites. So I said send me in handcuffs, at least. But the court just sat with my rights. That petition is with me. I [also] sent it to the [National] Human Rights [Commission]. But no road opened for me.

He also showed me a hand-written letter to the then–home minister and deputy prime minister, L. K. Advani (see Figure 2). It was written in English, and in the transcript that follows I have tried to be faithful to his original petition in the box that follows.

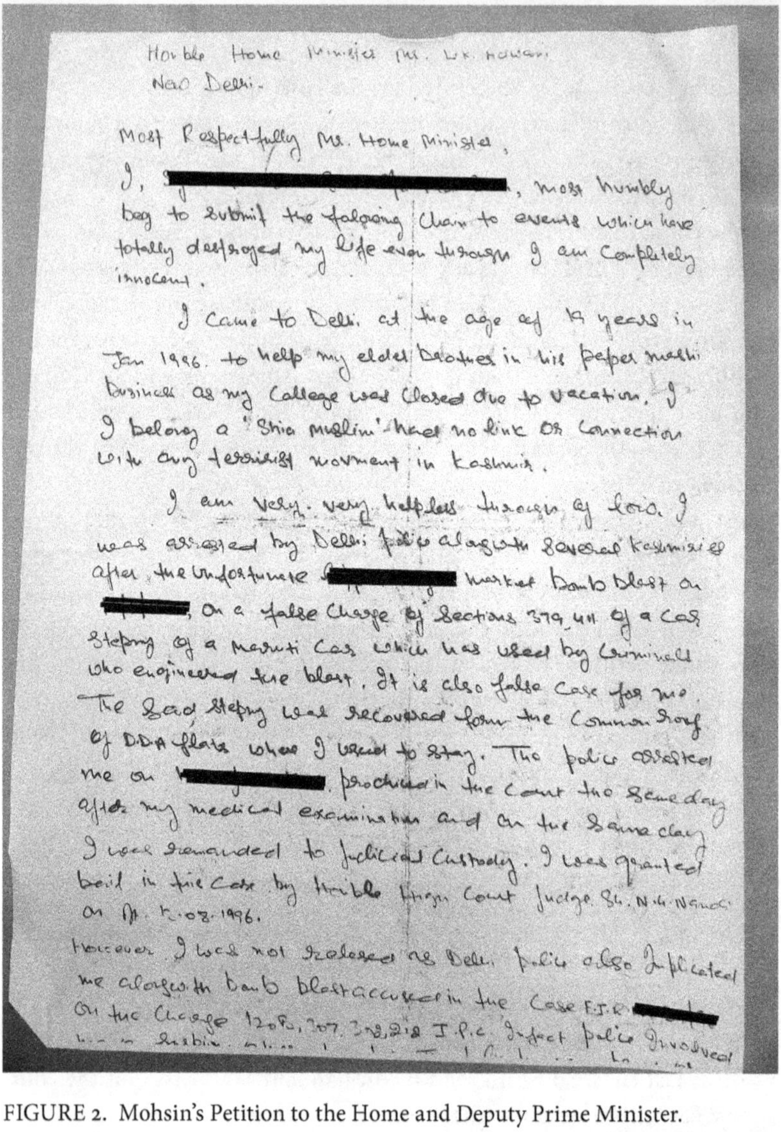

FIGURE 2. Mohsin's Petition to the Home and Deputy Prime Minister.

Hon'ble Home Minister Mr. L. K. Advani
New Delhi

Most Respectfully Mr. Home Minister,

I, Syed Mohsin Shah s/o Mohammed Shah, most humbly beg to submit the following chain to events which have totally destroyed my life even [though] I am completely innocent.

I came to Delhi at the age of 19 years in Jan 1996 to help my elder brother in his [papier maché] business as my college was closed due to vacation. I belong to a "Shia Muslim" had no line or connection with any terrorist movement in Kashmir.

I am very very helpless through of law. I was arrested by Delhi police along with several [Kashmiris] after the unfortunate . . . market bomb blast on . . . On a false charge of sections 379, 411 of car stepney of a Maruti car which was used by criminals who engineered the blast. It is also false case for me.

. . .

The charge against me was framed after 4 1/2 years under section 212 which clearly states that I harboured accused persons after having knowledge and belief that they [the other defendants] had entered into a conspiracy to cause explosion.

I am feeling the trial even after eight years when the charge under section 212 IPC harbouring the accused persons attracts 5 years of maximum sentence. . . .

The attitude of the [prosecution] and even the trial court is to [delay] the case indefinitely even though the Hon'ble High Court ordered a day-to-day trial and copy attached. The Court has ignored the same and there is no desire to speed up the case. Only 26 witnesses out of the huge list of 280 witnesses. Only 4 witnesses were to [testify] against me and three witnesses have already been examined and only one witness is yet to be examined. . . .

Sir, I have submitted [several] bail application to the trail court which me kept pending and unanswered/undecided. I have spent 8 years in Tihar jail. . . .

Sir, as a last resort to end my agony and endless stay in jail. I am [now] writing to kindly take necessary steps to at least grant of bail set me free on the charge. Now my father has died so my family destroy the life. Now my old mother totally blind and she waited me.

Sir, please in only my case. If I involved in this case then I accept all the punishment through the law and Court.

I am sure that this last effort of mine will not go unheard and through justice is delayed it will not be denied.

To make sure that the letter had been delivered, he sent it by registered post. The receipt for this letter, along with a receipt for a similar petition that he sent to the Red Cross' Delhi office on the same date, are reproduced in Figure 3.

From the trunk, Mohsin also pulled out five notebooks—diaries of his days in jail. Written in Urdu, with a smattering of English in tiny handwriting that covered the entirety of the pages, they reflected the scarcity of writing material in the jail.

Mohsin had an intimate connection to these documents. From witness statements, to petitions, to diaries—all these documents forced Mohsin to relive moments of his trial. When speaking about his petitions, Mohsin would tell me that "koi suna nahin" (no one listened) to his repeated petitions. It was not just that his petitions received no replies, but that his experiences were disregarded, as the authorities were unmindful of the "torture" of prison and turned a deaf ear on the many injustices he was put through.

At one level, repeatedly writing petitions was a mode of participating in the trial process. They were meant to influence his trial process—to shorten it or at least to help him to obtain bail. But if these petitions were viewed only as tactical, then it made no sense for Mohsin and others to repeatedly write and send them, since they knew there was little chance of a reply. Indeed, it made no strategic sense to write diaries.

In this chapter, I suggest three different ways to understand the writing done by Mohsin and other terror-accused individuals. First, if letters can be thought of as forms of indebtedness—as to send a letter is to expect a reply—then a petition can be thought of as a way to make demands of the law. As I explain later in this chapter, in looking at them in terms of Cavell's idea of passionate utterances (2005), I argue that petitions can help us understand legal language as a mode of claim-making. Second, I suggest that we can also regard these petitions as a mode of self-writing. Even though

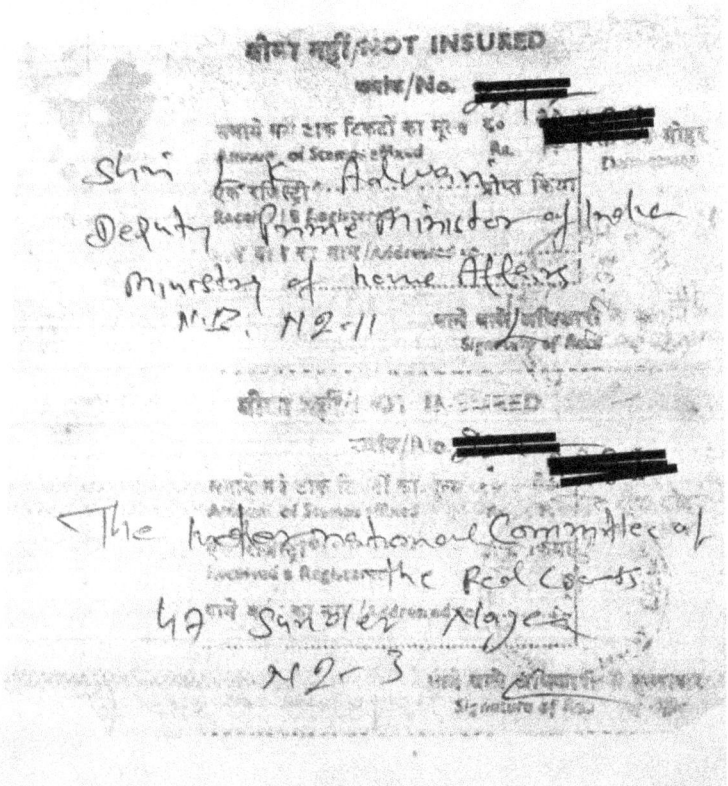

FIGURE 3. Postal receipts from two of Mohsin's petitions.

they are addressed to another, their primary function is to reclaim an account of oneself *for* oneself. Third, I read these petitions as a mode of inhabiting the world through the act of mourning. Mohsin's relentless, repetitive writing of petitions can be understand them as a way of grieving over a life spent in jail and all of the futures that he has lost. In the face of this overwhelming trauma, Mohsin did not seem to lose his words and become silent: rather he was abandoned *to* his writing.

THE GRAMMAR OF PETITIONS

Looking at the grammar of these petitions enables us to see these three approaches as facets of the ethics of writing. By looking at the confluence of the first, second, and third persons in these petitions, we can better apprehend why the terror-accused wrote so many petitions in the face of almost continuous silence on the part of the addressees.

While some of these petitions were written in the first person, the majority were written in the third person. This is the standard structure of the kind of official petition shown at the beginning of this chapter. Take for example, Mohsin's petition (which is English) to the chief minister of Jammu and Kashmir shown in the box:

Page no. 1

To, The Hon'ble Sh. Mufti Mohd. Syed
Chief Minister of Jammu and Kashmir

Subject: Mercy petition of [Syed Mohsin Shah, son of]
Syed Mehmood Shah, presently lodged in [Tihar Jail, ward no. 3]
Tihar Since 18/05/96. Case FIR no. 715/96
Trial Court: Shr. N. K. Kaustabh [Additional Sessions Judge)
Patiala House New Delhi

Hon'ble Sir,
The humble and helpless applicant most humbly wish to submit the following to the Hon'ble Chief Minister for Kind attention and adequate action in his case.

That the accused being a Kashmiri Muslim and was staying in Delhi at the time when some antisocial activist did the act of bomb blast at . . . central market and was implicated in this case on very flimsy grounds.

That the process of law in which the applicant has complete belief has now come to the conclusion that the delayed justice in his case will not only ruin his life but also the life of his family members.

That the charge as per the prosecution story is that the applicant sheltered criminals who did this deadly act and also helped them with "the car" of which one tyre was found in the common roof of the rented accommodation. That as per the allegation of the accused/applicant knowingly did the act of sheltering

Page no. 2
   the criminals, which is completely wrong and baseless and even if it is accepted as the truth the judicial custody of the accused has already surpassed the maximum prescribed imprisonment for the charge against the accused/applicant.
   That it is very clear from the attitude of the prosecution that they are not interested to conclude this case within any stipulated period because out of 201 witnesses only 17 witnesses have been examined so far and at this rate it is quite likely that this case will never be finished in the entire life of the applicant.

The petition carries on for four handwritten pages, in which Mohsin describes the injustices that he faced while waiting for his trial to come to proceed. He implores the chief minister of Jammu and Kashmir to intercede on behalf of the "applicant" and other "innocent Kashmiris are confined jail without trials or very slow trial." He provides the addressee with narrative of how "the accused/applicant was just a student" who had come to Delhi to help his brother with his business and was arrested by the police in a "false case." He ends his petition with the following plea shown in the box:

That in view of the above circumstances, the applicant has lost all the hopes that he will ever see freedom and get out of this jail . . . The applicant has already undergone the worst and has lost his youth and the golden period of his life. He has acquired no knowledge or practical working experience and has lost confidence due to long confinement in jail. Even in jail, the Kashmiri Muslims are treated with a different yard stick. They are subject of hate and often treated as enemy of India. For a young Indian, all these excess are to much to bear. The initiative of your esteem govt is highly appreciated by several patriotic Indians.

The humble applicant now prays request your good self to look into his case and help him get justice at your earliest.

Thanking you in anticipation
Yours sincerely

[Signature]
Syed Mohsin Shah
S/o Syed Mehmood Shah
Presently lodged in Jail no- 3
Tihar, New Delhi
Res. Address: [address in Srinagar, Kashmir]

On their surface, the petitions have a very simple grammatical structure. They are written by Mohsin, to his addressees, in this case the chief minister—the "you." Mohsin (the "I"), who signs his name at the end of the petition, is telling the addressee (the "you") of all injustices that have happened to him and asking the addressee to take mercy and to intervene on Mohsin's behalf. When read like this, Mohsin is the enunciator of the utterance and the chief minister, its addressee. Notice, however, how they are written in the third person: Mohsin refers to himself as the "applicant" or the "accused" and writes as if he is interceding on behalf of another person. There are three grammatical persons in this petition: the first person, "I," who writes this letter; the second person, the "you" to whom the petition is addressed; and the third person—that is, the petition is about a "him."

The place of pronouns has been central to some linguists' conceptions of the possibilities of human language. Benveniste's (1971) idea of language is dialogical and is constituted by an I-you polarity: The "I" is the enunciator of a discourse, and the "you" is the addressee, with the third person being an absent nonperson (197–98). While the third person is a nonperson because the third person is absent from dialogue that takes place between "I" and "you," the third person is simultaneously a condition of possibility of the first and second person. The third person is the foil upon which the subjectivity of the first and second person is established.

Das (2015), drawing upon Sanskrit grammar, questions the distance between the first, second, and third persons that Beneveniste's trichotomy implies.[12] Drawing on commentaries by Sanskrit grammarians, Das (2015) argues that the third person is not a nonperson, but is a person who can be "brought into sentience" (102) through different modes of address. Building on this and examples from her own ethnographic work, she points to a fluidity between personal pronouns, where the "I," "you," and "they" can change places or blend into one another. This discussion of grammar and pronouns, in the Sanskrit texts, is linked to questions in aesthetic theory of how I can be moved by an artistic or literary work and to feel the emotions in those texts as if they were mine. For Das (2015), the ethical implications of this grammatical structure are clear. Rather than thinking of ethics as the decisions one makes in relation to another, the ethical subject "is crafted as much out of the affective force of an attunement to this other, who is not wholly other, who could be me" (108).

In this chapter, I seek to bring a similar sensibility to a reading of Mohsin's petitions. The first, second, and third person are all at play in Mohsin's ethical constructions of himself. As he tries to establish a connection from himself to another through his letters, he is simultaneously crafting an ethical relation to himself. We can read these petitions as facets of a single, yet fluid, ethical process and thereby move away from reading them as constructing a relationship between political subjects and state authority (as historians have done) or as modes of performing political subjectivity (as anthropologists have done). Instead, we can attune ourselves to Mohsin's voice as it emerges in his legal petitions.

THE FIRST PERSON: PETITIONS AS
PASSIONATE DEMANDS FOR A FUTURE

In one of our conversations, Mohsin told me of the day that he was acquitted:

When the judge gave his decision, in 2010, I refused to leave the court. I told [the judge]: "I was absolutely innocent. How many times did I tell you? How many times did I tell you I was innocent? How many times did I tell you let me out on bail? If you can't give me bail, at least let me go to my father's funeral while in custody. Tell me, how many times did I tell you? Now where should I go? My life is ruined, my house has been destroyed. My daddy has died, my sister has died." Then the judge shouted, "Take him out of court!" Even though I had been acquitted, they had to drag me out of court.

In telling the story, he raised his voice and seemed to point at an imaginary judge in the room, channeling the second person and shouting as if the judge was in front of us. This is one way in which I read his petitions—as a demand upon and confrontation with the second person. Each of his petitions had asked for something, ranging from parole to attend his father's funeral, to be granted bail pending trial, to being acquitted. In the petitions he sent after his acquittal, he asked the state administration for a government job and compensation. Yet, none of these letters ever received a response. Mohsin's lament, "No one listened to anything," indicates that he felt that he was owed a reply to the letters that he sent.

Implicit in the idea of a letter is the logic of exchange (Schneider 2005, 59–62; Phipps 2015). To receive a letter is to be put under an obligation to reply, and to write a letter is to expect a response. The logic of the letter allows the first person to place a demand upon the second person. What does this idea of a demand, or a debt owed, do to our idea of legal language? What does the logic of the letter do to our idea of the law? Here, the law is not something that is declared, but something that is demanded. In order to better understand this idea of a petition-as-demand, we need to depart from constative or performative ideas of the petition (Cody 2009). As I stated in the introduction to this chapter, I want to focus on the perlocutionary, and so I take a different route to look at these petitions through Cavell's (2005) idea of a "passionate utterance."[13]

Cavell (2005) offers the phrase "passionate utterances" (176) to expand the effects of speech and to highlight the place of emotion, rather than convention, in understanding how speech acts. Passionate utterances neither describe nor report, as constative utterances do; nor do they only do something by saying something, as illocutionary speech does. Rather, they are aimed at moving another (Cavell 2005, 177). Thus while Austin (1962) thinks of saying "I do" at a wedding as a performative utterance (since in the saying of the statement "I do," I become someone who is married), but it is also to utter a desire—not only to be heard but also to have that commitment returned. To say "I do" is, as in the letters discussed above, to make a claim upon another.

In his discussion of passionate utterances, Cavell treats performative utterances as being confined to the realm of law, whereas passionate utterances as belonging to the realm of desire. But in characterizing passionate utterances as those that "make room for, and reward, imagination and virtuosity" (Cavell 2005, 173), he might equally be describing the recycling of legal forms that I wrote about earlier, since they too are about making legal language one's own and deploying it in creative forms.

Constable (2014) conceives of legal language as a conversation involving a series of passionate utterances. She argues that "even as legal acts seem to epitomise conventional offers and demands or even mandates and imperatives to participate in the 'order of law,' law also seeks to persuade 'you' and is 'persuadable' by you" (36). Legal utterances are not simply declarations, but modes of making claims. They are articulations of desire that seek a response from their addressees.

We can think of Mohsin's petitions, similarly, in terms of the language of persuasion and claim-making. They are framed as demands that he (the first person) places on addressees (the second person). He singles them out and seeks to move them either by an appeal for them to recognize his own plight ("Sir, as a last resort to end my agony and endless stay in jail . . . Sir, please [in] only my case") or on the basis of law ("applicant's right to life and liberty enshrined under [Article] 21 [of the Constitution] and his right to have fair trial stands violated"). In either case, the petitions presume that the addressee is attuned to the speaker and will be moved to respond. The petitions seek to single out particular addressees and place demands upon them. When speaking to me about his petitions, Mohsin often used words like *bataya* and *kaha* (both of which mean "told") to describe what he had written in the petition, as if through the petition he had made his demands orally, in person, to the addressee.[14]

His petitions and letters can be understood as a series of passionate utterances. They aim to persuade. It is almost as if they say: "I am here. You must hear my story. This is what I am owed and you must what I am due." This is one of the characteristics of petitions that I want to call attention to, beyond the performative, constative, and representational—namely, that in each utterance there is a potential, a confrontation, a claim, a demand.

These petitions also implicate the idea of time. Their narratives begin with chronological ordering of the past and end in the present. The sequential ordering is a way in which order becomes imposed on the events. The letter opens with a progressive description of "what happened" and narrates a series of events in succession; the sending of letter itself then marks the end of the narrative. The petition is hence both a container for a narrative and a part of the narrative.

The petition also links the past to the present and, importantly, also to *future* lifeworlds. Even as they are written from the temporal perspective of the present, such letters provide a window into the future (Ochs and Capps 1996, 24). They end with a demand or a desire. This is what the petitioner hopes for in the future; this is what he thinks ought to come to pass. Hence petitions letters inherently anticipate a world that could be. They lay claim upon their addressees to intercede in order for these futures to come to pass.

These petitions, then, can be read as enabling passionate claims to be made for a future. They show that the responsibility for effecting such futures lies with their addressees. Thus, Mohsin's petitions to various organizations and officials can be understood as making claims for a certain future for himself. He describes the agonizing experience of the courts, from the flimsy evidence to the endless delays, and points to all the life (births, deaths, marriages) that he has missed out on while he while he was incarcerated. He pleads with his addressees, asking them to ensure that his future is not blighted. He writes his petitions with the aim of moving his addressees to give him a future that is outside of prison.

THE SECOND PERSON: WRITING AS A RECOVERY OF THE SELF

The letter of petition is based on the idea that the supplicant (the first person) can access a politically superior person or institution (the second persons) without actually being physically present, since the letter carries the petitioner with it and creates his or her presence in the domain of the addressee. Letters are a way of mapping relationships over distance and are a mode of creating the presence of an absent person in the domain of the addressee (Goodrich 2013; Schneider 2005, 28–30).

The letter of petition therefore is a way of transcending the necessity of the presence of the petitioner and the addressee of the petition. It is this idea that allows one to send a letter from prison to the National Human Rights Commission or to the deputy prime minister of India. Some forms of the writ petition that I began the chapter with may state: "The Petitioner abovenamed most humbly showeth." The idea here is that the petition, *as* the petitioner, shows the court what is asked for and the reasons for it. The letter of petition stands in place of the petitioner.

This way of understanding the letter, however, imagines it only as a way of positioning the first person in relation to the addressee, the second person. Even though they are addressed to the second person (the "you"), I think there is another way of thinking about these letters, such that the second person is, additionally, oneself. Seen from this perspective, the letters and the diaries that Mohsin wrote in jail bear many similarities.

Since, I could not read Urdu, Mohsin read out portions of the diary to me. The first entry he read to me was dated June 17, 1996 (though it was written sometime in early 2000), the day he was picked up by the police. He described what he wrote in his diary:

I started from here. [I wrote] about the courts, who came to court, which witness came, what did he say, the witness name, what time he came.

This first entry is a detailed account of the day of his arrest: a description of the room in which he was staying with his brother, the people he met on that day, the time that he went to the mosque and returned, when he first met the police, and how they took him into custody. He guided me through a few of his notebooks. They contained details of his life in prison as well as what happened in court. One of the final entries named the twenty-six judges who had presided over the case under a heading "Judicial Hall of Shame," seemingly in order to recall the names of judges who left him in jail for fourteen years.

The following is the last entry he made before he was acquitted:

7/4/2010. Today is Wednesday. After morning teatime, head sahib told me, "Get ready quickly, you have a court date today." On that day, other people also had their court dates—all their names were written on a sheet. I told head sahib that my co-accused's names were not written on that sheet. I understood that perhaps the judge had sent a production warrant for me alone. I came back to my cell, I gave my clothes to the dhobhi and got them pressed quickly. Then head sahib came back and said, "It's not your court date today, you have an appointment [with the doctor] today. So at 9 A.M. I was taken to DDO hospital and there the doctors checked my legs. They wanted to do an ultrasound and a doppler test and they told me to come back on the 16th of April.

Many of the diary entries were populated with these kinds of details of everyday life. I asked Mohsin how he started keeping his diary. He replied:

> I had a friend Ishaaq Wani. He was from Kishtwar. He gave me a qur'an. He died. Since he came [to prison], he had a bad cough. I don't know what happened. They must have hit him very badly. But he used to write. He had a diary that was this big, it was thick. [He spread his forefinger and thumb two inches apart]. When I saw him, in 2001 I think, he was always writing. In the meeting room in jails, in court. He was always writing. When I saw him, I also thought that they won't release me so it's a good idea that I write a diary. Maybe people in the future will know what tortures happened here. From then I started writing.

I pressed him further and asked him why he wrote his diary. He replied,

> When Ishaaq Wani passed away, this idea came into my head. *Kyunki umid nahin the. Hamein nahin chod denge. Tab se.* [Because I had no hope that they would release me. I started writing since then]

Mohsin, wrote because he had no hope of release. Why did Mohsin write *because* had lost hope of an acquittal? One could argue that he and other terror accused persons had no choice but to write petitions, as there was no other medium through which to address the courts and other officials from jails. One could see the letters as tactical ways of influencing the trial. But, as we saw, most of the letters that were sent by Mohsin and others did not receive replies. In the face of this continuous epistolary silence, why did they continue to write? Part of the answer lies in the ethical implications of the act of writing.

Through the act of writing one's story, it is almost as if one can narrate a new form of the self into existence. (Foucault 1994; Goodrich 1997, 273; Deleuze and Guattari 1986, 593). For example, the former president of Czechoslovakia, Vaclav Havel (1990), in writing about his own letter writing during a period of incarceration, pointed to the ability of his letters to create a "new concept of life" (43). Writing from jail—when the horizon of one's physical world does not extend beyond the prison walls, when one has no hope of release—paradoxically allows for the development of new forms of the self through writing.

The reconstitution of the self via petitions and diaries becomes all the more urgent in the context the terror-accused's first encounter with prosecution documents. The terror-accused do not know the charges against them at the time that they are first arrested by the police. Given that anti-terror laws allow a period of pre-charge detention of up to six months, which can be and is often extended beyond this, many terror-accused will learn of the charges against them only six months or more after the date of their official arrest. Mohsin had no idea of what he was accused of until fourteen months after his official arrest date, which was fifteen months after he was initially (illegally) arrested. As I outlined in Chapter 4, many terror-accused reacted to a reading of the narrative contained in the charge sheet with a sense of vertigo—they were made dizzy by the stories told about them.

While official files narrated their lives in ways that were unrecognizable to the terror-accused, petitions and diaries were ways of recovering and re-claiming their lives. It is for this reason that much of their writing is in dialogue with the prosecution's narrative or events that happened in court. As Mohsin would tell me later on, the petitions and diaries reflected the truth in contrast to "all the lies" contained in the prosecution's documents.

The petitions were more obviously framed against the prosecution's narrative of Mohsin's life. Recall that they provided the alternate narrative of him as an innocent person falsely accused of a heinous crime and trying to rebuild his life in prison through education. They invoke the registers of liberal citizenship and the violation of constitutional rights. Simultaneously they ask for certain things, on the basis of the image of himself that Mohsin has built for his addressees, through the letter. Further, most of the petitions I saw were written in English, not in Hindi or Urdu. There was a certain premium placed on being seen as being able to write in English, not just because, as we saw with Qayoom's argument, the Delhi courts use English, but also because the ability to write English signifies education and economic prosperity. This can be seen as asserting the logic that if one were educated and well off, one would have no "reason" to turn to terrorism.

One of the functions of the petitions that Mohsin and others wrote, even though they were formally addressed to others, was to reclaim the account of oneself *for* oneself. The second person that was being addressed in these letters was simultaneously the state and the self. In this this doubling of the "you" of the petitions, it is almost as if Mohsin (the you) first ventriloquizes the narrative of the state and then Mohsin (the I) responds to this narrative. In this way, Mohsin is writing the truth of what happened to him, for himself.

In the highly restricted confines of prison, writing provided Mohsin and others a way of reconceiving their lives. Even as there was a desire for a reply, it was their writing of their narratives against those of the state that sustained the authors of these petitions. The act of writing allowed them to reclaim a position for themselves in the world. In the face of a loss of hope, through the act of writing, they slowly recreated themselves in the world.

THE THIRD PERSON: MOURNING AND THE ABANDONMENT TO ONE'S WORDS

In writing these petitions Mohsin was placing a claim for a certain future on his addressees. They were aimed at showing the other the pains and injustices that he, as the third person, has had to endure and to persuade the other to intercede on his behalf. These are instances of perlocutionary utterances. Mohsin's claims were meant to move his addressees—whether by sympathy for his plight or by a regard for upholding rules and a sense of justice—to release him from jail, to end the criminal case, and to put a halt to his suffering. They were invitations to respond to Mohsin's passionate claims. But as he repeatedly said to me, "Koi suna nahin" (No one listened). Given the state's silence and the failure of judges and ministers to respond to, let alone acknowledge, his pain, the question for us is, then, what happens when perlocutionary utterances are, to use Austin's terminology (1962), infelicitous?

The answer, I suggest, is a form of mourning. This is not the quiet, transformational form of mourning in the face of skepticism that Cavell (1992) has described elsewhere, but is a relentless, piercing form of mourning that borders on madness. The sheer volume of Mohsin's letters was overwhelming. Their relentlessness conveyed a sense of mourning, not only for what had happened to him in the past, but also for futures that had been stolen from him. In this endless cycle of writing and waiting for a reply, his words took on an amplified quality and a certain insistence that they be heard. One cannot help but be struck by the tone of the letters—pleading, melancholy, shrill with desperation.

Through all our interactions, a melancholy air surrounded Mohsin. In contrast, his nephews who were with us sometimes exuded a teenage querulousness and embarrassment. Though they helped me go through Mohsin's various papers, pointing things out and giving me copies of letters, every time Mohsin recounted an experience or asked a question, they sniggered, rolled their eyes, let out barely muffled sighs of exasperation. They had definitely heard his story, not once, not twice, but many times before.

His nephews were clearly embarrassed by their uncle's desperation. At one of our meetings in Kashmir, one of them looked downward as Mohsin asked me, "Is it possible to meet Manmohan Singh [then prime minister of India] or Sonia Gandhi [president of the then-ruling Congress Party]? Do I need to make an appointment, or can I just go in to their office? I've written them a letter telling them how my life was spoiled." At that time, he was a guard at a bank, while his peers from school were earning much more than him as doctors and teachers.

They have destroyed the time for my progress. They should know how they have ruined my life, my family. My nephew was very small when I was arrested; he used to pee on my lap. Now look at him. When I was released, I did not recognize anyone, only my brother. I did not recognize my own mother. One day in jail is like ten years on the outside. My time has been destroyed. I could have become anyone. I could have become a *hurriyat* [political] leader. I now can't be a Nelson Mandela. I was so young when I was arrested. If I had a Ram Jethmalani [a famous criminal lawyer], I might have come out of jail in one or two court hearings. But I need money for that. If I had money, my life would not have been ruined. I could have become a big person. But by God's will this was not my path.

He wanted the world to know how much he had suffered, how his youth and his future were taken from him. He told me that he had met a professor from Jamia Milia Islamia (the national Islamic university) in Delhi who said that his diaries could be published. He struggled to remember the professor's name, but after some time we figured that Mohsin was referring to Khushwant Singh—a journalist and award-winning novelist. Soon evening approached, and I had to leave Mohsin's brother's house. I promised him that we would be in touch.

Several months later, on a muggy Delhi afternoon, a human rights organization held a public meeting to release a report about fabricated terrorism cases.[15] I had arranged for Mohsin to speak of his experiences at this event. Mohsin and one of his nephews were flown down to Delhi.

I spent the evening prior to the event with Mohsin and his nephew. He was staying with a friend of the organization, in a Muslim area of south Delhi of called Batla House, the site of the 2008 shoot-out where several alleged terrorists and one police officer were killed. We walked around the crowded, sweaty market to buy jeans for his nephew from one of the pushcarts. He tried to help out his nephew—an offer that was quickly rebuffed. "When he was a child, he would listen" Mohsin said, "but our bond has been broken." I tried to change the subject away from his nephew's disrespect for him and asked him if he had heard back about his petition for a government job. He told me that he was still working as a bank guard, "I am still a burden on my brother . . . they have ruined my future." I told him about another terror-accused in Delhi, who had received compensation from the Delhi government for the false accusations and who had also spent 14 years in jail only to be acquitted. I told Mohsin that we could ask him on how he went about it. "I also need a job and compensation," he said again.

He asked me about the next day's meeting, "What is the use? Will I get anything?" I was embarrassed, because I knew my reply would be inadequate. I told him that the meeting was to draw public attention to the injustices perpetrated by the Special Cell. Mohsin again said that he needed to be compensated and given a proper job. He wanted to bring himself "up to a particular level" so that he could cease to be a burden on his brother and establish himself in the world.

In the evening heat, Mohsin, his nephew, and I passed by a large gathering protesting the Batla House shoot-out. A man on a stage shouted into a microphone, "They say that we should not act violently against the law or police . . . but we want justice." One poster on stage commemorated the shoot-out with silhouettes and the names of the deceased (see Figure 4); another highlighted a "signature campaign against the Batla House encounter asking for judicial inquiry"; a third announced a march from Batla House to the home minister's residence demanding a judicial inquiry. Mohsin and I spoke about the Batla House encounter, and he again asked what could be done—"So much injustice has happened." He asked me about his own case again. And again he asked if he could meet the prime minister, Manmohan Singh, or Sonia Gandhi or Rahul Gandhi. I told him that a man who was then in the Indian government would be at the event and that we could speak with him to figure out a way to go about setting up a meeting.

After we returned to where Mohsin was staying, he said he would telephone Khushwant Singh to see if he could get his diaries published. Mohsin pulled out a small telephone diary and dialed a number. He introduced himself several times, "Sir, I am Mohsin, from Srinagar. We'd met there"; "Sir, I am Mohsin, from Srinagar . . ." Suddenly, Mohsin went quiet, and it was evident that the person at the other end of the line had hung up on him.

FIGURE 4. A large poster about the Batla House encounter in the Batla House area, naming the people killed by the police and asking, "Agla number kiska?" (Who is next?)

A parched, heart-breaking silence hung in the air. He first said, "Unke pas time nahin hai" (He did not have time). Then a few moments later, "Log darte hai" (People are afraid). His nephew let out a cruel snigger. I did not want to say anything that would heighten Mohsin's embarrassment. Eventually I awkwardly suggested that we go for a cup of tea. He declined, saying he needed to prepare himself for *namaz.*

Mohsin seemed to inhabit the world through mourning for it (Das 2007, 4). Mohsin lamented all the injustices done to him in the past—the false case, the flimsy evidence, the almost never-ending, withering trial process. Mohsin seemed to have been ground down by what has happened to him. His life, his world lay in ruins. In this sense, his diary and his letters were an accounting that was also an act of mourning for all that he had lost.

Mohsin's letters written from prison asked that he be released on bail, acquitted, or at least allowed to perform the last rites for his father and sister. I imagine that these were also labors of immense grief. Insofar as Mohsin's narratives are peppered with what could have been—he could have been a doctor, he could have been a teacher, he could have been a leader like Nelson Mandela—they simultaneously lament the future lifeworlds that never came to pass.

Mohsin narrated his life in terms of abandonment: "No path opened for me," "this was not god's will," "no one listened." He felt stranded in a world in which he was left to relive the past trauma repeatedly. Whether shouting at the judge during his acquittal, shopping for jeans for his nephew, or being slighted by the journalist, these everyday events were framed by the trauma of incarceration. The injury of his trial was reconfigured and reinvented on a daily basis as if everyday events could be read only through the trauma of his arrest and trial, and now he was perennially being cast adrift in the world.

Mohsin seemed abandoned, not just to his trauma, which seeped into everyday life, but also to his petitions. After his acquittal he continued to send petitions to legal authorities, central government ministers, and human rights commissions demanding compensation and a job. Back in Srinagar, he had showed me copies of two of the petitions he had sent to the state's chief minister and the home minister in which he narrated, again and again, how he had been picked up as a teenager and kept in jail for fourteen long years. He told the ministers of the trauma's he had faced at the hands of the police, the flimsy accusation, the hostile witness, and finally, after fourteen years, the eventual acquittal. In these letters he told of the injustices of being denied the ability to live his life—to get a university education, to be present for the birth of nephews and nieces, and to perform funeral rights for family members who died while he was in prison. Along with these letters he included copies of the last page of the trial court judgment, which declared him acquitted. He had taken a yellow highlighter to the words in the trial court judgment that declared him innocent.

In the face of his overwhelming trauma, Mohsin's words had not been rendered lifeless; rather, they seemed to barely be able to contain his emotion. It was almost as if he was abandoned to them, as if he could not help but write. When I first encountered his petitions, I was amazed by the relentlessness of his writing. Soon after, I felt, perhaps as his nephews did, overwhelmed by their staggering number and their tone. As he told me some years after I first met him, "If I was to fully open up my heart to you, you would not be able to bear the pain."

The tone of the petitions was amplified and intense, because they were attempting to express the inexpressible pain of having one's past ground down, and one's present and future lived only through past injuries. They were attempts to express the unsayable pain of constantly living in a present that is defined by and narrated through a past trauma. Each letter sent out into the world amplified the intensity of his words, like the lines of a tragic opera.

Cavell (1994) imagines the voice within tragic opera as a judgment on the world "called forth by pain beyond a concept" (149), as an attempt to express an inexpressible pain, requiring "understanding without meaning"(144), that words cannot convey the depth of pain. This voice, attempting to express the inexpressible, is in a "mad state; as if opera is naturally pitched at this brink" (149). Like voices in opera, the innumerable letters that Mohsin sent out, the obsessive writing of his diaries, and the endless repetition of his narrative were on the brink of madness. But how else could Mohsin mourn for murdered pasts and futures? How else could he possibly attempt express the pain of reliving the time of his trial? Mohsin spoke about his pain with the knowledge that his words could never express the true depth of this injury. These letters are testament to the fact that Mohsin was abandoned to the inadequacy of his words to bear the true depth of his pain.

CONCLUSION

An Acquittal?

During the course of my fieldwork I followed the case of a Kashmiri man I call Shamsher. He was very tall and he cut an imposing, yet gentle and reserved, figure. As he was on bail pending trial, he came to each hearing from Srinagar. He was evidently better off than the other terror-accused whom I met, as he was well-dressed and spoke to me mostly in English, with a smattering of Hindi. At his court hearings every two weeks, he wore an expressionless exterior and did not seem to like the small talk that occupied most people at the back of the courtrooms. When I met him at each of his hearings, he smiled, made very polite conversation, and engaged with my questions about his case in a very factual, restrained manner.

From these short conversations and from the arguments made during the hearings, I managed to piece together an initial picture of the case against Shamsher. Shamsher, originally from Kashmir, lived in the Middle East in the early 2000s. The Special Cell accused Shamsher of sending satellite phones and other electronic communications equipment from the Middle East to India. This shipment was destined, according to the Special Cell, to a banned terrorist organization in Kashmir. Special Cell officers allegedly intercepted the shipment at the Delhi Airport after a tip-off from a "secret informer" and then filed a case against Shamsher and two others for various offenses, including members of a banned terrorist organization.

The fact that the police alleged that Shamsher was supporting a terrorist organization barely came up in the trial. Instead, as I stated in the introduction to this book, technicalities were at the heart of the proceedings. As we have seen in other trials, Shamsher's was marked by police ineptitude in the paperwork and other technicalities they were required to follow during the investigation and the trial. For instance, while the police are expected to file first information reports (FIRs) immediately after learning about an offense, in this case, the Special Cell filed the FIR seven days after they purportedly intercepted the shipment at the Delhi airport. As we saw in Bharucha's and Kumar's case and in Keshav's and Sonia's case (in Chapter 3), here too the prosecution had not followed the two-step process required to file terrorism charges. In filing the charge sheet against him, the police had not followed the certificatory processes to bring the world into the court file—a process that I detailed in Chapter 5—as they had not filed the consignment bill (which they say was attached to the consignment that allegedly contained the electronic equipment) or the seizure memo through which they seized the consignment. The main evidence against Shamsher was an alleged telephone conversation that took place in Kashmiri between Shamsher and the head of the terrorist group. This conversation had been allegedly intercepted by the Special Cell and translated by a native Kashmiri speaker. The Special Cell had not obtained the necessary permissions to intercept the telephone call, and the person who purportedly translated the conversation was never even called to testify.

Confusions reigned all around, not just with the police. As we saw with cases discussed in this book, uncertainty lies at the heart of any engagement with legal technicalities. Thus, in January 2013, during the final day of arguments in Shamsher's case, a question arose about a significant technical detail. The judge, prosecutor, and defense lawyer were momentarily confused as to whether Shamsher ought to have been prosecuted under the Unlawful Activities Prevention Act (UAPA), or the Prevention of Terrorism Act (POTA), which was in the process of being repealed when the case was first registered. For about half an hour, the judge, defense lawyer, and prosecutor floundered around looking for the exact date of registration of the case and the exact date of the repeal of POTA and the enactment of the UAPA Amendment Act of 2004. If the case was improperly registered under the UAPA, this would mean the entire trial was invalid. Years after the case was first filed, on the last date of hearing, they all came to the conclusion that the case was properly registered under the UAPA.

Shamsher's case was listed for judgment in February, some weeks before I was to return to London from my fieldwork. I went to the courtroom where his case was being heard, but could not find Shamsher. I checked the case list outside the court and noticed that his case was listed for arguments, not for judgment. I stayed there till Shamsher showed up. He was evidently worried and asked me if I knew why his case was listed under arguments and not for judgment. Since I was not sure either, we asked the *naib* court. The naib court also said he was not sure why it was listed for arguments. He telephoned his lawyer, who told him to stay there and that in the event the case was called, Shamsher was to tell the judge that his lawyer was on his way. Confused and nervous, Shamsher began pacing up and down the short corridor outside the courtroom.

He was obviously and understandably very uneasy. While he was previously reticent about discussing his case, his nervousness seemed to have broken any hesitancy. At times in our conversation that day, it seemed as if he was so nervous that he had to continuously speak. At other times, his anxiety seemed to force him into a deep silence.

He said that after the last date of hearing, he did not dare to go back to Srinagar. He feared that heavy snow fall might have blocked off transport links between Srinagar and Delhi, and he didn't want to take the risk not being in Delhi. He told me that he suffered from such anxiety that his family took him to the doctor to check his blood pressure. His parents wanted to come for the "day of judgment," but he stopped them as travel from Srinagar was too difficult. More importantly, he did not want them to be present in court if he was convicted. He did not want the last memory they had of him to be of him being led away by the police.

He told me that he was originally from Srinagar, Kashmir, and that he had moved to the Middle East in his early twenties. At first he worked as a waiter in a restaurant, but by the mid-2000s Shamsher had become the manager of an industrial food production company that catered meals for thousands of construction workers every day.

He became aware of the Special Cell's case against him only when he went to the local Indian consulate to renew his passport. There, he was told that that the consulate was unable to renew his passport as there was a "notice" against his name. The consulate also told him that his then current passport was also invalid because of this notice. He was told that if he wanted to renew his passport, he would have to go back to India to figure out what had gone wrong. But he could not return, as he no longer had any valid travel documents. He asked friends and relatives in India to conduct some inquiries, to figure out what exactly this "notice" was about, but to no avail. He said he was trapped: He could not renew his passport, and he could not travel back to India. Because he no longer had a valid passport, he could no longer work and was fired from his well-paid job. Ultimately he was sent back to India and was arrested upon his arrival in Delhi. Because he had been deported from the Middle Eastern country, he would not be let back into that country. "The Special Cell," he told me, "ruined my career, my life, my family—everything."

After his arrest at the airport, he was taken to a magistrate. He said, "Okay I said to myself, now that I am here, I need to fight it." He was in police custody for nine days. He said that the police could not do "their illegal custody business [because] there was paper, the ticket, saying that [he] had arrived in India on that date." He said that was also the reason why they could not torture him. He said, "If I'd been in India, they would have tortured me for ten, fifteen, days, one month, and then waited for the wounds to heal and then produced me in court."

He believed that if the court looked at the documents in his case, then he would be acquitted. Like other terror-accused individuals whom I met, he seemed comfortable in using legal language. He told me that the Special Cell had only told some *kahaaniyan*, or stories, about him in their charge sheet. As we saw in Chapters 4 and 5, he knew that the narrative of a case crucially depended on the file. "They cannot prove anything against me," he told me.

> They said I have sent this phone and other electronics—but where is the receipt? They did not even seize it and did not submit a seizure memo [to the court]. Under Section 45, of the Unlawful [Activities Prevention] Act, they did not even have permission to file this case against me, but still they went on *gair kanoon* [outside the law]. They said I spoke on the telephone with some man and that they have a recording of it. But they do not have the any translator for it. They said that my voice matched the voice on the recording, but my lawyers destroyed the expert they had brought. It is an absolutely fake case against me.

Echoing the idea of the vulnerability of the state to its words (Chapter 3), he said that "the law that they themselves have written says do things this way. Then why did they do things another way? It is only because they have made this false case against me."

While he was convinced the case against him was weak, he conceded that this did not mean he would be acquitted. He knew that uncertainty was at the heart of an intimate encounter with the law. "You never know what kind of pressures they put on a judge," he said. I asked him what he meant by this. As we saw in Chapter 1, he, too, had heard rumors about the powers of the police. He said that he had heard that the Home Ministry would send word, through the Special Cell, to a "judge to *keencho* [stretch] the case for as long as possible" and could even tell a judge to convict a person. The Special Cell, according to Shamsher, followed the orders of the Home Ministry. He said that a "judge who doesn't want to convict will sometimes stretch the case for as long as possible" so as to "not piss off the Home Ministry by giving an acquittal."

I asked him what he thought about the judge in his case. He claimed an intimate familiarity with him and said that he was very good. (This was the same judge who presided over Kumar and Barucha's case.) "He's done work on every date, and he doesn't waste time. The only time this judge has taken leave was when his father passed away, but apart from that he's done work on every date." Shamsher said that it was this judge who had granted him bail. Shamsher told me that after the hearing, when he was sitting outside the court, the judge walked past, smiled, and said, "Abhi khush ho?" (Are you happy now?) The reason he was granted bail was that, as in Bharucha's case (discussed in Chapter 3), the prosecution had not followed the two-step process to file UAPA charges. Shamsher was told about this vital technical detail by Kumar, with whom he shared a cell. Shamsher then told his lawyer to ask the judge to dismiss the terrorism charges (as he had done in Kumar's and Bharucha's case). Instead of dismissing the case because of a faulty sanction to prosecute, the judge let Shamsher out on bail (as was done in Keshav's case).

At that time he had been out on bail for about six months. "I thought I could restart my life," he said. But with the fortnightly hearings and monthly trips to "mark attendance" at the Special Cell, he was not able to plan anything. "I try to think about the future, but I cannot do anything because of this case." As we saw with Mohsin in Chapter 6, Shamsher seemed stuck in time as he worried about the afterlife of his trial. He worried aloud about the repercussions of the case on his future: "Even if I am acquitted, once people hear that there was this accusation against me, they will not speak with me. I can't go back to the [Middle East] for work. Who will give me a passport now? I have to start everything from the beginning here."

While we waited on a bench outside the courtroom, he asked what I would do next since my fieldwork was almost at an end. I told him that I had volumes of material that I needed to go through and make sense of. Shamsher began to rattle off the cases that he knew of that had ended in acquittals. It turned out that he had been imprisoned with several people we have encountered in this book. In addition to Kumar, he knew Shahid (whom he seemed to like), Bharucha (whom he seemed to respect for his wide reading), and Irfan (who he thought was *pagal*, or mentally ill). He said that only a handful of people charged under anti-terror laws were actually involved in terrorist activities. "Most people," he said, "are completely innocent. The police have created false cases against so many people, including me."

I told him about a human rights association called the Jamia Teachers Solidarity Association and its recently released report about how the Special Cell fabricates terrorism cases (Jamia Teachers Solidarity Association 2014). He said that he would want to read the report, to see the cases of people whom he knew in jail. I asked for his email address to send him a copy, but he immediately said no. Lika many of my interlocutors, he believed that the Special Cell was monitoring his activities, including his email. As I took down his postal details, I asked if he thought the Special Cell was monitoring his cell phone. He said yes, though he added that "the Special Cell isn't concerned about minor things. They don't care if you are crossing a red light or if you are fucking a girl. They are only interested in the major things that they can give a different meaning to. Like if you say that you have a lot of currency or anything like that."

As the morning wore on, his nervousness mounted. The case had not yet been called, and there was no sign of his lawyer. Several times, he held his head in his hands as he rocked back and forth on the bench. He said that he had not been able to do anything in Srinagar with this case still looming. He had not been able to think about the future. He wanted to start a tour company to arrange trips to a ski resort in Kashmir. But "I can't do anything," he said. "I can't do any job or get married because this case has stopped my life."

Shamsher's anxiety was stretched out further as the court broke for lunch without calling his case. We waited outside the courtroom for his lawyer. While we waited, the judge presiding over his case walked by. Shamsher stood, bowed slightly, smiled and said, "Hello sir" as the judge passed by wordlessly. "He's a very good man," Shamsher said hopefully.

After we were finally joined by Shamsher's lawyer, the three of us went to the court canteen for lunch. I ordered food for the three of us. Shamsher's lawyer told him that he would definitely be acquitted and that he had nothing to worry about. The lawyer spoke brashly, not mindful of Shamsher's nervousness. He said that unlike other lawyers who "only shout in court to impress their clients, but do little work," he worked hard for his cases. Shamsher quietly said that many terror-accused he knew were represented by the lawyer named Sheikh (whom we met in Chapter 1). The lawyer responded that unlike Sheikh, he was not corrupt and did not cut deals with the Special Cell.

After lunch, we went back to court. Shamsher's lawyer was inside the courtroom, and Shamsher and I waited outside for his case to be called. A man walked by whom I recognized him as a Special Cell officer. I asked Shamsher if this was the police officer in his case. He said no, and that "this judge has many Special Cell cases with him, so he must have come for some other case." Giving voice to forms of custodial intimacy I wrote about in Chapter 1, he said that he knew several Special Cell officers. He seemed to excuse the officers for prosecuting him. While it was wrong for them to file this case against him, "They also had very little choice since pressure on them was coming from above." Nonetheless, he seemed to abhor one of officers in his case. The officer he named was involved in fabricating the case against Qayoom (discussed in Chapter 2). This officer was recently involved in car accident, which left him with a permanent facial disfigurement. While the courts might excuse the Special Cell's fabrication of cases, Shamsher believed that this police officer had been found guilty by a different order of justice. Shamsher said:

> Allah is so big, and he has given his judgment. He was going on the highway and he had an accident. He's got an inch-deep scar on his forehead. His eyes have become like this like this [he pointed his fingers in opposite directions]. Judgment has come against him.

After about half an hour, the naib court came outside and told Shamsher that his case was about to be called. Shamsher looked extremely distressed, and he began sweating even in the cold. As we entered the courtroom, he could not bring himself to sit in back. He stood close to the front and nervously shifted weight from one leg to the other. I stood right behind him.

Finally, the reader called Shamsher's case, and his lawyer approached the judge's desk. Shamsher took his place behind the lawyer, and I stood behind Shamsher. The judge began to read the conclusion of the judgment very softly. From where we were standing, I could hear only the words "guilt," "failed," "reasonable doubt." Suddenly, I saw Shamsher's knees buckle, and he fell backward on to me. I tried to hold him up, and the naib rushed in to help me. Shamsher steadied himself and asked, "Bari kiya hai na?" (It is an acquittal, right?) A smiling judge said, "Haan, bari kiya hai" (Yes, yes, it is an acquittal). I suddenly realized that Shamsher was sobbing, and I began tearing up as well. There were hugs and smiles all around, as the lawyer embraced Shamsher and the naib court first hugged me and then Shamsher. The naib held Shamsher in an embrace and said, "Pata tha ki tumko bari kardenge" (I knew you would be acquitted). The Special Cell officer who was still in court came and patted Shamsher on the back.

As we left the courtroom, tears continued to roll down Shamsher's face. He gave his lawyer and me a hug each, and said he needed to call his family. He said that he would call me later. The naib and the Special Cell officer came into the corridor, and we discussed what had just happened. The naib court told us he thought Shamsher was a very decent and honest person, as if to say that he thought the case should never have been filed in the first place. The lawyer teased the Special Cell officer: "If you are going to file false cases, at least do so in the proper way." The Special Cell officer smiled and, not wanting to engage, responded, "It is good you did your job so well."

I telephoned Shamsher the next day and asked him how he was feeling. He said for the first time in years, he was able to sleep. He was very relieved and could not wait to get back to Srinagar to be with his family. However, an anxiety crept back into his voice as he wondered aloud whether this case would continue to haunt him. He did not know if he could get his old job back. If he could not, he did not know what he would do in Kashmir. "Even [though] I am acquitted, they will find some way to get me," he said. I could never clarify what he meant, as he pushed away any uncertainty about the future: "At least for now, I am out of jail." I asked him if there was any chance to meet before he left Delhi and whether he would come to Tis Hazari so that I could give him a copy of the Jamia Teachers' Solidarity Association's report that I had promised him. "Post mein bhejo" (Send it in the post), he said. "I never want to set foot in Tis Hazari again."

At the end of this book, I would like to think about the way most terrorism trials conclude: in acquittals. The overwhelming majority of terrorism trials end with the defendants being found innocent of the terrorism charges brought against them. And as we saw in Chapter 2, on occasion courts will go even further to hold that the police fabricated evidence and falsely prosecuted innocent people. But what is meant by an acquittal?

At one level, this question draws our attention to what these acquittals turn on. They do not depend on grand statements of law, but rather on humble technicalities. To a distant eye, it may seem strange that technical details can occupy such an important place in a trial. But as we have seen, technicalities lie at the heart of a trial as important consequences can flow from something as trifling as the certification of a signature or a misfiled document or a grainy image on a computer screen. In drawing attention to the law as a process, this book provides an opening to those legal scholars who locate the law solely in judgments and legislations to pay attention to aspects that are too often dismissed as mere technicalities. This book sheds light on what every legal practitioner knows: that technicalities lie at the heart of the law. While they may seem unimportant and mundane, without them legal meaning could not be produced, and judgments could never be written, as cases would be left without facts.

The importance of technicalities to the outcome of trials also explains why the terror-accused invest time and energy in understanding how they are meant to function. Legal technicalities emerge as materials that can be worked with. Like a potter who works clay or a carpenter who works wood, those who work the law seek an intimate relationship with it, to feel it, to see what forms can emerge, to understand what it can do. For the terror-accused who worked with technicalities, the law came to be conceived not as distant, but as close at hand. In drawing attention to the everyday, inspirational work that terror-accused individuals undertook in order to maintain their lives through the trial process, this book has focused on the technicalities of the law as tools with which the terror-accused craft their lives in courtrooms. Living and working with legal technicalities enables them to forge friendships and communities within the courtroom. There is much riding on these technicalities, which is why so much activity and emotion is invested in them. What is at stake in each of these "minor" technicalities is nothing short of one's life.

The idea that technicalities engender forms of life has prompted my effort in this book to recover the world of courtrooms, and the law more generally, from dismissal by critical legal scholars. Rather than imagine the law solely as forms of epistemic and material violence, I have argued that the law engenders forms of life. In addition to being experienced as overwhelming and violent, the law also emerges as vulnerable, confused, and at times, even friendly. In this book, the law is a mode through which to inhabit the milieu of courtrooms, and to imagine a future. It is a site of tenacious creativity that is invested with hopes and desires.

This is why I imagine this book as an attempt to bring human voice into the law. One has only to keep one's ear close to the ground to hear the depth and intensity of emotion behind every detail of the trial process. In every faulty document filed by the police, one can hear a claim that the case has been fabricated and that the terror-accused have been framed. In every procedural step missed by the prosecution, one can hear an accusation of hypocrisy that the state is not following its own law. Behind every petition, one can hear vulnerability and a cry for justice.

To be acquitted, then, is not merely to have been declared innocent by a court of law. For some, like Shamsher, it is a moment of relief and doubt: relief that one does not need to spend more time in jail and doubt as to what the future holds. For people such as Qayoom, it is a vindication that the slow work that he and his co-accused had put into learning legal language had borne fruit. For others, like Mohsin, it is a moment when his anger burst forth—anger that he had protested his innocence for fourteen long years and that only at the judgment did the court finally listen to him. As symbolized by these acquittals, law is not merely a set of rules or a series of judgments or an expression of state power. It is an affective terrain in which lives are lived.

The word "acquittal" refers to a judgment or verdict that a person is not guilty of the crime with which he or she has been charged. To be acquitted of a crime is to be set free from a criminal charge by a judgment of a court of law. The etymological path of the word can be traced back through old from medieval Latin *acquitare*, meaning to "pay a debt," to the old French *acquiter*, to "pay, pay up, settle a claim" (Onions, 1966, 9). To be acquitted, then, is to be discharged of a debt, to have all claims against oneself settled, to have repaid what one owes.

Most of the terror-accused I met never voluntarily took on this debt. Rather, the burden of a terrorism trial was forced upon them. In an increasingly authoritarian contemporary India, a similar burden has been placed on hundreds more people. The UAPA and other special security legislation has been used to target democratic rights activists and people from Muslim and Dalit communities. The police have used the cover of anti-terror legislation to torture, illegally detain, and falsely charge innocent people. They have fabricated evidence and have painted the exercise of democratic rights as a terrorist activity. Those accused of terrorist crimes face months of pre-charge detention. If their cases go to trial, they can face years—potentially close to a decade—waiting for their cases to come to a close. While many of those charged will most likely be acquitted, the trial will exact a heavy price.

The freedom that an acquittal brings is a tainted one. As one recently acquitted terror-accused individual, who had spent more than a decade in jail and was finally acquitted, said to me, "When I went in to jail, there was no internet or mobile phones, all of this is a new magic to me. Everything is different, everything is changed. I feel lost in this new world." This feeling of being lost in one's freedom is echoed in the prison memoirs written by Arun Ferreira (2014), a human rights activist who describes fifty-four months of being incarcerated for terrorist crimes. Toward the end of his book, he depicts his life after he was acquitted:

> For the longest time, I found it difficult to deal with my life as a free man. Persistent phone calls from the media left me in a daze. In prison, the only person I would meet was my lawyer and we would always jot down in advance what was to be discussed with him. Technology, too, was a big challenge. In the world of apps, mobiles and other gizmos, I felt challenged. . . . The occasional hustle or noise at home or at get-togethers soon makes me irritable. (157–58)

Recall that after his acquittal, Mohsin seemed similarly caught in time, trapped by the injury inflicted by the trial. Even though these men have been acquitted and have been set free, the trial visits them as a continuing tragedy. Parts of their past lives will never return, and they will be tormented by visions of what could have been: more time spent with families and friends who passed away during their time in jail; life events that could have taken place—marriages, children, and a career. The lives that they could have lived will cast a shadow on the life that they have lived. It is these still-born lives—these forms of death—that will haunt those acquitted of terrorist crimes.

As Mohsin's and Shamsher's narratives remind us, their imaginations of their futures will also be cursed. Despite their freedom, the experience of the trial will make them look over their shoulders for years after their trials have ended. Shamsher and others like him imagine that the Special Cell will continue to monitor email accounts and cellphones. They will see signs of the police hidden behind the most innocent of objects. Further, as Mohsin believes, people are scared to be associated with former terror-accused. Questions about the trial will continue to reverberate through their lives: What will their futures look like? Will potential employers be wary of these past accusations? Who would marry a person who had such a run-in with the police?

Even as the law opens new modes of living during the trial, it continues to exact a steep price outside the prison walls, turning freedom itself into a curse. Though these former terror-accused have discharged the debts that were forced upon them, the law has yet to acquit itself.

And what of those who are convicted? As I had no access to jails, I could only hear their narratives second hand from those still on trial or from people like Yaseen bhai, who had been let out on bail while their appeals were being heard. From what I was told, those convicted also continued to work with technicalities. Either through their lawyers or state legal aid, they filed appeals against their conviction, in which they pointed to all the flaws in the police's investigation and the errors that the trial courts had been led into. They sent petitions to judges, ministers, and other authorities, pleading for mercy and protesting their innocence.

I once asked a terror-accused what he would do if he were convicted. "I have full faith that I would be released," he said. "I knew that if the magistrate convicted me, I would go to the Sessions Court. If the Sessions Court went against me, then I would go to the High Court. After that there is the Supreme Court. I always knew that I would be released and that I would just have to survive prison." Maybe those who had been convicted would exhibit a similar tenacity, despite their experiences of the trial. They would continue to work with the law, in the hope that they would eventually be released.

It is time, then, to revisit the opening page of this book—the excerpt from Anne Carson's (2013) *Red Doc>*. The text itself is from a play within Carson's verse-novel. The story within the story retells the tragedy of Prometheus: the fire he steals from the gods is rethought of as hope. To have hope, then, is perhaps an act of theft from vengeful gods. It is to steal life back from those who take it from us, to find life where there ought to be only death. But Prometheus steals hope only to gift it to human beings. Hope is also then a gift to be exchanged, and it is this exchange that gives us life. It is hope's shared blindness that protects us from seeing only death before us.

The excerpt stands out from the rest of Carson's verse-novel primarily because of most of the book's text is set justified in a two-inch column that runs down the middle of the page. By contrast, in this excerpt the words seem to pull away from the center, toward the edges of the page. What is also distinctive about this page is that, unlike the rest of the book, its text lacks punctuation and capitalization. Our eyes then take up the slow labor of returning syntax and grammar to it. Perhaps this is another way of imagining hope in the face of tragedy: as the work done to bring back meaning to words, as the work done to put the words, our lives, back in order.

ACKNOWLEDGMENTS

An experienced criminal lawyer whom I know once reflected on the risks involved in her daily practice. What was a simple legal mistake for her could have life and death consequences for her clients. In that introspective moment she told me, "We learn off of the lives of others." The stakes involved in a book are of far less consequence, yet the adage remains valid. This book would not have been possible if the people and families whom I met had not entrusted the stories of their lives to me. They opened their hearts to me, gave me their time, and allowed me a glimpse into the grinding world of courtrooms, and for this I am eternally indebted. I can only hope that I have narrated the stories of their trials and of their inspirational lives in ways that do them justice. I hope this book can express the depth of my gratitude to and affection for Yaseen bhai, Mohammed Amir Khan, Syed Maqbool Shah, and the other unnamed people who appear in this book. I would also like to thank the many lawyers—Rebecca Mammen John, Shomona Khanna, Ashok Agrwaal, and Nitya Ramakrishnan, among others—who gave me insights into their cases.

For their help with this book and more importantly, their continued commitment to the idea of justice, I thank the members and friends of the People's Union for Civil Liberties, the People's Union for Democratic Rights, and the Jamia Teachers' Solidarity Association. In the face of an increasingly authoritarian India, they continue to chip away at the edifice of violence and injustice. Through their meticulous and painstaking research, they provide hope where there is increasingly little.

The origins of this book owe much to the patient camaraderie of Piyel Haldar. Piyel has an excitement about concepts—and this, I hope, is reflected here. Birkbeck has supported a diversity of ideas, and I am grateful to the School of Law, Birkbeck for expressing its confidence in my research project through the Ronnie Warrington Studentship, which enabled me to undertake fieldwork in India. I would like to thank Raghab Dash, who helped me navigate the Parliament of India Library, and Nawazgul Kanungo, who helped me on my field visit in Kashmir. It would be remiss of me to not thank M. P. Karthik for hosting me during my research trip to Srinagar. I would like to thank Veena Das and Alain Pottage for their continued support of this project.

My colleagues at SOAS have given me much support. The introduction of this book was drafted on a writing retreat that was generously funded by the School of Law, SOAS. Other research trips to India were funded by SOAS through the School of Law and the Faculty of Law and Social Sciences. Thanks to Petra Mahy for being such a pal during our first year at SOAS, to Grace Mou for her tips on book publishing, and to Anne Street whose generous teaching notes helped me find the time to complete this book.

Parts of this book were written while I was a Future of Change (India) Research Fellow at the Faculty of Law, University of New South Wales, Sydney. It was a real privilege to have gone to UNSW at Sydney, to have had the space to write, and to have been part of such an intellectually stimulating milieu. Parts of this book were presented at an Ethnography Forum organized by Melissa Crouch and at a workshop titled *The Judiciary and Public Policy* co-organized by Gabrielle Appleby. The feedback I received at both these events was invaluable.

The editorial process at Fordham University Press has been fantastic. From the early days of conceiving the book to this finished project, Bhrigupati Singh has been immensely supportive. He and Clara Han, as series editors, organized an incredibly constructive prepublication workshop where I received very helpful comments from them and from Tobias Kelly, Matthew Hull, Sameena Mulla, Pratiksha Baxi, and Francis Cody. I am very grateful for their considered feedback, which has immeasurably improved this book. From reviewing the book proposal in 2018, to meeting me in New York to discuss the book in 2019, and to finding exacting anonymous reviewers, Tom Lay at Fordham University Press has been an efficient friend to this book. I would also like to thank the two anonymous reviewers for their helpful comments.

Versions of two chapters of this book have appeared in the *Law & Society Review* and *Contributions to Indian Sociology*. The editors of those journals, Susan M. Sterett and Pratiksha Baxi, respectively, pushed me to clarify the arguments that are developed in this book.

Several friends have been a great support through the writing process. Laura Lammasniemi has been a careful reader of this manuscript. Kanika Sharma and Victoria Mitchell have read and helped me clarify the book chapters. More significantly, Kanika, Laura and Victoria have made the writing process a fun and social one. Through the months of the pandemic, I could not have asked for better neighbors than Gautam and Tonusree, who have been a source of companionship, cocktails, and delicious food. Prashant Iyengar has generously used his critical eye to go over several chapters in this book, and his comments have helped me sharpen my arguments.

My interest in ethnography as a way of understanding the world was first piqued thanks to an undergraduate fellowship from Sarai/CSDS. From that first presentation I made in 2003 on practices surrounding VHS technology, Ravi Sundaram has been a constant source of intellectual energy and excitement.

This book would not have been possible without the support of my second family in Delhi, centered in an area we affectionately call "B'nags." Anita Abraham, Iram Ghufran, Fatima Nizaruddin, Shahrukh Alam, Parvati Sharma, Philippe Cullet, and Naveen T. K.—my life and this book are richer because of you. Monica Kohli, Malavika Vartak, and Bikramjeet Batra were the extension of this home in London and brought with them the laughter and warmth of Delhi.

Subasri Krishnan has always been willing to bounce ideas back and forth with me, discuss serious ethical issues relating to fieldwork, and importantly, provide opportunities for me to laugh at myself. I know this stand-alone paragraph (that she so subtly asked for) will not do justice to the amount of love I have for her, but one can only try.

In Bangalore and Delhi, I've made some of the best friends who—through their hitherto unknown excellent editing skills (Sameer), or their ability to send intercontinental comfort mangoes in high-stress times (Jiti), or their superhuman power of finding beauty in everything you write (Sruti), or through their "proper" efforts to make everything seem easier than it is (Sidey), or even through their well-intentioned, yet brutally honest advice (Vishnu)—have made writing this book a whole lot more enjoyable.

This book owes much to two people: Lawrence Liang and Jawahar Raja, who have been more than friends. In some senses, they are present through the entirety of this book. From 2002 when he was my teacher in my final year of law school to the present moment, Lawrence has been a friend and mentor and has led me into ever-expanding intellectual worlds. While Jaws is a much better lawyer than he is a DJ, from him I learned that the law has a rhythm, a tune, a life. Through his stubborn passion, I came to appreciate what was at stake in the minute details of the everyday practice of law. Working with him, Anand Singh, Rajat Kumar, and Sahana Manjesh was one of the best times I have had, and I hope this book reflects an enthusiasm for the law that that experience has left me.

Many friends have been intellectual companions through various moments of this book. For their friendship and their help through the different stages of writing, I thank Anuj Bhuwania, Anand Taneja, Rahul Rao, Başak Ertür, Akshay Khanna, Eddie Bruce-Jones, Paul O'Connell, Nimer Sultany, Kate Grady, Carol Tan, Fareda Banda, Ernest Caldwell, Lucy King, Shri Singh, Hannah Franzki, M. S. Prashant, Preeti Ramdasi, Tarunabh Khaitan, and Alex Bubb. A big heartfelt thank you to Julia Eckert and Sneha Krishnan for their careful, incisive, and generous reading of earlier versions of chapters. Jinee Lokaneeta has been a source of both professional and intellectual support. I cannot not thank her enough for her mentorship and all the intellectual inspiration and advice that she has given me. Thanks to Chinmay Kanojia, Praavita Kashyap, and Anushrut Agrwaal for their help in transliterating some of the documents used in this book. Danielle McClellan provided excellent editorial assistance. I would also like to express my gratitude to Dayanita Singh for graciously allowing me to use one of her photos as the cover image of this book.

I could not have wished for a more supportive family. I knew Natalina for too short a time, and I hope this book reflects her curiosity about the world. I hope it also reflects the influence of my grandmother, Vasantha Devi, who loved telling her grandchildren stories. Padma Aunty has always encouraged me to publish and has been an enthusiastic reader of my work. My aunt and uncle, Sri Periamma and Rangaraj Periappa, and my brother and sister-in-law, Prashanth and Anagha, have always been a supportive presence, even if they always seem too far away. My father's eldest sister, Vijaya Athe, has had a strong influence in my life, and through her I now know the strength and compassion one must have to live life differently.

My parents have given me music, joy, and love. With their tender support, they have given me the space to explore life.

And finally, to my partner Roberto. It is difficult to put down in words, the depth of gratitude and love that I have for him. His patience, creativity, ability to plan, and infectious enthusiasm have helped me in writing this book. He has read every chapter with the most careful eye and showed confidence in me when I was consumed with doubt. He has shown me the wondrous possibilities of life.

NOTES

INTRODUCTION

1. Thompson reaches this conclusion even though the entirety of his *Whigs and Hunters* (1990) tells us that the rule of law was used to entrench and then mask class inequalities in eighteenth-century England. For a discussion of the debates generated by this conclusion, see Peluso (2017).

2. The epithet *bhai* means brother.

3. This is often translated as a rule by a caliph or rule by Islamic principles. Despite its framing by the police in this case as emblematic of an Islamic movement aimed at overthrowing the state, the Khilafat movement played an important part in India's nationalist movement. With the defeat of the Ottoman Empire at the end of the First World War, the victorious European powers divided the empire and removed the Ottoman sultan from his role as the caliph, or spiritual leader, of Sunni Muslims. In 1919, a movement was launched to restore the caliph. It was joined by Gandhi and the Indian National Congress. See Minault (1982).

4. This number has been compiled from the National Judicial Data Grid, https://njdg.ecourts.gov.in/njdgnew/?p=main/index&state_code=7~26&dist_code=9&est_code=undefined (accessed November 5, 2019).

5. I use the term "terror-accused" as a shorthand for people accused of terrorist crimes. In Indian courts and public discourse, people charged with crimes are referred to as "accused" rather than "defendants." Often in legal and media discussions, people charged with terrorist offences are referred to as "terror-accused." I have used this term here as an abbreviated form of "people accused of a terrorist crime" rather than an identity category.

6. This metaphor comes up regularly in scholarship (e.g., Clarke's [1938] essay titled the "The Handmaid of Justice") as well as cases in the UK (e.g., *Coles v. Ravenshear* [1907] 1 KB 1). The metaphor is regularly employed by courts in India to justify a deviation from procedural rules.

7. This is what Ingold (2010) has called the "hylomorphic model of creation"(92), wherein the creative process is imagined as the imposition of a pre-imagined form on a substance. Instead, Ingold proposes an "ontology that assigns primacy of the process of formation against the final products, and to the flows and transformations of materials as against states of matter" (92).

8. As Baxi's (2014) work on rape trials in Gujarat reminds us, legal technicalities can be ways in which violence is perpetuated and reinscribed on the bodies of rape survivors. Investigative and trial processes, such as the forensic examination after the rape and the defense lawyers' cross-examination, force rape survivors to relive their trauma. Further, it is through these very technicalities that the testimony of the rape survivor is delegitimized: Through forensic examinations, the body of the rape survivor is made to speak against her words, and cross-examinations in courts are used to terrorize rape survivors into turning against their earlier statements recorded by police officials.

9. Cavell (2005, 187–88) questions this association between the illocutionary and performative that is implicit in Austin's text. In particular, he asks in what sense the illocutionary can be thought of as conventional.

10. As Hussain (2003, 65–66) has argued, the colonial state defined the "rule of law" in terms of predictable and regular procedure. In doing so, the colonial state was able to maintain its argument that it brought the rule of law to the colonies, while masking the "despotic" elements of colonial law.

11. The second part of the 1908 act allowed for the government to declare an association and membership of that organization illegal by executive fiat. The 1908 act was the immediate precursor to the current anti-terror law—the Unlawful Activities (Prevention) Act, 1967. For a discussion of the link between the two statutes, see Suresh and Raja (2012).

12. McQuade (2021, 125–62) argues that this committee was set up in the context of colonial anxieties over the stability of their rule in India, which grew against the backdrop of the First World War, the Irish Easter Uprising, and revolutionary networks that developed around the empire.

13. This was recommended as it was "of the utmost importance that punishment or acquittal should be speedy both in order to secure the moral effect which punishment should produce and also to prevent the prolongation of the excitement which the proceedings may set up" (Sedition Committee 1918, 201).

14. The act was popularly known as the Rowlatt Act. Its enactment was followed by mass protests and reprisals by the colonial state. Most infamously, the Jallianwala Bagh Massacre, in which protesting civilians were killed by armed troops, took place in the context of protests against this law. See Wagner (2019).

15. Sections 3, 21, 33 of the Anarchical and Revolutionary Crimes Act, 1919.

16. Section 4 of the Anarchical and Revolutionary Crimes Act, 1919.

17. Schedule, Anarchical and Revolutionary Crimes Act, 1919.

18. A similar tactic of prescribing special rules of evidence and procedure for general crimes in specific areas is followed in the Bengal Suppression of Terrorist Outrages Act, 1932. This act prescribed a summary trial procedure for people accused of certain offenses under the Indian Penal Code, 1860, the Explosive Substances Act, 1883, and the Arms Act, 1878, before a special magistrate (instead of a more senior Court of Sessions), "if in the opinion of the appropriate Government . . . there are reasonable grounds for believing that any person has committed a scheduled offense . . . in furtherance or in connection with the terrorist movement" (Section 25 of the Bengal Suppression of Terrorist Outrages Act, 1932). The legislation gave the provincial government the authority to designate special magistrates to hear the case but gave the district administration the power to determine which cases should be tried before these special courts.

De (2014, 266–67) points out that laws similar to these did not go unchallenged. For example, in the Lahore Conspiracy case, Bhagat Singh and his co-accused refused both to recognize the legitimacy of the colonial court and to defend themselves. In 1930, the governor general, using his emergency powers under the Government of India Act, 1919, issued Ordinance No. 3, which set up a tribunal just for this particular case. The ordinance allowed for the tribunal to pass any sentence authorized by law, including a death sentence, and Section 9(1) gave the tribunal the power to try the defendants in absentia. Unsurprisingly, a judgment was issued convicting all of the accused and the death sentence being issued to some—Bhagat Singh among them. His legal team took their case to the privy council, where they argued that ordinance setting up the special tribunal was *ultra vires*, or outside the scope of the governor general's powers under the Government of India Act. The privy council dismissed this appeal.

De points out that there were different legal challenges to special courts from the 1920s to the 1940s. Most of these challenges were based on the limitations on power placed upon the executive by the Government of India Acts of 1919 and 1935.

19. See De (2014, 2018), who argues that the enactment of the constitution created a new juridical field in which power had to be recalibrated.

20. While prior colonial legislations have used "terror" as a justification for special procedures, this is the first time that a definition of terrorism had been legislated into existence in Indian law. McQuade (2021) argues that for the colonial state "terrorism" became a useful way of delegitimizing the widening nationalist movement and simultaneously to justify the creeping expansion of executive rule (203). He observes that the British colonial development of discourses of terrorism ultimately fed into the first definition of terrorism in international law, in the Convention for the Prevention and Punishment of Terrorism, as violence that is primarily against the state and the symbolism of sovereignty (204–39).

See also Stampnitzky (2013), who looks at the fundamental uncertainty of the meaning "terrorism." In looking at the rise of "terrorism experts," she argues that forms of political violence became "terrorism" via conflicts over the production of knowledge about it. "Terrorism" and "terrorism experts" co-created each other.

21. The act was subsequently renewed in 1987 and then was allowed to lapse in 1995. While there were attempts to legislate TADA into permanency (*Economic and Political Weekly* 2000), the proposed legislations did not pass Parliament. India did not have a specific anti-terror legislation until 2001, when the Prevention of Terrorism Ordinance (POTO) was promulgated.

22. The act was first promulgated as an executive ordinance called the Prevention of Terrorism Ordinance in 2001, soon after the 9/11 attacks in the United States. Following the attacks, the United Nations Security Council passed Resolution No. 1373 (2001), which required all states to "combat . . . threats to international peace by terrorist acts" (United Nations Security Council Resolution No. 1373 [2001]). For a criticism of Resolution No. 1373 and consequent resolutions, see Galloway (2011.) This quickly became the most cited justifications for an anti-terror law not only in India, but around the world.

This ordinance was ostensibly promulgated in response to this "new" international obligation, the coalition government lead by the Hindu right-wing Bharatiya Janata Party (BJP), which subsequently introduced a bill in Parliament to permanently enact this ordinance. On December 13, 2001, while Parliament was in session, five gunmen made their way through the security cordon at Parliament House and killed several people. As a result of the "attack on Parliament," the chorus of the global war on terror became shriller. As the bill could not be passed—Parliament was adjourned after the attack—a second ordinance was issued on December 30, 2001. The bill was presented in the budget session of Parliament in 2002, amid opposition from the opposition Congress Party and the communist parties, which cited the effect that TADA previously had had on the rights of minority groups. The lower house passed the bill, but it was rejected by the upper house. The government fell back on its option to call a joint sitting of both houses of Parliament, the bill was passed by a vote of 425 to 296, and the Prevention of Terrorism Act (POTA) became law in 2002.

23. Both legislations define the act of terrorism in terms of the intent to strike fear into the people; threatening the unity security or sovereignty of India; using bombs, dynamite, lethal weapons; causing or likely to cause the destruction of life or property.

24. Section 25 of the Indian Evidence Act, 1876.

25. The UAPA became the primary terrorism law because of an amendment effected in 2004. In 2004, the Hindu right-wing BJP-led government was voted out of power and a Congress Party–led coalition was elected. Citing POTA's selective application against Muslims, tribal populations, Dalits, and other minority

groups, one of the coalition's main promises during the election was a dismantling of the BJP's communal politics through a repeal of POTA (Singh 2007, 13). The Congress-led government, however, performed a sleight of hand and along with the repeal of POTA, enacted the Unlawful Activities Prevention (Amendment) Act, 2004, which added most of POTA's provisions to the Unlawful Activities Prevention Act, 1967. Notably, it did not transport the provision allowing confessions made to a police officer admissible as evidence.

26. Referring to the government's repeal of POTA and its refusal to make a decision on a clemency petition filed by a person convicted in the Parliament attack case, L. K. Advani, the BJP's former home minister stated: "In all, these things send a message to all terrorist groups that this country is soft on terrorism. You can get away with it." Statement of L. K. Advani, Leader of the Opposition, in the Lok Sabha, December 17, 2008, http://loksabhaph.nic.in/Debates/result14.aspx ?dbsl=10813; translation by author.

27. Statement of Kapil Sibal, Minister of Science and Technology, in the Lok Sabha, December 17, 2008, http://loksabhaph.nic.in/Debates/result14.aspx?dbsl =10813. See also statement of Kirip Chaliha, MP (Congress), in the Lok Sabha, December 17, 2008: "There are moments when you have to emerge to secure the lives and property of every Indian national whose lives are endangered because of terror" (http://loksabhaph.nic.in/Debates/result14.aspx?dbsl=10813).

28. While statistical data is varied, they point to the fact that the vast majority of terror-accused are discharged or acquitted. According to one report, in the decade of TADA's existence, 76,036 individuals were arrested for committing acts of terrorism. Of these, 25 percent were dropped by the police without framing charges; trials were completed in only 35 percent of the cases, and of these, only 1.5 percent ended in a conviction. This means that out of a total number of 76,036 arrests, only about four hundred people were ever convicted (Ministry of Home Affairs, Government of India, Memorandum to the full Commission of National Human Rights Commission Annexure 1, December 19, 1994, cited in Kumar et al. 2003, 99). National Crimes Record Bureau (2017) data about UAPA investigations and trials paint a similar picture. Only 56 percent of all UAPA investigations actually result in a charge sheet under the UAPA. Of those UAPA cases that make it to trial, only 33 percent end in a conviction. Recent data shows that below 2 percent of those arrested under the UAPA between 2015 and 2019 were eventually convicted (Tripathi 2021).

29. This argument is not confined to "extraordinary" laws such as the UAPA; it also pertains to "ordinary" laws such as sedition. See Singh (2018).

30. Singh (2007) harnesses Agamben's (2005) ideas about the state of exception to argue that anti-terror laws and ordinary criminal laws form an interlocking system through which exceptional laws are increasingly normalized, so that what was seen as temporary would become permanent. This, to my mind, is a misreading

of Agamben's argument, as the state of exception is defined by its lack of law—it operates as a zone of anomie. Thus, to speak of "exceptional laws" is a contradiction in Agamben's terms, since what defines the state of exception is the absence of law and the persistence of its force.

31. In constructing their arguments against anti-terror laws, human rights organizations have created a genealogy of these laws that goes back to colonial statutes. Through these statutes, the colonial state sought to oppress populations by banning associations by executive fiat, imprisoning people without trial, and using emergency powers. Present-day anti-terrorism statutes are compared to laws from the colonial era, which allowed "no *vakil*, no appeal, no *daleel*" (no lawyer, no appeal, no evidence) (People's Union for Civil Liberties 1985, 4). These organizations aim to delegitimize present day anti-terrorism laws as a return to the oppressive laws of the colonial state, since they are marked by the absence of a fair trial and due process, which is wholly antithetical the values of democracy and constitutionalism. They argue that the expansive nature of power granted to the police and the procedural deviations contained in these statutes reflect a form of colonial control.

32. For example, special courts were constituted by virtue of Section 9 of the Terrorist and Disruptive Activities (Prevention) Act (1987) and under Section 23 of the Prevention of Terrorism Act (2002).

33. Legal processes have been understood as providing such a clear view of society that some scholars have questioned whether the "legal" in the field of legal anthropology has any conceptual purchase (Comaroff and Roberts 1981, 243). If legal processes are not much more than social structures masquerading as law, what is the point of studying the law?

34. This argument tracks Winner's (1980) argument about the politics of artifacts, in which he criticizes social scientists who suggest that technologies are nothing but manifestations of social power, as if the technologies in themselves do not matter.

35. Specifically, I asked for details about the cases that were currently pending before Delhi's trial courts, in which the accused were charged with offenses under the UAPA (India's current anti-terrorism statute), TADA, and POTA (UAPA's predecessors). TADA and POTA are currently not in force, but trials that had commenced under those acts continue to be governed by those provisions, leading to what Singh (2007) describes as the "afterlife" of terror statutes.

36. Through my time working with Jawahar and throughout my fieldwork, I never once saw a case from start to finish. The cases described in this book were encountered at various stages of completion. Some of the trials were just beginning and were going through their pretrial motions before a magistrate, while others had been committed to the sessions courts for trial and I was able to see the recording of witness testimony. I caught two cases when final arguments were

underway and was able to be there for the moment when judgments were pronounced. One of the cases I tried to follow, which was about a bomb blast at a cinema in Delhi in 2005, had one substantive hearing in the entire fourteen months of my fieldwork. At this hearing, the sole accused was produced by the police, his presence was noted by the judge, and the case was adjourned. In most of the trials, the case would merely be adjourned on many dates that were scheduled for hearing. This could happen for a number of reasons: The witnesses had not turned up, the judge was unwell, the lawyers were on strike, the defense lawyers could not make it to court, the police had failed to bring the accused person from the jail to the court, or because the judge simply did not have the time for the case.

37. My aim here was not to get a factually accurate account of their experiences, since I recognized that these accounts relied on memory, were partial, and were situationally produced and interpreted (Ewick and Silbey 1995). Rather, my aim was to get a sense of their affective states while inhabiting the world of the courtroom and of how these experiences continued to impact their lives.

1. CUSTODIAL INTIMACY

1. For a brief, if journalistic, account of the history of the Special Cell, see Mishra (2013).

2. The court had an option to release the accused on bail, but that could almost never be done for UAPA cases as the rules under the UAPA made bail virtually impossible.

3. Scholars are deeply ambivalent regarding police violence. It is well known that for Benjamin (1978), the police are the meeting point of creating law and preserving violence. Some scholars (Arnold 1986; Fassin 2013), in pointing to the contextual and embedded nature of police violence, have highlighted the tension between the police's position of enforcers of the law and their role in reinforcing a social order based on systems of racial and economic discrimination, if not segregation.

4. In proposing this idea of custodial intimacy, I join other scholars who have recently looked at the ambiguous nature of the police to understand the nature of state power. Eckert (2005), in tracking the "double life of the killing state" (2) in India, argues that police killings symbolize a state in crisis and decay as well as a remedy for that very decay. Similarly Lokaneeta (2020) frames the state in terms of contingency where the police emerge as both repressive and pastoral. In describing the police as having a "provisional authority," Jauregui (2016) views the split nature of the police through the tension between Weberian ideas of legality and legitimacy. Similarly, Khanikar (2018) argues that the legitimacy of the police in India is contingent on both violence and legality.

Comaroff and Comaroff (2006) frame the dual nature of the police in terms of a movement between Foucauldian governmentality and post-Foucauldian theatricality. Das (2007) gives us the phrase "paradox of illegibility" (162) to show that the state as manifested through police violence oscillates between its magical and rational forms.

5. Take for example, the case of *State v. Maurif Qamar and Mohammed Irshad Ali* (https://indiankanoon.org/doc/86786615/), which involved three police forces. The Central Bureau of Investigation accused the Special Cell of arresting and fabricating the case against two alleged informers of a central intelligence agency, the Intelligence Bureau. Here one police organization is accusing a second of arresting the informers of a third. Case on file. See also Jamia Teachers Solidarity Association (2014: 131–43).

6. "Encounter" deaths follow a well-known formula used by Indian security forces to justify killing. In the documentation relating to these deaths the police often narrate the following sequence of events: They apprehend a "militant"; the militant says he can lead them to an arms cache; the arms cache is rigged with explosives; the militant dies. Other variations on this script include the "militant" trying to escape or managing to grab a gun and shoot at the police, and the police then firing back to prevent the escape or in self-defense. These narratives all end with the security personnel killing the "militant." Such narratives pepper documentary records of extrajudicial killings in many parts of India (International Peoples' Tribunal on Human Rights and Justice in Indian-Administered Kashmir and Association of Parents of Disappeared Persons 2015; Kumar et al. 2003; Andhra Pradesh Civil Liberties Committee 1985).

7. *Naxal* refers to a member of the Maoist party. The word comes from Naxalbari, the name of the subdistrict in West Bengal, where the armed peasant revolt began in 1967. For a review of the history and literature about the Maoist movement in India, see Shah and Jain (2017).

8. Lashkar-e-Taiba has been designated a terrorist organization by India, as well as other countries. For a history of this organization see, Fair (2018) and Sikand (2007).

9. A *maulvi* is a scholar who advises on matters of Islamic law.

10. In April 2001, East Delhi was gripped by reports of an attack by a *kala bandar* (black monkey) or the monkey-man. The beast was described variously as "a bounding black bear and a masked superhero, but most often it is described as half monkey, half man . . . with long, poisoned metal claws" (Dugger 2001). Between May 10 and 25, 397 people made calls to the police control room in Delhi claiming to have been attacked by this bizarre creature (Verma and Srivastava 2003). Some newspaper reports suggested that the police began keeping a separate register to monitor all monkey-man complaints (Singh 2001). The Delhi police issued sketches of the monkey-man, even though descriptions of the creature

varied wildly and changed over time. Mental health professionals described the event as an instance of "mass hysteria" (Verma and Srivastava 2003, 355) or "mass psychogenic illness" (Chowdhury and Brahma 2005, 106). Crucial to the monkey-man rumor is that the story spread, like a "contagion" (Dugger 2001), first (if we believe one news report) from the suburbs of eastern Delhi to the old city of Delhi (Singh 2001).

11. Coombe (1997) documents some of these rumors. For instance, the man-in-the-moon logo of some of the products manufactured by Proctor and Gamble were said to link the brand to satanism (253)

12. Guha (1999) argues with more nuance than I have been able to articulate above. He argues that rumors against the immediate colonial officers were coupled with rumors that invoked the support of a higher sovereign. Thus, even as the rumors helped mobilize insurgents against their immediate colonial oppressors, these rumors also fueled the idea that Queen Victoria would come to their aid against the colonial officials. Rumors would then be a form of resistance to a lesser form of sovereign power, but at the same time, invoke the protection of a higher form.

2. RECYCLED LEGALITY

1. This question of how to determine whether the rule applies in a given fact situation opened a debate between two of the stalwarts of Anglo-American legal philosophy, Hart and Dworkin. While the larger debate focuses on the nature and scope of law (Shapiro 2007) and on the question of legal interpretation, both scholars agree on the point that there are some scenarios that trouble the rule. In Chapter 3, I engage with the ethnographic implications of this debate.

2. De (2018) provides a similar account of early constitutional litigation in India in the 1950s. He documents how the independent Indian state used laws to regulate economic activity, while the newly enacted constitution provided new avenues to challenge state action and to put the state itself on trial.

3. Gluckman (1955) refers to the law as "flexible" when it can be stretched to cover various new circumstances and notes that legal concepts are "permeable" in that "circumstances which are extrinsic to the concepts themselves can pervade them, diffuse into them and be channeled into them" (293).

4. "When they (my elders) named some object, and accordingly moved towards something, I saw this and I grasped that the thing was called by the sound they uttered when they meant to point it out. Their intention was shewn by their bodily movements, as it were the natural language of all peoples: the expression of the face, the play of the eyes, the movement of other parts of the body, and the tone of voice which expresses our state of mind in seeking, having, rejecting, or avoiding something. Thus, as I heard words repeatedly used in their

proper places in various sentences, I gradually learnt to understand what objects they signified; and after I had trained my mouth to form these signs, I used them to express my own desires."

5. "The language is meant to serve for communication between a builder A and an assistant B. A is building with building stones: there are blocks, pillars, slabs and beams. B has to pass the stones, and that in the order in which A needs them. For this purpose they use a language consisting of the words 'block,' 'pillar,' 'slab,' 'beam.' A calls them out;—B brings the stone which he has learnt to bring at such-and-such a call."

6. Kripke (1982) argues that rules are central to Wittgenstein's idea of how we come to acquire language—that we are judged on whether we have used language properly or not. In Kripke's view, what is at stake in knowing the rule is the ability to follow it correctly. One learns a rule by instruction: A teacher teaches, and the student learns the rule. The teacher can judge if the student has correctly learned the rule, if the student applies the rule the teacher would have applied or if the student obtains the same result the teacher would have obtained.

7. This is what Cover (1983) would call an interpretive commitment—to make a norm one's own, to give it one's own meaning, and to project this understanding of a norm into future worlds (45).

8. A Sikh temple.

9. The state filed an appeal against these acquittals before the Delhi High Court, and police officials filed an appeal against the trial court's direction that they be prosecuted for fabrication of evidence. The Delhi High Court dismissed the state's appeal and upheld the acquittals of Qayoom and his co-accused. But it also quashed the trial court's direction that the police officials be prosecuted. The last time I spoke to Qayoom he was planning to file an appeal in the Supreme Court against the High Court's order quashing the prosecution of the police officials.

3. LAW AND THE VULNERABLE STATE

1. A number of anthropologists have similarly put forward a bipolar conception of state power. Rutherford (2009), for example, takes as her starting point for colonial governmentality in New Guinea not domination or control, but sympathy, which "encompasses empathy, pity and compassion but . . . can spawn hostility as easily as love" (4). Fassin (2005), in his ethnography of refugee camps in Calais, complicates Agamben's theorization of bare life and the state of exception and puts forward an idea of state power as simultaneously marked by compassion and repression. Das (2007), in her study of post-Sikh riots Delhi, paints a picture of the state that is "instituted through sporadic, intermittent contact, rather than an effective panoptic surveillance" (167). Here, the state oscillates between rational rule-bound bureaucratic avatar and magical, spectral

forms and thus emerges as both threat and possibility. Singh (2011, 2015) provides us a conception of sovereignty that oscillates between violence and contract.

2. Dworkin (1982, 1986) draws a strong distinction between creating and interpreting. He argues that in interpreting legal precedent, the judge refines the proposition of law. Fish (1982b) notices the inherent contradiction in this distinction asks whether interpreting legal precedent can ever be anything other than a creative process.

He argues that what gives a text its meaning are "interpretive communities" rather than the author, the text itself, or the solitary reader (Fish 1980, 14) and that legal interpreters are constrained "by their tacit awareness of what is possible and not possible to do, what is, and is not a reasonable thing to say, and what will and will not be heard as evidence in given enterprise" (Fish 1982b, 211). In Fish's understanding, an interpretation of a legal text will be constrained by the judge's understanding of what his or her interpretive community—presumably other judges and lawyers—will think is a possible interpretation. Unlike Dworkin (1986), however, Fish does not understand judges as being constrained by precedent. Instead the judge recreates this doctrinal history in the act of interpretation.

3. In contrast to Dworkin's judging model, Fish (1982a) offers a "lawyer's model" of legal interpretation, wherein arguments lie at the center of understanding the law, and not a judge's decisions.

4. Cognizance is a stage of the judicial process in which a magistrate (the lowest judicial officer in the court hierarchy) reads the police charge sheet and determines whether the facts narrated in the charge sheet state that the accused persons committed an offense. Cognizance is the first step toward a criminal trial. The underlying policy of this process is to ensure that there is a judicial check on the police and prosecution.

5. Though charge sheets are filed before magistrates, magistrates often lack subject-matter jurisdiction to conduct the trial in these cases. Therefore, the magistrate must commit the case for trial before a senior court, i.e., the Sessions Court.

6. "S. 45. Cognizance of offences.—(1) No court shall take cognizance of any offence . . . without the previous sanction of the Central Government.

(2) Sanction for prosecution under sub-section (1) shall be given within such time as may be prescribed only after considering the report of such authority appointed by the Central Government or, as the case may be, the State Government which shall make an independent review of the evidence gathered in the course of investigation and make a recommendation within such time as may be prescribed to the Central Government or, as the case may be, the State Government."

7. "Written Submissions on Point of Charge," on file with author.

8. Quoted from the charge sheet, on file with author.

9. He said this phrase—"null and void"—in English. The rest of the quotations from our conversations have been translated by me from Hindi to English.

4. HYPERTEXT

1. This is a memo prepared by the police that records that a particular witness, during the investigation, pointed out an object or place of some relevance to the investigation.

2. Witness deposition. On file with the author.

3. Lowenkron and Ferreira (2014) draw attention to the methodological issues that an engagement with documents entails. They argue that the content and mode of production of documents co-produce each other and that studying reading and writing practices of these documents helps reveal power structures.

4. Moore and Singh (2018) extend the idea that the technology employed in the legal process creates a version of reality through their idea of the "data double." By analyzing the use of visual images and video-taped testimony in domestic violence cases, they argue that the virtual image of the victim of domestic violence comes to stand in for the actual person.

5. *Masooda Parveen v Union of India* (2007) 4 SCC 548.

6. Page C of the Supreme Court file, Writ Petition No. 275/1999, hereafter referred to as "Court file." On file with the author.

7. The People's Union for Civil Liberties notes that the "'encounter' . . . [is the] unique contribution of the police in India to the vocabulary of human rights. . . . [It involves the] taking into custody of an individual or a group, torture and subsequent murder. The death generally occurs as a result of brutal torture or a stage-managed extermination. . . . An official press release then elaborately outlines a confrontation, an encounter where the police claim to have fired in 'self-defence.'" (People's Union for Civil Liberties 1982, n.p.).

8. Court file 49–50 (counter-affidavit filed by the Union of India).

9. Court file 62 (Rejoinder-affidavit filed by Masooda Parveen).

10. Supreme Court order dated March 3, 2006, on file with author.

11. Supreme Court order dated April 19, 2006, on file with author.

12. Supreme Court order dated April 19, 2006, on file with author.

13. The table is adapted from People's Union for Democratic Rights (2007, 11).

14. Court file 68 (affidavit on behalf of the State of Jammu and Kashmir).

15. Court file 145 (affidavit of the district magistrate of Pulwama).

16. Court file 144 (affidavit of the district magistrate of Pulwama).

17. Court file 151–52 (affidavit of the district magistrate of Pulwama).

18. *Masooda Parveen v. Union of India* (2007) 4 SCC 548, para 12.

19. Judgment, paragraph 6, on file with the author.

5. CERTIFICATION AND THE FABRICATION OF TRUTHS

1. This idea of evidence-as-a-process also is present in the Indian Evidence Act, 1872. Its main author argued that the word confuses the distinction "between the testimony on which a fact is believed and the fact itself" (Stephen 1872, 6). Hence, under the act, "evidence" was not proof, and nor was it a fact, but rather it was a process to prove or disprove the existence of a fact.

2. From the eighteenth century onward, English law began to experiment with a number of ways to ensure the truth of the facts found by the trial process. Bentham (1843) thought the probity of the testimony presented in court could be ensured by making the trial more public. Schneider (2015) describes methods employed by Victorian courts in England and India— from increased perjury prosecutions, to punitive tattooing for lying in court, to testing testimony against the reputation of classes of people. Singha (1998, 46–47) investigated oaths and truth-telling in courts in early colonial India.

3. Latour's failure to consider how legal facts are created by material processes is probably because he is focused on an appellate court where "facts" are less in contention and because he was not present during the birth of the file (as he was in his scientific work mentioned above).

4. This idea that the file can produce its own regime of facts has been noted by a number of scholars such as Tarlo (2003), Dery (1998), and Vismann (2008).

5. See also Vismann (2008, 7, 77–78).

6. I have not discussed these documents in the interest of being concise.

7. In common law jurisdictions in the United States and the UK these types of testimonies may be referred to as "stipulations," where both parties agree, or stipulate, to certain facts, so that they do not have to argue them.

8. See Inoue (2018), who argues that ethnographic attention to verbatim technologies can reveal important political characteristics of institutions. Here, I contend that transcription practices in the courtroom point to the primacy of written documents over orality.

9. "ExPW" translates to "exhibit prosecution witness." This is followed by the witness number (10) and the number of the document being exhibited (A, B, etc.)

10. As Berti (2015) notes, these types of negative sentences "are aimed at providing the lawyer's version of the story through the witness's denial of what he [the lawyer] appears to be stating" (31).

6. PETITION WRITING

1. My effort here is not so much to look at the idea of writing through speech act theory—though this has been done, notably by Derrida (1977) and Das (2004)—but rather to trace the perlocutionary through these forms of writing.

2. Historians have pointed to the centrality of the letter to the legal systems of Europe (Bazerman 2000; Goodrich 1997; Schneider 2000; van Voss 2001) and South Asia (Mohiuddin 1971; Bayly 2000; Raman 2012). The letter was a key mode of operation of power, and epistolography was a key form of the state's writing. The state and legal practices were mediated by a "culture of epistolarity" (Schneider 2000), in which where relations between officials *inter se* and between the state and its subjects were governed by proper forms of epistolary behavior. Recent ethnographies have also highlighted the centrality of the letter to everyday governmentality (Hull 2012; Mathur 2016).

3. See, for example, the job card in Mathur's (2016) ethnography of lower bureaucracy in northern India or the *parchi* (chits, or slips of paper) in Hull's (2012) ethnography of the bureaucracy in Islamabad.

4. Indian law students will know that the ability to petition the Supreme Court for the enforcement of a fundamental right is itself a fundamental right. Hagiographies of India's higher judiciary will often speak of the courts' "epistolary jurisdiction." In a case titled *People's Union for Democratic Rights v. Union of India* (1982) 3 SCC 235, the Indian Supreme Court justified the creation of an "epistolary jurisdiction" in the following terms:

> Where judicial redress is sought of a legal injury or legal wrong suffered by a person or class of persons who by reason of poverty, disability or socially or economically disadvantaged position are unable to approach the court and the court is moved for this purpose by a member of a public by addressing a letter drawing the attention of the court to such legal injury or legal wrong, court would cast aside all technical rules of procedure and entertain the letter as a writ petition on the judicial side and take action upon it. (para 10)

5. *Arzdasht* is a combination of two words: *arz,* Arabic for "submission," and *dasht*, Farsi for "to have" or to "possess" (Zaidi 2005, 9).

6. Mohiuddin (1971) argues that *arzdasht* "referred to a petition (i.e. letter) submitted to the Emperor by any person from a prince to a plebeian. . . . As a matter of fact, every letter, whether private or official addressed to the Emperor is termed an *arzdasht*" (151).

7. Petitions during the Mughal period, as in England during the medieval period, were also framed in deferential, supplicatory tones and encapsulated a relationship of lordship and dependence between the author of the letter and its addressee. Petitions in these periods were a metaphor for thinking about the

relationship between the monarch and subject: "Monarchs ruled and humble subjects petitioned" (Zaret 1999, 81).

8. There are similarities between petitions written to officials and prayer-petitions written to jinns and gods. Taneja (2017) provides a fascinating account of letters written to jinns and gods in Delhi. Supplicants would write letters to jinns in terms reminiscent of legal cultures, describing places where jinns resided as *kachari* or *adalat*—words that translate as "court." Malik (2015) provides another account of the link between prayer and legal letter writing and looks at letters written on government-issued stamp paper to Golu Devta, a deity in northern India.

9. One can think of the colonial idea of petitioning as one that emerged in seventeenth- century revolutionary England. Zaeske (2003) argues that in medieval England petitions were used to deal with local problems and to redress private grievances. Prior to the English Civil War, the process of petitioning was considered a secret privilege of Parliament (Siddiqui 2005; Zaret 2000). Thereafter, the petition came to be imbued with additional significance: it became a right, and as such dovetailed with the emergence of a nascent public sphere. (Siddiqui 2005). Zaeske (2003) describes the emergence of collective petitioning by those who sought to democratize the government, especially the Levellers, who claimed an ancient and natural right to petition by all people.

10. This duality between author and addressee has enabled scholars to look at the political valences of petitions. Historians of South Asia have looked at petitions to conceptualize the shifting nature of political subjectivity, the form of political rule, and the relationships between the two (Balachandran 2019; De 2019; Raman 2019; Travers 2019; Stephens 2019). Anthropologists of South Asia have looked at petitions as modes of performing political subjectivity (Cody 2009; Mathur 2019).

11. In the late 1980s a popular movement for Kashmiri independence gathered momentum. Simultaneously, an armed insurrection also spread through the state. For a history of the freedom movement in Kashmir, see Puri (1995) and Ali (2011). At the height of the insurgency in the late 1990s many of the terrorism cases in Delhi involved Kashmiri accused. Zia (2019) has recently written about the arrests, killing and forced disappearances of men taking place under the military occupation of Kashmir, and the work of mourning by Kashmiri women.

12. Both Das and Benveniste refer to Sanskrit grammar's tripartite division of pronouns. The Sanskrit terms for the first, second, and third person are *uttam purusha* (supreme person), *madhyam purusha* (intermediate person), and *pratham purusha* (literally first person), respectively. While Benveniste (1971) transposes this structure on to the Indo-European structure of pronouns (I, you, he) (195), Das points out that the *pratham purusha* is first because the *pratham purusha* can be brought into being through discourse.

13. This is not to argue that the performative and the perlocutionary are discrete categories. Even though Austin (1962) seems to relate the performative to the illocutionary, as Laugier (2020) suggests, both "the illocutionary and the perlocutionary are two aspects of the performative" (8).

14. According to Altman (1982), the letter can be perceived both as metaphor—that is, as a trope of the author and addressee of the letter—and as a metonym, such that the letter literally stands in for the parties to the epistolary exchange (19). Here Mohsin draws attention to the metonymic quality of his letters.

15. Jamia Teachers Solidarity Association 2014.

REFERENCES

Agamben, Giorgio. 1998. *Homo Sacer: Sovereign Power and Bare Life*. Translated by Daniel Heller-Roazen. Stanford: Stanford University Press.

Agamben, Giorgio. 2005. *State of Exception*. Translated by Kevin Attell. Chicago: University of Chicago Press.

Ahmad, Irfan. 2014. "Kafka in India: Terrorism, Media, Muslims." In *Being Muslims in South Asia: Diversity and Daily Life*, edited by Robin Jeffrey and Ronjoy Sen, 289–329. New Delhi: Oxford University Press.

Ali, Tariq. 2011. "The Story of Kashmir." In *Kashmir: The Case for Freedom*, edited by Tariq Ali, Hilal Bhatt, Angana P. Chatterji, Habbah Khatun, Pankaj Mishra, and Arundhati Roy, 7–56. London: Verso.

Altman, Janet Gurkin. 1982. *Epistolarity: Approaches to a Form*. Columbus: Ohio State University Press.

Andhra Pradesh Civil Liberties Committee. 1985. *"Encounter" Deaths in Andhra Pradesh*. Hyderabad: Andhra Pradesh Civil Liberties Committee.

Aretxaga, Begoña. 2005. *States of Terror: Begoña Aretxaga's Essays*. Edited by Joseba Zulaika. Reno: Center for Basque Studies, University of Nevada.

Arnold, David. 1986. *Police Power and Colonial Rule: Madras 1859–1947*. Delhi: Oxford: University Press.

Austin, J. L. 1962 *How to Do Things with Words*. Oxford: Clarendon Press.

Balachandran, Aparna. 2019. "Petitions, the City and the Early Colonial State in South India." *Modern Asian Studies* 53, no. 1: 150–76.

Balagopal, K. 1989. "Drought and TADA in Adilabad." *Economic and Political Weekly* 24, no. 47: 2587–91.

Balagopal, K. 1994. "In Defence of India: Supreme Court and Terrorism." *Economic and Political Weekly* 29, no. 32: 2054–60.

Baxi, Pratiksha. 2014. *Public Secrets of Law: Rape Trials in India*. New Delhi: Oxford University Press.

Baxi, Upendra. 1992. "The State's Emissary: The Place of Law in Subaltern Studies." In *Subaltern Studies VII*, edited by Partha Chatterjee and Gyanendra Pandey. Delhi: Oxford University Press.

Baxi, Upendra. 1999. "Constitutionalism as a Site of State Formative Practices." *Cardozo Law Review* 21, no. 4: 1183–210.

Bayly, C. A. 2000. *Empire and Information: Intelligence Gathering and Social Communication in India, 1780–1870.* Cambridge: Cambridge University Press.

Bazerman, Charles. 2000. "Letters and Social Grounding of Different Genres." In *Letter Writing as a Social Practice.* Edited by David Barton and Nigel Hall, 15–30. Amsterdam: John Benjamins.

Benjamin, Walter. 1978. "Critique of Violence." In *Reflections: Essays, Aphorisms, Autobiographical Writings*, edited by Peter Demetz, 277–300. New York: Harcourt Brace Jovanovich.

Bentham, Jeremy. 1843. *The Works of Jeremy Bentham, Vol. 6. Published under the Superintendence of his Executor, John Bowring.* Edinburgh: William Tait, 1843. http://oll.libertyfund.org/titles/1923#Bentham_0872-06_239.

Benveniste, Emile. 1971. *Problems in General Linguistics.* Miami, FL: University of Miami Press.

Bernstein, Anya. 2018. "Democratizing Interpretation." *William & Mary Law Review* 60, no. 2: 435–506.

Berti, Daniela. 2009. "Hostile Witnesses, Judicial Interactions and Out-of-Court Narratives in a North Indian District Court" *Contributions to Indian Sociology* 44, no. 3: 235–63.

Berti, Daniela. 2011. "Courts of Law and Legal Practice." In *A Companion to the Anthropology of India*, edited by Isabelle Clark-Decès, 353–70. Oxford: Blackwell.

Berti, Daniela. 2015. "Technicalities of Doubting: Temple Consultations and Criminal Trials in India." In *Of Doubt and Proof: Ritual and Legal Practices of Judgment*, edited by Daniela Berti, Anthony Good, and Gilles Tarabout, 19–38. Farnham: Ashgate.

Bix, Brian. 1991. "H. L. A. Hart and the 'Open Texture' of Language." *Law and Philosophy* 10, no. 1: 51–72.

Boltanski, Luc. 2014. *Mysteries and Conspiracies: Detective Stories, Spy Novels and the Making of Modern Societies.* Translated by Catherine Porter. Cambridge: Polity Press.

Bourdieu, Pierre. 1987. "The Force of Law: Towards a Sociology of the Juridical Field." *Hastings Law Journal* 38, no. 5: 814–53.

Bunt, L. 2008. "A Quest for Justice in Cuzco, Peru: Race and Evidence in the Case of Mercedes Corimanya Lavilla." *Political and Legal Anthropology Review* 31, no. 2: 286–302.

Burns, Robert P. 1999. *A Theory of the Trial.* Princeton, NJ: Princeton University Press.

Carson, Anne. 2013. *Red Doc>*. London: Jonathan Cape.

Cavell, Stanley. 1976. *Must We Mean What We Say?* Cambridge: Cambridge University Press.

Cavell, Stanley. 1990. *Conditions Handsome and Unhandsome: The Constitution of Emersonian Perfectionism*. Chicago: University of Chicago Press.

Cavell, Stanley. 1992. *The Senses of Walden: An Expanded Edition*. Chicago: University of Chicago Press.

Cavell, Stanley. 1994. *A Pitch of Philosophy: Autobiographical Exercises*. Cambridge, MA: Harvard University Press.

Cavell, Stanley. 1995. *Philosophical Passages: Wittgenstein, Emerson, Austin, Derrida* Oxford: Blackwell.

Cavell, Stanley, 2004. *Cities of Words: Pedagogical Letters on a Register of the Moral Life*. Cambridge, MA: Harvard University Press.

Cavell, Stanley. 2005. *Philosophy the Day after Tomorrow*. Cambridge, MA: The Belknap Press of Harvard University Press)

Chatterjee, Moyukh. 2017. "The Impunity Effect: Majoritarian Rule, Everyday Legality, and State Formation in India." *American Ethnologist* 44, no. 1: 118–30.

Chomsky, Noam. 2005. "Manipulation of Fear." In *December 13: Terror over Democracy*, edited by Nirmalangshu Mukherji, ix–xvii. New Delhi: Promilla.

Chowdhury, A. N., and A. Brahma. 2005. "An Epidemic of Mass Hysteria in a Village in West Bengal." *Indian Journal of Psychiatry* 47, no. 2: 106–8.

Clarke, Charles E. 1938. "The Handmaid of Justice." *Washington University Law Quarterly* 23, no. 3: 298–320.

Cody, Francis. 2009. "Inscribing Subjects to Citizenship: Petitions, Literacy Activism and the Performativity of Signature in Rural Tamil India." *Cultural Anthropology* 24, no. 3: 347–80.

Cohn, Bernard. 1965. "Anthropological Notes on Disputes and Law in India." *American Anthropologist* 67, no. 6: 82–122.

Comaroff, Jean, and John Comaroff. 2006. "Criminal Obsessions, after Foucault: Postcoloniality, Policing and the Metaphysics of Disorder." In *Law and Disorder in the Postcolony*, edited by Jean Comaroff and John Comaroff, 273–98. Chicago: University of Chicago Press.

Comaroff, John. 2013. "Foreword." In: *Policing and Contemporary Governance: The Anthropology of Police in Practice*, edited by William Garriott, xi–xxii. New York: Palgrave Macmillan.

Comaroff, John, and Simon Roberts. 1981. *Rules and Processes: The Cultural Logic of a Dispute in an African Context*. Chicago: University of Chicago Press.

Conley, John, and William O'Barr. 1990. *Rules versus Relationships: The Ethnography of Legal Discourse*. Chicago: University of Chicago Press.

Conley, John, and William O'Barr. 2005. *Just Words: Law, Language and Power*. Chicago: University of Chicago Press.

Constable, Marianne. 2014. *Our Word Is Our Bond: How Legal Speech Acts.*
Stanford, CA: Stanford University Press.

Coombe, Rosemary. 1997 "The Demonic Place of the 'Not There': Trademark
Rumours in the Postindustrial Imaginary." In *Culture, Power, Place: Explorations
in Critical Anthropology*, edited by Akhil Gupta and James Ferguson, 249–76.
Durham, NC: Duke University Press.

Coordination of Democratic Rights Organisations. 2012. *The Terror of Law: UAPA
and the Myth of National Security.* Pamphlet.

Cover, Robert. 1983. "Nomos and Narrative." *Harvard Law Review* 97, no. 1: 3–68.

Das, Veena. 1998. "Wittgenstein and Anthropology." *Annual Review of Anthropology* 27: 171–95.

Das, Veena. 2004. "The Signature of the State: The Paradox of Illegibility." In
Anthropology in the Margins of the State, edited by V. Das and D. Poole,
225–52. Santa Fe, NM: School of American Research Press.

Das, Veena. 2007. *Life and Words: Violence and the Descent into the Ordinary.*
London: University of California Press.

Das, Veena. 2015. "What Does Ordinary Ethics Look Like?" In *Four Lectures on
Ethics: Anthropological Perspectives*, 53–126. Chicago: Has Books.

Das, Veena. 2018. "Ethics, Self-Knowledge, and Life Taken as a Whole." *HAU:
Journal of Ethnographic Theory* 8, no. 3: 537–49.

De, Rohit. 2014. "Rebellion, Dacoity and Equality: The Emergence of the
Constitutional Field in Postcolonial India." *Comparative Studies in South Asia,
Africa and the Middle East* 34, no. 2: 260–78.

De, Rohit. 2018. *A People's Constitution: The Everyday Life of Law in the Indian
Republic.* Princeton, NJ: Princeton University Press.

De, Rohit. 2019. "Cows and Constitutionalism." *Modern Asian Studies* 53, no. 1:
240–77.

Deccan Herald. 2012. "Monkeys in Tis Hazari Courts Guilty as Charged."
September 25. http://www.deccanherald.com/content/280937/monkeys-tis
-hazari-courts-guilty.html.

Deleuze, Giles, and Felix Guattari. 1986. *Kafka: Toward a Minor Literature.*
Translated by Dana Polan. Minneapolis: University of Minnesota Press.

Delhi District Courts. 2014. "Judicial Officers at Delhi District Courts." http://
delhicourts.nic.in/thc_08.htm.

Derrida, Jacques. 1977. "Signature Event Context." In *Limited Inc.* , edited by
Gerald Graff. Evanston, IL: Northwestern University Press.

Derrida, Jacques. 1992. "Force of Law: The 'Mystical Foundations of Authority.'"
In *Deconstruction and the Possibility of Justice*, edited by Drucilla Cornell,
Michel Rosenfeld, and David Gary Carlson, 3–67. London: Routledge.

Dery, David. 1998. "'Papereality' and Learning in Bureaucratic Organisations."
Administration and Society 29, no. 6: 677–88.

Dirks, Nicholas. 2015. *Autobiography of an Archive: A Scholar's Passage to India.* New York: Columbia University Press.

Duffy, Maureen. 2018. *Detention of Terrorism Suspects: Political Discourse and Fragmented Practices.* Oxford: Hart Publishing.

Dugger, Celia. 2001. "Delhi Journal; Beware Monkey-Man, Scourge of the Gullible." *New York Times*, May 19. http://www.nytimes.com/2001/05/19/world /delhi-journal- beware-monkey-man-scourge-of-the-gullible.html.

Dworkin, Ronald. 1982. "Law as Interpretation." *Critical Inquiry* 9, no. 1: 179–200.

Dworkin, Ronald. 1986. *Law's Empire.* Cambridge, MA: Harvard University Press.

Eckert, Julia. 2005. *The Trimurti of the State: State Violence and the Promises of Order and Destruction.* Max Planck Institute for Social Anthropology Working Papers, no. 80. http://www.eth.mpg.de/cms/de/publications/working _papers/w p0080.html.

Eckert, Julia. 2009. "Law for Enemies." In *The Social Life of Anti-Terror Laws: The War on Terror and the Classification of the "Dangerous Other*, edited by Julia Eckert, 7–31. London: Transaction Publishers.

Economic and Political Weekly. 2000. "TADA: Hard Law for a Soft State." *Economic and Political Weekly* 35, no. 13: 1066–71.

Engelke, Matthew. 2009."The Objects of Evidence." In *The Objects of Evidence: Anthropological Approaches to the Production of Knowledge*, edited by Matthew Engelke, 1–20. Oxford: Blackwell.

Ertür, Basak. 2015. "Spectacles and Spectres: Political Trials, Performativity and Scenes of sovereignty." PhD diss., Birkbeck, University of London.

Ewick, Patricia, and Susan Silbey. 1995. "Subversive Stories and Hegemonic Tales: Towards a Sociology of Narrative." *Law & Society Review* 29, no. 2: 197–226.

Fair, C. Christine. 2018. *In Their Own Words: Understanding the Laskhar-e-Taaba.* Oxford: Oxford University Press.

Fassin, Didier. 2005. "Compassion and Repression: The Moral Economy of Immigration Policies in France." *Cultural Anthropology* 20, no. 3: 362–87.

Fassin, Didier. 2013. *Enforcing Order: An Ethnography of Urban Policing.* Cambridge: Polity Press.

Felman, Shoshana. 2002. *The Juridical Unconscious: Trials and Traumas in the Twentieth Century.* Cambridge, MA: Harvard University Press.

Ferguson, James. 1994. *The Anti-Politics Machine: "Development," Depoliticization, and Bureaucratic Power in Lesotho.* Minneapolis: University of Minnesota Press.

Ferreira, Arun. 2014. *Colours of the Cage: A Prison Memoir.* New Delhi: Aleph Book Company.

Fish, Stanley. 1980. *Is There a Text in This Class? The Authority of Interpretive Communities.* Cambridge, MA: Harvard University Press.

Fish, Stanley. 1982a. "Interpretation and the Pluralist Vision." *Texas Law Review* 60, no. 3: 495–505.

Fish, Stanley. 1982b. "Working on the Chain Gang: Interpretation in the Law and in Literary Criticism." *Critical Inquiry* 9, no. 1: 201–16.

Foucault, Michel. 1994. "Self Writing." In *Ethics: Subjectivity and Truth*, edited by Paul Rabinow, 207–22. New York: The New Press.

Galanter, Marc. 1968–69. "The Study of the Indian Legal Profession." *Law and Society Review* 3, no. 2/3: 201–17.

Galanter, Marc. 1992. *Law and Society in Modern India*. Oxford: Oxford University Press.

Galloway, Fraser. 2011. "Anti-Terrorism Resolutions: The Security Council's Threat to the UN System." *Journal of Terrorism Research* 2, no. 3: 105–25.

Ghosh, Durba. 2017. *Gentlemanly Terrorists: Political Violence and the Colonial State in India, 1919–1947*. New York: Cambridge University Press.

Gluckman, Max. 1955. *The Judicial Process among the Barotse of Northern Rhodesia*. Manchester: Manchester University Press.

Goodale, Mark. 2017. *Anthropology and Law: A Critical Introduction*. New York: New York University Press.

Goodman, Ryan. 2001. "Beyond the Enforcement Principle: Sodomy Laws, Social Norms, and Social Panoptics." *California Law Review* 89: no. 3: 643–740.

Goodrich, Peter. 1987. *Legal Discourse: Studies in Linguistics, Rhetoric and Legal Analysis*. London: Macmillan.

Goodrich, Peter. 2013. "Epistolary Justice: The Love Letter as Law." *Yale Journal of Law and the Humanities* 9, no. 2: 245–95.

Greene, Jody. 2008. "Hostis Humani Generis." *Critical Inquiry* 34, no. 4: 683–705.

Guha, Ranajit. 1999. *Elementary Aspects of Peasant Insurgency in Colonial India*. Durham, NC: Duke University Press.

Gupta, Akhil. 1995. "Blurred Boundaries: The Discourse of Corruption, the Culture of Politics and the Imagined State." *American Ethnologist* 22, no. 2: 375–402.

Gupta, Akhil. 2012. *Red Tape: Bureaucracy, Structural Violence and Poverty in India*. Durham, NC: Duke University Press.

Haldar, Piyel. 1994. "In and out of Court: On Topographies of Law and the Architecture of Court Buildings (a Study of the Supreme Court of Israel)." *International Journal for the Semiotics of Law* 7, no. 20: 185–200.

Han, Clara. 2013. "A Long-Term Occupation: Police and the Figures of the Stranger." *Social Anthropology* 21, no. 3: 378–84.

Hart, H. L. A. 1958. "Positivism and the Separation of Law and Morals." *Harvard Law Review* 71, no. 4, 593–629.

Hart, H. L. A. 2012. *The Concept of Law*, 3rd ed. Oxford University Press.

Hastrup, Kirsten. 2004. "Getting It Right: Knowledge and Evidence in Anthropology." *Anthropological Theory* 4, no. 4): 455–72.

Havel, Vaclav. 1990. *Letters to Olga: June 1979—September 1982*. Translated by Paul Wilson. London: Faber and Faber.

Hayden, Robert M. 2002. "Antagonistic Tolerance: Competitive Sharing of Religious Sites in South Asia and the Balkans." *Current Anthropology* 43, no. 2: 205–31.

Heidegger, Martin. 1977. *The Question Concerning Technology and Other Essays.* Translated by W. Lovitt. New York: Harper & Row.

Herbert, Bob. 2006. "The Kafka Strategy." *New York Times*, September 18. https://www.nytimes.com/2006/09/18/opinion/18herbert.html.

Hull, Matthew. 2003. "The File: Agency, Authority, and Autography in an Islamabad Bureaucracy." *Language and Communication* 23, no. 3: 287–314.

Hull, Matthew. 2012. *Government of Paper: The Materiality of Bureaucracy in Urban Pakistan.* Berkeley: University of California Press.

Human Rights Watch. 2011. *The "Anti-Nationals:" Arbitrary Detention and Torture of Terrorism Suspects in India.* https://www.hrw.org/sites/default/files/reports/india0211W.pdf.

Hussain, Nasser. 2003. *The Jurisprudence of Emergency: Colonialism and the Rule of Law.* Ann Arbor: University of Michigan Press.

Hussain, Nasser. 2007a. "Beyond Norm and Exception: Guantanamo." *Critical Inquiry* 33, no. 4: 734–53.

Hussain, Nasser. 2007b. "Hyperlegality." *New Criminal Law Review* 10, no. 4: 514–31.

Indorewalla, Sharmeen Hakim. 2013. "7/11 Accused Uses RTI to Pick Holes in ATS Theory." *Mumbai Mirror*, May 7. http://www.mumbaimirror.com/mumbai/crime/7/11-accused- uses-RTI-to-pick-holes-in-ATS-theory/articleshow/19922381.cms.

Ingold, Tim. 1995. "Building, Dwelling, Living: How Animals and People Make Themselves at Home in the World" In *Shifting Contexts: Transformations in Anthropological Knowledge*, edited by M. Strathern, 57–80. London: Routledge.

Ingold, Tim. 2010. "The Textility of Making." *Cambridge Journal of Economics* 34, no. 1: 91–102.

Ingold, Tim. 2011. *Being Alive: Essays on Movement, Knowledge and Description.* Oxon: Routledge.

Ingold, Tim. 2013. *Making: Anthropology, Archaeology, Art and Architecture.* Oxon: Routledge.

Inoue, Miyako. 2018. "Word for Word: Verbatim as Political Technologies." *Annual Review of Anthropology* 47: 217–32.

International People's Tribunal on Human Rights and Justice in Indian-Administered Kashmir and Association of Parents of Disappeared Persons. 2015. *Structures of Violence: The Indian State in Jammu and Kashmir.* Srinagar: Jammu Kashmir Coalition of Civil Society.

Jaleel, Muzamil. 2015. "Hurriyat: Its History, Role and Relevance." *Indian Express*, August 31. https://indianexpress.com/article/explained/hurriyat-its-history-role-and-relevance/.

Jamia Teachers Solidarity Association. 2014. *Damned, Framed and Acquitted: Dossiers on a "Very" Special Cell.* Delhi: n.p.

Jammu and Kashmir Coalition of Civil Society. 2014. *The Anatomy of a Massacre: The Mass Killings at Sailan August 3–4, 1998.* Srinagar: Jammu and Kashmir Coalition of Civil Society.

Jauregui, Beatrice. 2011. "Law and Order: Police Encounter Killings and Routinized Political Violence." In *A Companion to the Anthropology of India*, edited by Isabelle Clarke-Deces, 371–88. Oxon: Blackwell.

Jauregui, Beatrice. 2016. *Provisional Authority: Police, Order and Security in India.* Chicago: University of Chicago Press.

Judicial Committee District Courts of Delhi. 2008. *District Courts of Delhi: Annual Report.*

Kafka, Ben. 2012. *The Demon of Writing: Powers and Failures of Paperwork.* New York: Zone Books.

Kalhan, Anil, Gerald Conroy, Mamta Kaushal, Sam Miller, and Jed Rakoff. 2006. "Colonial Continuities: Human Rights, Terrorism and Security Laws in India." *Columbia Journal of Asian Law* 20, no. 1: 93–234.

Kannabiran, K. G. 2004. *The Wages of Impunity: Power, Justice and Human Rights.* Hyderabad: Orient Longman.

Kannabiran, Kalpana. 2014. *Tools of Justice: Non-Discrimination and the Indian Constitution.* New Delhi: Routledge.

Kelly, Tobias. 2012. "Sympathy and Suspicion: Torture, Asylum and Humanity." *Journal of the Royal Anthropological Institute* 18, no. 4: 753–68.

Khan, Mohammad Amir. 2016. *Framed as a Terrorist: My 14-Year Struggle to Prove My Innocence.* Delhi: Speaking Tiger Books.

Khanikar, Santana. 2018. *State, Violence and Legitimacy in India.* New Delhi: Oxford University Press.

Khorakiwala, Rahela. 2020. *From the Colonial to the Contemporary: Images, Iconography, Memories, and Performances of Law in India's High Courts.* London: Hart Publishing.

Kripke, Saul. 1982. *Wittgenstein on Rules and Private Language: An Elementary Exposition.* Cambridge, MA: Harvard University Press.

Krishnan, Jayant. 2004. "India's Patriot Act: POTA and the Impact on Civil Liberties in the World's Largest Democracy." *Law and Inequality* 22, no. 2: 265–300.

Kumar, Ram Narayan, Amrik Singh, Ashok Agrwaal, and Jaskaran Kaur. 2003. *Reduced to Ashes: The Insurgency and Human Rights in Punjab.* Kathmandu: South Asia Forum for Human Rights.

Latour, Bruno. 1999. "Circulating Reference: Sampling the Soil in the Amazon Forest." In *Pandora's Hope: Essays on the Reality of Science Studies*, 24–79. Cambridge, MA: Harvard University Press.

Latour, Bruno. 2010. *The Making of Law: An Ethnography of the Conseil d'Etat.* Translated by Marina Brilman and Alain Pottage. Cambridge: Polity Press.

Laugier, Sandra. 2020. "Encounters of the Third Kind: Performative Utterances and Forms of Life." *Inquiry: An Interdisciplinary Journal of Philosophy.* doi: 10.1080/0020174X.2020.1784785.

Lefebvre, Alexandre. 2005. "A New Image of Law: Deleuze and Jurisprudence." *Telos* 130, Spring: 103–26.

Lefebvre, Alexandre. 2008. *The Image of Law: Deleuze, Bergson, Spinoza.* Stanford, CA: Stanford University Press.

Lefebvre, Alexandre. 2011. "Law and the Ordinary: Hart, Wittgenstein, Jurisprudence." *Telos* 154, Spring: 99–118.

Lessig, Lawrence. 1998. "The New Chicago School." *Journal of Legal Studies* 27, no. S2: 661–91.

Liang, Lawrence. 2005. "Porous Legalities and Avenues of Participation." In *Sarai Reader 05: Bare Acts,* edited by Monica Narula, Shuddhabrata Sengupta, Jeebesh Bagchi, Geert Lovink, and Lawrence Liang. Delhi: Sarai/CSDS.

Lokaneeta, Jinee. 2020. *Truth Machines: Policing, Violence and Scientific Interrogations in India.* Ann Arbor: University of Michigan Press.

Lorenzini, Daniele. 2015. "Performative, Passionate and Parrhesiastic Utterance: On Cavell, Foucault and Truth as an Ethical Force." *Critical Inquiry* 41, no. 2): 254–68.

Lorenzini, Daniele. 2020. "From Recognition to Acknowledgement: Rethinking the Perlocutionary." *Inquiry: An Interdisciplinary Journal of Philosophy.* https://doi.org/10.1080/0020174X.2020.1712231.

Lowenkron, Laura, and Leticia Ferreira. 2014. "Anthropological Perspectives on Documents: Ethnographic Dialogues on the Trail of Police Papers." *Vibrant—Virtual Brazilian Anthropology* 11, no. 2. http://www.vibrant.org.br/issues/v11n2/laura-lowenkron-leticia-ferreira-anthropological-perspectives-on-documents-ethnographic-dialogues-on-the-trail-of-police-papers/.

Main, Thomas O. 2009–10. "The Procedural Foundation of Substantive Law." *Washington University Law Review* 87, no. 4: 801–41.

Malik, Aditya. 2015. "The Darbar of Goludev: Possessions, Petitions and Modernity." In *The Law of Possession: Ritual, Healing and the Secular State,* edited by William S. Sax and Helen Basu, 193–225. New York: Oxford University Press.

Malimath, V. S., S. Varadachary, Amitabh Gupta, Madhava Menon, Subba Rao, and Durgadas Gupta. 2003. *Report of the Committee on Reforms of Criminal Justice System.* Bangalore: Government of India. https://mha.gov.in/sites/default/files/criminal_justice_system.pdf.

Mathur, Nayanika. 2016. *Paper Tiger: Law, Bureaucracy and the Developmental State in Himalayan India*. Cambridge: Cambridge University Press.

Mathur, Nayanika. 2019. "A Petition to Kill: Efficacious Arzees Against Big Cats in India." *Modern Asian Studies* 53, no. 1: 278–311

Mbembé, Achille. 2003. "Necropolitics." Translated by Libby Meintjes. *Public Culture* 15, no. 1: 11–40.

McQuade, Joseph. 2021. *A Genealogy of Terrorism: Colonial Law and the Origins of an Idea*. New York: Cambridge University Press.

Merry, Sally Engle. 1990. *Getting Justice and Getting Even: Legal Consciousness among Working-Class Americans*. Chicago: University of Chicago Press.

Mertz, Elizabeth. 1994. "Legal Language: Pragmatics, Poetics and Social Power." *Annual Review of Anthropology* 23: 435–55.

Mertz, Elizabeth. 2007. *The Language of Law School: Learning to "Think like a Lawyer."* Oxford: Oxford University Press.

Mertz, Elizabeth, and Jothie Rajah. 2014. "Language-and-Law Scholarship: An Interdisciplinary Conversation and a Post-9/11 Example." *Annual Review of Law and Social Sciences* 10: 169–83.

Minault, Gail. 1982. *The Khilafat Movement: Religious Symbolism and Political Mobilization in India*. New York: Columbia University Press.

Mishra, Abhinandan. 2013. "The Curious Case of Delhi's Controversial Special Cell." *Sunday Guardian*, March 30. http://www.sunday-guardian.com /investigation/the-curious-case-of-delhis-controversial-special-cell.

Mody, Peervez. 2008. *The Intimate State: Love-Marriage and the Law in Delhi*. New Delhi: Routledge.

Mohiuddin, Momin. 1971. *The Chancellery and Persian Epistolography under the Mughals: From Babur to Shah Jahan, 1526–1658*. Calcutta: Iran Society.

Moir, Martin. 1996. "*Kaghazi Raj*: Notes on the Documentary Basis of Company Rule, 1773–1858." *Indo-British Review: A Journal of History* 21, no. 2: 185–93.

Montfort, Nick. 2003. "Introduction: The Garden of Forking Paths." In *The New Media Reader*, 29–30, edited by Noah Wardrip-Fruin and Nick Montfort. Cambridge, MA: MIT Press.

Moore, Dawn, and Rashmee Singh. 2018. "Seeing Crime, Feeling Crime: Visual Evidence, Emotions, and the Prosecution of Domestic Violence." *Theoretical Criminology* 22, no. 1: 116–32.

Mukherji, Nirmanlangshu. 2005. *December 13: Terror over Democracy*. New Delhi: Promilla.

Mulcahy, Linda. 2007. "Architects of Justice: The Politics of Courtroom Design" *Social and Legal Studies* 16, no. 3: 383–403.

Nader, Laura. 1965. "The Anthropological Study of Law." *American Anthropologist* 67, no. 6, part 2: 3–32.

Nader, Laura. 2002. *Life of the Law: Anthropological Projects*. Berkeley: University of California Press.

National Crimes Record Bureau. 2017. *Crime in India 2016*. New Delhi: Ministry of Home Affairs.

Navlakha, Gautam. 2003. "POTA: Freedom to Terrorise." *Economic and Political Weekly* 38, no. 29: 3038–40.

Nigam, Chander. 2004. "Tis Hazari Diaries." In *Sarai Reader 05: Bare Acts*, 360–98. edited by Monica Narula, Shuddhabrata Sengupta, Jeebesh Bagchi, Geert Lovink, and Lawrence Liang. New Delhi: Sarai/CSDS.

Nugent, David. 2010. "States, Secrecy, Subversives: APRA and Political Fantasy in Mid-20th-Century Peru." *American Ethnologist* 37, no. 4: 681–702.

Ochs, Elinor, and Lisa Capps. 1996. "Narrating the Self." *Annual Review of Anthropology* 25: 19–43.

Onions, C. 2006. *The Oxford Dictionary of English Etymology*. Oxford: Clarendon Press.

Parmar, Pooja. 2015. *Indigeneity and Legal Pluralism in India: Claims, Histories, Meanings*. Cambridge: Cambridge University Press.

Pandey, Shikha. 2020. "Anti-Terrorism Courts and Procedural (In)justice: The Case of the National Investigation Agency (NIA) Special Courts in South Chhattisgarh, India." *Socio-Legal Review* 16, no. 1: 109–39.

Peluso, Nancy Lee. 2017. "Agrarian Classics Review Series: *Whigs and Hunters: The Origins of the Black Act*, by E. P. Thompson" *Journal of Peasant Studies* 44, no. 1: 309–21.

People's Union for Civil Liberties. 1982. *Murder by Encounter*. Delhi.

People's Union for Civil Liberties. 1985. *Black Laws*. Delhi.

People's Union for Democratic Rights. 2007. *Missing in Action: A Report on the Judiciary, Justice and Army Impunity in Kashmir*. New Delhi: People's Union for Democratic Rights.

Philips, Susan. 1994. "Local Legal Hegemony in the Tongan Magistrate's Court: How Sisters Fare Better than Wives." In *Contested States: Law, Hegemony and Resistance*, edited by M. Lazarus-Black, S. F. Hirsch, and S. Hirsch, 59–88. New York: Routledge.

Philips. Susan. 2000. "Constructing a Tongan Nation-State through Language Ideology in the Courtroom." In *Regimes of Language: Ideologies, Polities and Identities*, edited by P. Kroskrity, 229–57. Santa Fe, NM: School of American Research Press.

Phipps, Alison. 2015. "What Is Revealed by the Absence of a Reply? Courtesy, Pedagogy, and the Spectre of Unanswered Letters in Mandela's Trial." In *The Courtroom as a Space of Resistance: Reflections on the Legacy of the Rivonia Trial*, edited by Awol Allo, 241–62. Oxon: Routledge.

Pottage, Alain. 2012. "The Materiality of What?" *Journal of Law and Society* 39, no. 1: 167–83.

Pottage, Alain. 2014. "Law after Anthropology: Object and Technique in Roman Law." *Theory, Culture & Society* 31, no. 2/3: 147–66.

Pound, Roscoe. 2002. *Social Control through Law.* London: Transaction Publishers.

Power, Michael. 1997. *The Audit Society: Rituals of Verification.* Oxford: Oxford University Press.

Puri, Balraj. 1995. *Kashmir: Towards Insurgency.* Hyderabad: Orient Longman.

Raman, Bhavani. 2012. *Document Raj: Writing and Scribes in Early Colonial South India.* Chicago: University of Chicago Press.

Raman, Bhavani. 2019. "Civil Address and the Early Colonial Petitions in Madras." *Modern Asian Studies* 53, no. 1: 123–49.

Ran-Rubin, M. 2008. "Keeping the Peace: A Tale of Murder and Morality in Post-Apartheid South Africa." *Political and Legal Anthropology Review* 31, no. 2: 243–63.

Richland, Justin. 2013. "Jurisdiction: Grounding Law in Language." *Annual Review of Anthropology* 42: 209–26.

Riles, Annelise. 2000. *The Network Inside Out.* Ann Arbor: University of Michigan Press.

Riles, Annelise. 2004. "Property as Legal Knowledge: Means and Ends." *Journal of the Royal Anthropological Institute* 10, no. 4: 775–95.

Riles, Annelise. 2005. "A New Agenda for the Cultural Study of Law: Taking on the Technicalities." *Buffalo Law Review* 53, no. 3: 973–1033.

Riles, Annelise. 2011. *Collateral Knowledge: Legal Reasoning in the Global Financial Markets.* Chicago: University of Chicago Press.

Risinger, D. Michael. 1982. "'Substance' and 'Procedure' Revisited with Some Afterthoughts on the Constitutional Problems of 'Irrebuttable Presumptions.'" *UCLA Law Review* 30, no. 2: 189–216.

Roy, Arundhati. 2006. "Introduction: Breaking the News." In *December 13: A Reader. The Strange Case of the Attack on the Indian Parliament*, edited by Arundhati Roy, ix–xxi. New Delhi: Penguin.

Rubin, J. 2008. "Adjudicating the Salvadoran Civil War: Expectations of the Law in *Romagoza*." *Political and Legal Anthropology Review* 31, no. 2: 264–85.

Rutherford, Danilyn. 2009. "Sympathy, State Building and the Experience of Empire." *Cultural Anthropology* 24, no. 1: 1–32.

Sadiq, Kamal. 2008. *Paper Citizens: How Illegal Immigrants Acquire Citizenship in Developing Countries.* Oxford: Oxford University Press.

Samaddar, Ranabir. 2006. "Law and Terror in the Age of Colonial Constitution Making." *Diogenes* 53, no. 4; 18–33.

Sanín-Restrepo, Ricardo, and Gabriel Méndez Hincapíe. 2018. "The Encrypted Constitution: New Ways of Emancipation from Global Power." In *Decrypting Power*, edited by Ricardo Sanín-Restrepo. London: Rowman & Littlefield.

Sarat, Austin, and Thomas Kearns. 1995. "Beyond the Great Divide: Forms of Legal Scholarship and Everyday Life." In *Law in Everyday Life*, edited by Austin Sarat and Thomas Kearns, 21–62. Ann Arbor: University of Michigan Press.

Scheffer, Thomas. 2004. "Materialities of Legal Proceedings." *International Journal for Semiotics of Law* 17, no. 4): 356–89.

Scheffer, Thomas. 2010. *Adversarial Case-Making: An Ethnography of English Crown Court Procedure*. Leiden: Brill.

Schmitt, Carl. 1985. *Political Theology: Four Chapters on the Concept of Sovereignty*. Translated by George Schwab Cambridge, MA: MIT Press.

Schneider, Gary. 2005. *The Culture of Epistolarity: Vernacular Letters and Letter Writing in Early Modern England, 1500–1700*. Newark: Delaware University Press.

Schneider, Wendie Ellen. 2015. *Engines of Truth: Producing Veracity in the Victorian Courtroom*. New Haven, CT: Yale University Press.

Scott, James C. 1988. *Seeing like a State: How Certain Schemes to Improve the Human Condition Have Failed*. New Haven, CT: Yale University Press.

Sedition Committee. 1918. *Report*. Calcutta: Superintendent Government Printing, India.

Sengupta, Shuddhabrata. 2006. "Media Trials and Courtroom Tribulations." In *December 13: A Reader. The Strange Case of the Attack on the Indian Parliament*, edited by Arundhati Roy, 29–56. New Delhi: Penguin.

Sethi, Manisha. 2014. *Kafkaland: Prejudice, Law and Counterterrorism in India*. Gurgaon: Three Essays Collective.

Shah, Alpa, and Dhruv Jain. 2017. "Naxalbari at Its Golden Jubilee: Fifty Recent Books on the Maoist Movement in India." *Modern Asian Studies* 51, no. 4: 1165–1219.

Shapiro, Scott. 2007. "The 'Hart-Dworkin' Debate: A Short Guide for the Perplexed." In *Ronald Dworkin*, edited by Arthur Ripstein, 22–55. Cambridge: Cambridge University Press.

Siddiqui, Majid. 2005. *The British Historical Context and Petitioning in Colonial India*. New Delhi: Jamia Milia Islamia.

Sikand, Yoginder. 2007. "Islamist Militancy in Kashmir: The Case of the Laskhar-e-Taiba." In *The Practice of War: Production, Reproduction and Communication of Armed Violence*, edited by Aparna Rao. New York: Bergahn Books.

Singh, Bhrigupati. 2011. "Agonistic Intimacy and Moral Aspiration in Popular Hinduism: A Study in the Political Theology of the Neighbour." *American Ethnologist* 38, no. 3: 430–50.

Singh, Bhrigupati. 2015. *Poverty & The Quest for Life: Spiritual & Material Striving in Rural India*. Chicago: University of Chicago Press.

Singh, Onkar. 2001. "It's a Man! It's a Monkey! It's a . . ." Rediff.com, May 18. http://www.rediff.com/news/2001/may/18mon2.htm.

Singh, Ujjwal Kumar. 2006. "The Silent Erosion: Anti-Terror Laws and Shifting Contours of Jurisprudence in India." *Diogenes* 53, no. 4: 116–33.

Singh, Ujjwal Kumar. 2007. *State, Democracy and Anti-Terror Laws in India*. New Delhi: SAGE.

Singha, Radhika. 1998. *A Despotism of Law: Crime and Justice in Early Colonial India*. New Delhi: Oxford University Press.

Skocpol, Theda. 1985. "Bringing the State Back In: Strategies of Analysis in Current Research." In *Bringing the State Back In*, edited by Peter Evans, Dietrich Rueschemeyer, and Theda Skocpol, 3–38. Cambridge: Cambridge University Press.

Smith, Richard Saumarez. 1985. "Rule-by-Records and Rule-by-Reports: Complementary Aspects of the British Imperial Rule of Law." *Contributions to Indian Sociology* 19, no. 1: 153–76.

Stampnitzky, Lisa. 2013. *Disciplining Terror: How Experts Invented "Terrorism."* Cambridge: Cambridge University Press.

Starr, June, and Jane Collier. 1989. *History and Power in the Study of Law: New Directions in Legal Anthropology*. Ithaca, NY: Cornell University Press.

Stephen, James Fitzjames. 1872. *The Indian Evidence Act: With an Introduction on the Principles of Judicial Evidence*. London: Macmillan.

Stephens, Julia. 2019. "A Bureaucracy of Rejection: Petitioning and the Impoverished Paternalism of the British-Indian Raj." *Modern Asian Studies* 53, no. 1: 177–202.

Stoler, Ann. 1992. "'In Cold Blood': Hierarchies of Credibility and the Politics of Colonial Narratives." *Representations* 31: 151–89.

Sundaram, Ravi. 1999. "Recycling Modernity: Pirate Electronic Cultures in India." *Third Text* 13, no. 47: 59–65.

Sundaram, Ravi. 2010. *Pirate Modernity: Delhi's Media Urbanism*. Oxon: Routledge.

Sunstein, Cass R. 1996. "On the Expressive Function of Law." *University of Pennsylvania Law Review* 144, no. 5: 2021–53.

Suresh, Mayur. 2007. "Dead Man Walking: Sovereignty and the Supreme Court in the Age of Terror." In *Sarai Reader 07: Frontiers*, edited by M. Narula, S. Sengupta, J. Bagchi, and R. Sundaram, 121–33. Delhi: Centre for the Study of Developing Societies.

Suresh, Mayur. 2019. "The Slow Erosion of Fundamental Rights: How *Romila Thapar v. Union of India* Highlights What Is Wrong with the UAPA." *Indian Law Review* 3, no. 2: 212–23.

Suresh, Mayur, and Jawahar Raja. 2012. "'Detrimental to the Peace, Integrity and Secular Fabric of India' The Case against the Students' Islamic Movement of India.'" Jawaharlal Nehru Working Paper Series, no. 14. https://www.jnu.ac.in/sites/default/files/u63/14-Detrimental%20%28Mayur%20Suresh%29.pdf.

Taneja, Anand Vivek. 2017. *Jinnealogy: Time, Islam, and Ecological Thought in the Medieval Ruins of Delhi.* Stanford, CA: Stanford University Press.

Tarlo, Emma. 2003. *Unsettling Memories: Narratives of India's "Emergency."* New Delhi: Permanent Black.

Taussig, Michael. 1987. *Shamanism, Colonialism and the Wild Man: A Study in Terror and Healing.* Chicago: University of Chicago Press.

Taussig, Michael. 1988. "The Injustice of Policing: Prehistory and Rectitude." In *Justice & injustice in Law & Legal Theory,* edited by A. Sarat and T. Kearns, 19–34. Ann Arbor: University of Michigan Press.

Thompson, E. P. 1990. *Whigs and Hunters: The Origin of the Black Act.* London: Penguin.

Tomlins, Christopher, and John Comaroff, 2011. "'Law As . . .': Theory and Practice in Legal History." *UC Irvine Law Review* 1, no. 3: 1039–80.

Travers, Robert. 2019. "Indian Petitioning and Colonial State-Formation in Eighteenth-Century Bengal." *Modern Asian Studies* 53, no. 1: 89–122.

Tripathi, Rahul. 2021. "Below 2% of Those Arrested under UAPA Convicted in 2015–19: NCRB." *Economic Times,* June 18. https://economictimes.indiatimes.com/news/politics-and-nation/below-2-of-those-arrested-under-uapa-convicted-in-2015-19-ncrb/articleshow/83624754.cms?utm_source=contentofinterest&utm_medium=text&utm_campaign=cppst.

Twining, William. 2006. *Rethinking Evidence: Exploratory Essays,* 2nd ed. Cambridge: Cambridge University Press.

Van Oorschot, Irene, and Willem Schinkel. 2015. "The Legal Case File as a Border Object: On Self-Reference and Other-Reference in Criminal Law." *Journal of Law and Society* 42, no. 4: 499–527.

Van Voss, Lex Heerma. 2001. "Introduction" to "Petitions in Social History." Special issue, *International Review of Social History* 46, no. 9: 1–10.

Verma, S. K., and D. K. Srivastava. 2003. "A Study on Mass Hysteria (monkey men?) Victims in East Delhi." *Indian Journal of Medical Science* 57, no. 8: 355–60.

Vismann, Cornelia. 2008. *Files: Law and Media Technology.* Translated by Goeffrey Winthrop-Young. Stanford, CA: Stanford University Press.

Wagner, Kim. 2019. *Amritsar 2019: An Empire of Fear and the Making of a Massacre.* New Haven, CT: Yale University Press.

Wax, Stephen. 2008. *Kafka Comes to America: Fighting for Justice in the War on Terror.* New York: Other Press.

Weber, Max. 1991. "Politics as a Vocation." In *From Max Weber: Essays in Sociology*, edited and translated by H. H. Gerth and C. Wright Mills, 77–128. New York: Routledge Classics.

Weber, Samuel. 1989. "Upsetting the Set Up: Remarks on Heidegger's Questing after Technics." *MLN* 104, no. 5: 977–92.

Weissbourd, Bernard, and Elizabeth Mertz. 1985. "Rule-Centrism versus Legal Creativity: The Skewing of Legal Ideology through Language." *Law & Society Review* 19, no. 4: 623–60.

Winner, Langdon. 1980. "Do Artefacts Have Politics?" *Daedalus* 109, no. 1: 121–36.

Wittgenstein, Ludwig. 2009. *Philosophical Investigations*. Translated by G. E. M. Anscombe, P. M. S. Hacker, and Joachim Schulte, and edited by P. M. S. Hacker and Joachim Schulte, 4th ed., Chichester: Blackwell.

White, James Boyd. 1984. *When Words Lose Their Meaning: Constitutions and Reconstitutions of Language, Character and Community*. Chicago: University of Chicago Press.

White, James Boyd. 1985. *Heracles' Bow: Essays on the Rhetoric and Poetics of Law*. Madison: University of Wisconsin Press.

Yngvesson, Barbara, and Susan Coutin. 2006. "Backed by Papers: Undoing Persons, History and Return." *American Ethnologist* 33, no. 2: 177–90.

Zaeske Susan. 2003. *Signature of Citizenship: Petitioning, Antislavery and Women's Political Identity*. Chapel Hill: University of North Carolina Press.

Zaidi, S. Inayat A. 2005. "Introduction." In *The British Historical Context and Petitioning in Colonial India*. New Delhi: Jamia Milia Islamia.

Zaret, David. 1999. *Origins of Democratic Culture: Printing, Petitions and the Public Sphere in Early Modern England*. Princeton, NJ: Princeton University Press.

Zia, Ather. 2019. *Resisting Disappearance: Military Occupation and Women's Activism in Kashmir*. Seattle: University of Washington Press.

INDEX

committal, 99, 229n5

confession made to a police officer, 20–21, 222n25

Congress Party, 22, 193, 219n3, 222n22, 222n25, 223n27

Conley, John, and William O'Barr, 75, 106

Constable, Marianne, 92, 140, 187

constitution: and anti-terror laws, 22–23, 176, 224n31; as a new juridical field, 20, 221n19; separation of powers, 22

conviction rate under anti-terror laws, 223n28

courtrooms: conceptualisation of, 6, 9, 11, 26–29; Tis Hazari, 8–9

Cover, Robert, 30, 72–73, 77, 90, 228n7

Criminal Law Amendment Act 1908, 19, 220n11

culture of epistolarity, 172–73, 232n2

custodial intimacy, 37–39, 62, 69–70, 205. *See also* intimacy

custody, 9, 21, 36, 48, 60, 88, 126, 170, 185, 202; illegal, 35, 58, 61, 64, 176, 189, 202, 230n7. *See also* custodial intimacy

Das, Veena: on the circulation of documents, 139, 232n1; "descent into the ordinary," 49; on ethical work, 96; on grammatical persons, 184–85, 233n12; on learning language, 79–80; on mourning, 195; on rumors, 67; on state power, 225n4, 228n1

De, Rohit, 19, 221nn18–19, 227n2

deposition. *See* transcription

Derrida, Jacques, 52, 94, 232n1

Dworkin, Ronald, 97–98, 227n1, 229nn2–3

Eckert, Julia, 24, 54, 225n4

encounter death, 55, 57, 125, 194–95, 226n6, 230n7

ethics, 13, 59, 79–80, 90, 96, 181–85

evidence: meaning of, 231n1; special rules in anti-terror laws, 19–22, 221n18, 221n25, 224n31

examination-in-chief, and cross examination, 141, 151–55, 157–58, 159–63, 167–68, 220n8, 231n10

files: and colonial state, 119–20, 138; and court processes, 2–4, 7–9, 12–13, 33–34, 84, 118–19, 122, 133–34, 143–44, 150; and ensuring certainty and accountability, 119, 121, 138–39; and the production of narratives, 140–41; and production of truths, 117–24, 135–36, 137, 139, 191, 202, 231n5

Fish, Stanley, 229nn2–3

Foucault, Michel, 190

friendship, 37–40, 52, 54–56, 59, 70; and togetherness, 60–61, 207–8

grammatical person, 184–85, 186, 188, 191, 192, 233n12

Gupta, Akhil, 4, 58, 92, 120

Han, Clara, 54

Hart, H. L. A., 97–98, 227n1

Heidegger, Martin, 15

Hindu nationalism, 1, 27, 29, 62, 222n22, 222n25

Hull, Matthew, 119–21, 133, 135, 139–41, 148, 232nn2–3

Hussain, Nasser, 18, 24, 220n10

hyperlegality, 24

hypertext, 122–24. *See also* files

illegal detention, 22, 25, 35–36, 39, 42, 44, 49, 53–54, 61, 66, 69, 82, 95, 137

Indian Penal Code, 1860, 3, 12, 20, 24, 25, 99, 102, 106, 107, 179, 221n18

Ingold, Tim, 14–15, 220n7

interpretation *See* legal language

intimacy: and approach to law, 2, 15–16, 20, 33, 69–70, 77, 89–91, 172–73, 203, 207; custodial, 37–39, 52, 53–54, 62, 69–70, 203, 205, 225n4; and opacity, 38, 52, 70

Jamia Teachers Solidarity Association, 23, 204, 206, 226n5, 234n15

Jammu and Kashmir independence movement, 124, 136, 233n11

Jauregui, Beatrice, 37, 225n4

jurisgenesis, 73, 77

Kafkaesque, 30–31

Khilafat, 2, 219n3

Kripke, Saul, 228n6

Lashkar-e-Taiba, 63, 226n8

Latour, Bruno, 12, 139, 147

Laugier, Sandra, 17–18, 80, 169, 234n13

law and society approaches: law as society, 28; law in society, 26–27

Lefebvre, Alexandre, 97–99

legal language: abandonment to the inadequacy of, 196–97; as a debt, 186–87; and form of life, 72–74, 77, 79–81, 89–91, 227n4, 228n5; as form of self-writing, 190–91; and interpretation, 74, 77, 97–99, 228n6; opacity and openness, 2–4, 15, 71, 74–75, 77; as strategic resource, 78–79; as tekhne, 5, 73; and violence, 4, 95. *See also* state

Letters, 16, 85, 125, 127, 169–70, 172–74, 177, 180, 184, 186–90, 192, 196–97, 232n2, 232n4, 232n6, 233n8, 234n14. *See also* petitions

Liang, Lawrence, 78

Lokaneeta, Jinee, 225n4

magistrate, 22, 43, 99, 101, 143–44, 149–50, 221n18, 229nn4–5

Maoist movement, 226n7

Masooda Parveen case, 124–27, 134–36

Mathur, Nayanika, 120, 232n2, 233n10

Mbembé, Achille, 4

McQuade, Joseph, 19, 220n12, 221n20

Memo, 115, 117, 119, 126, 140, 144–47, 149, 159–64, 167, 175, 200, 202, 230n1. *See also* files

Mertz, Elizabeth, 15, 75, 94, 98, 114, 140

Metropolitan Magistrate. *See* magistrate

mourning, 181, 192, 195–96, 233n11

Nader, Laura, 27

narrative: around law and state, 30, 92–93; fabrication through file, 29, 116, 119, 121, 124, 126, 129, 134–36, 139–43, 149–51, 166–68, 202; in law, 76, 78, 140, 170, 173, 175, 183, 187–88, 191–92, 195, 197

National Investigation Agency, 22, 40–41, 66

Navlakha, Gautam, 23

Naxal. *See* Maoist movement

paperwork. *See* files

paranoia, 62, 67

People's Union for Civil Liberties, 224n31, 230n7

People's Union for Democratic Rights, 230n13, 232n4

petitions, 34, 50–52, 83, 123, 125, 174, 176–80, 208, 210, 223n26, 232n4, 233n8, 233n10; grammar of, 181–84, 187, 188, 190–92; history of, 172–73, 232nn5–7, 233n9; structure of, 170–71, 187

Terrorist and Disruptive Activities
(Prevention) Act, 1985, 21–22, 24–25,
222nn21–22, 224n35. *See also* anti-
terror laws
testimony. *See* transcription
Thompson, E. P., 1, 219n1. *See also* rule
of law
Tis Hazari Courts Complex, 6–8.
See also courtrooms
torture, 22, 36, 39, 53–54, 64, 66, 96, 125,
173, 180, 202, 209, 230n7
transcription, 87, 116, 139, 151–55,
231n8
trial, conceptions of, 5, 11, 13–15, 19, 23–24,
26–29, 30. *See also* courtrooms

Unlawful Activities Prevention Act,
1967: deviations from "ordinary"
procedural and evidentiary laws,
21–22; history of, 220n11, 222n25;
sanction to prosecute under, 93,
100–2; and "state of exception,"
22–23. *See also* anti-terror laws

utterances: illocutionary and perfor-
matives, 17, 169, 186, 220n9, 234n13;
passionate, 17, 173, 180, 185–88, 192;
perlocutionary, 17–18, 67, 80, 169, 186,
192, 232n1, 234n13

voice, 16–18, 30, 80, 169, 185, 197. *See also*
Cavell, Stanley
vulnerability and language, 16–18, 80,
91–96, 112–14, 135, 169, 202, 208.
See also voice

war on terror, 27, 222n22
Weber, Max, 95, 225n4
Weber, Samuel, 16
Winner, Langdon, 224n34
Wittgenstein, Ludwig, 72–73, 79–80, 97,
227n4, 228nn5–6
writing: and ethics, 72, 81, 89–91, 169–70,
173, 180, 184–85, 190; and producing
truths (*see* files); as way of understanding legal language, 72, 81,
85–87, 89

Mayur R. Suresh is Senior Lecturer in Law at SOAS, University of London.

www.ingramcontent.com/pod-product-compliance
Lightning Source LLC
Chambersburg PA
CBHW020249030426
42336CB00010B/682